MULTICULTURAL PICTUREBOOKS

ART FOR ILLUMINATING OUR WORLD, SECOND EDITION

SYLVIA AND KEN MARANTZ

THE SCARECROW PRESS, INC.

Lanham, Maryland • Toronto • Oxford

2005

SCARECROW PRESS, INC.

Published in the United States of America
by Scarecrow Press, Inc.
A wholly owned subsidiary of The Rowman & Littlefield Publishing Group, Inc.
4501 Forbes Boulevard, Suite 200, Lanham, Maryland 20706
www.scarecrowpress.com

PO Box 317
Oxford
OX2 9RU, UK

British Library Cataloguing in Publication Information Available

Library of Congress Cataloging-in-Publication Data
Marantz, Sylvia S.
  Multicultural picturebooks : art for illuminating our world / Sylvia Marantz,
Kenneth Marantz.— 2nd ed.
    p. cm.
  Includes bibliographical references and index.
  ISBN 0-8108-4933-X (pbk. : alk. paper)
  1. Children—Books and reading—United States. 2. Children's literature,
English—Bibliography. 3. Picture books for children—United States—Bibliography.
4. Minorities—United States—Juvenile literature—Bibliography. I. Marantz, Kenneth A.
II. Title.
Z1037.M267 2005
011.62—dc22
                                                    2004013640

♾™ The paper used in this publication meets the minimum requirements of American National
Standard for Information Sciences—Permanence of Paper for Printed Library Materials,
ANSI/NISO Z39.48–1992.
Manufactured in the United States of America.

CONTENTS

PREFACE

We believe in the importance of educating children about the world beyond their classroom. In this age of "globalization," what happens anywhere in the world affects everyone. Every year, in schools all over the United States and Canada, children arrive from many places speaking many languages. They deserve respect for the background or "culture" they bring with them, while the children they encounter here need help to better understand them. Although they can help us only to lift a corner of a curtain, picturebooks, we are convinced, can aid this process in both words and pictures, in all areas of the curriculum. The illustrations, in particular, are an all-too-often ignored source.

Since the publication of our *Multicultural Picturebooks: Art for Understanding Others* in 1997, hundreds of relevant picturebooks have been published. From these, we have selected those that we feel meet our criteria: telling a story that will appeal to children while including illustrations displaying some artistic competency and reflecting some aspect of the culture concerned. If the art style is "translated" for Western European eyes, the cultural sensibilities should still be apparent. Finally, the text and the pictures should work together, as in any successful picturebook, to make an effective entity. The grade levels suggested are, of course, subjective, and only suggestions, because students vary so widely.

Since many books included in volumes I and II have gone out of print, we have tried to include only those that we found "in print," although this situation is constantly changing. Others may well still be available in public libraries or online. We have not, of course, seen every picturebook published from 1997 to early 2004 but have made every effort to search out whatever we could find that might prove useful through both text and art to accomplish the aim of mutual understanding and respect.

The arrangement used in the first two volumes, we have been told, is a useful one, so we have retained it. Broad areas of the world are divided into what we feel are logical divisions. But it is important to convey to youngsters that there are no generic "Africans" or "Native Americans" as such but members of distinctive groups with their own cultures. We have mentioned these in the annotations and have listed these groups, along with individual countries, in the index. Although there have been changes over the years in the amount of material in various areas, we have been pleased to find that there is something about almost everywhere for student use. We have kept our selections to picturebooks, so there are no comprehensive collections. But in the appendix, we have included books of background information along with other resources.

We have not included illustrations. We feel that the tiny black-and-white reproductions possible would do little more than decorate the pages, while full-color samples of jackets and sometimes inside pages are readily available on many publishers' Web sites as well as on the sites of those who sell books online, such as amazon.com. We have also not included biographies in picturebook format. The ever-growing number, primarily of African Americans and Latin Americans, became more than we could cover in this volume.

Finally, we look back over fifty years of experience with books, art, and children and extensive travel visiting friends all around the world with hope that picturebooks can in some way help our children to better understand and get along in this rapidly changing world.

Sylvia and Ken Marantz

INTRODUCTION PART 1

SELECTING AND EVALUATING A MULTICULTURAL PICTUREBOOK

The field of children's literature is replete with attempts to define picturebooks, all of some merit. We consider the picturebook as one that tells a story either in pictures alone or in almost equal partnership with some text. How many words are too many? Only our instinctive response to a specific book permits an answer. Our approach, therefore, is to examine candidates as somewhere on a continuum from the totally textless work to one with only a handful of illustrations. The potency of the pictures in contributing to the story rather than the number of pictures per page becomes the test. Note that we spell "picturebook" as a single word to identify these special qualities as well as to differentiate this genre from other books with illustrations. The latter include most books about art; those on most any other subject in which visual information is included; and finally the oversize "coffee-table" books filled with illustrations and designed for casual browsing. The single-word spelling is being adopted more and more to designate the kind of book we have defined above. We use it also to call attention to our claim that picturebooks are art objects rather than literary artifacts.

Our concerns center around the means by which the visual qualities of picturebooks affect their abilities to tell stories about people who may hold values and practice behaviors different from those of the readers, as well as those who have those values or behaviors. Part of our analyses deals with the informational content and part with the feelings generated about that information, what is often referred to as the "emotional content." In their efforts to convey aspects of an existing or past society, picturebooks have been labeled with words like "factual," "genuine," "real," "honest," "true," "verifiable," "accurate," "authoritative," or the really difficult to define, "authentic." It is particularly difficult to come up with a working definition of "authentic" because human society is not some neat theoretical abstraction but rather a mixture defying precise specificity. "Culture" refers to the way people behave in specific circumstances; what they value and believe. How can we describe a culture "authentically?" If we give it a name, such as African American, does that mean it really exists as such? In what ways could we provide an "authentic" picture of American "culture?" Are there values, beliefs, behaviors that we all have in common? If the American population is too large for that, then how many people make a "culture" about which we can make statements that can be supported by others or by "facts?" And who is providing these "facts?"

Although the notion of "culture" is so tenuous, it has been used for political purposes, most recently for ethnic cleansing in Serbia and Rwanda. Other possible categories of groupings are national, regional, ethnic; perhaps these should be used instead of "culture" to differentiate among groups of people. On the positive side, there is a need to help specific groups of Americans achieve a greater feeling of self, an identification with the potency of achievements associated with past or present members of their social or ethnic group. The proliferation of books in which strong women star must help young females perceive a future of greater possibilities than their grandmothers could. So the aims of "multiculturalism" have included emphasizing the positive attributes of human societies, for example, the grandeur of the Mayan temples rather than the ritual murders, the outstanding rather than the stereotype. We have searched for the means by which author, artist, and designer have approached this aim in picturebooks.

We must recognize the impossibility of replicating a total "culture" in one book. The act of book making is a bit like that of translation; it is an artistic process that involves constant compromise. The success, perhaps the "authenticity," of a book depends on the skill of its makers in abstracting a message from the myriad materials available, a message that we, who may be foreigners, can understand. The message must also correspond in spirit with the life qualities of the message makers with whom the book is concerned, that is, the group or "culture." This is why we urge the use of many different books to reflect as many points of view as possible.

In addition, a picturebook is also an art object. The artists and designers have the responsibility to interpret the spirit of the story even if they don't always have complete freedom of expression. If a story is about a religious rite that involves a traditional object such as a Hanukkah menorah, the shape can have many variations, but it still must have spaces for nine lights or candles. Mickey Mouse may have only four fingers, but we expect King

Arthur to have five. Critics have criticized Mercer Mayer's illustrations for Jay Williams's *Everybody Knows What a Dragon Looks Like* because they were a mere pastiche of "Oriental" and Western art styles. If he had used them in an art history text, such criticism would be proper. But since of course all "Oriental" paintings are not in the same style, does his translation of the spirit of some periods of such paintings do such a disservice, or does his inventiveness strengthen the visual message of the book? Does this break with "authenticity" deny the book's use as a resource?

Because it embodies the sum of the stories that are the spiritual underpinning of any group of people, the picturebook has great potential for bridging the differences among us. The concept of story is one common to all of us, a shared experience that sets the stage for communication. Most young children have been introduced to some of the myths and fables that are part of their personal heritage. So picturebooks based on similar legends, as well as those based on daily life, can be absorbed and enjoyed. But what is learned depends a great deal on the insights and craftsmanship of those producing the picturebooks that contain them. We have done our best in assessing these qualities, hoping that you will find them useful.

We suggest here that picturebooks can help at least somewhat to give children at least the flavor of another way of perceiving life, a peek under the curtain. We adults working with children and books must in some cases not only help them understand the meaning of the words but also seek ways to "translate" the pictures. Dealing with cross-cultural learning in classrooms is never easy. But we believe in the potential of some picturebooks to get us involved with issues, concerns, values, and problems common to all humans, if rendered differently across the city or around the world. Those who create these books must understand the people on *both* sides of the bridge they are trying to build and think about what is appropriate for them. If they are successful, they have used their artistic skills to interpret what they want to convey so that the reader can value and be moved by the message. We have tried to select books that succeed in these aims. We hope that teachers, librarians, and parents can use them to build a curriculum that will suit their situation while offering as wide a variety of visual experiences from the selected "cultures" as possible.

Although we stopped our selection in January 2004, many new "multicultural" picturebooks have already been and will continue to be published. As you look these over for possible use, we suggest you ask some of the same questions we did as we chose the books in this volume:

Does the book tell an engaging story?

Are the illustrations competent? Are the representations of objects, humans, and animals convincingly portrayed? Is the use of the media consistent?

Do the text and the pictures work together to form a cohesive unit, each telling part of the story?

Are the characteristics of the group reflected in the story and the art?

Have the author and/or illustrator identified the sources used for the "cultural" background of that story and art?

NOTE

This part of the introduction has been adapted from volume I of our *Multicultural Picture Books: Art for Understanding Others.*

INTRODUCTION PART 2

MULTICULTURAL EDUCATION AND MULTICULTURAL LITERATURE

The concepts of "multicultural literature" and "multicultural education" deserve consideration here as the bases for the incorporation of selected picturebooks into school curricula. The phenomenal rise of interest in and discussion of these concepts became evident as we searched online to prepare this book. There are literally thousands of references to the subjects in books and periodicals dating just from the publication of volume II in 1997. All this is for an area of education that was not even recognized as a category in *Education Index* until 1978. Reese notes that it was from the start of the Civil Rights Movement that concern began for the self-esteem of the nondominant group, the so-called minorities, while realizing the need for the dominant group to become sensitized to cultural differences and varying historic perspectives. Perhaps because of the so-called ethnic studies of the 1960s and 1970s, characters finally began to appear in children's literature that were not exclusively "white," that African American children, for example, could finally find themselves in the books in their libraries. Before the 1960s, Mendoza reminds us, they were "invisible." There have been increases and decreases in both the number of "multicultural" books and the numbers dealing with particular areas and groups. For example, Lindsay notes that the Cooperative Children's Book Center in Madison, Wisconsin, has found fewer books about Native Americans in recent years to recommend, and so have we. But as the pressure to educate students with global perspectives rises, and as the flow of immigrants into the United States continues along with the demands from "minorities" for recognition, educators acknowledge that "multicultural education" is here to stay and that "multicultural literature" is an essential element.

There are many definitions of "multicultural education"; in fact there are also several alternative names and types suggested by Cai (pp. xvi–xvii). Ramsey offers another example from the National Council for the Accreditation of Teacher Education: multicultural education is "a process of preparing individuals for the social, political, and economic realities that they will experience in culturally diverse and complex human encounters." Finazzo incorporates the ideas of the seminal name in the field, James Banks, with her own extensive discussion (pp. 99ff.). Tiedt notes that "educators agree on defining the general parameters" but that "there remain differences in interpretation of theory and how theory should inform practice" (p. 14).

There is general agreement, however, on the aims of this education. In her foreword to Steiner, Alma Flor Ada reminds us of the importance of the child's own culture and notes that other cultures deserve respect as well. "Schools must do more to give students the crucial skills and knowledge they need to make sense of international developments," states Dunn (2002, p. 10). Clark describes the reasons for his projects: to clarify images of the world for his students and to discover how our images affect our views of "the other." We study "for self-knowledge, for moral redemption, to avoid hubris" (Clark 2000, p. 451). "Cultural diversity is just as important as biodiversity," he finds, in this "self-serving endeavor" (Clark 2000, p. 451).

Banks, in his "Diversity within Unity," summarizes a project that reviewed and synthesized the research related to diversity. He feels that diversity in the nation's schools is both an opportunity and a challenge. "Students must also develop the knowledge, attitudes, and skills needed to interact positively with people from diverse groups and to participate in the civic life of the nation" (Banks 2001, p. 202–3). Téllez states his case: "Multicultural education, in its widest goals, should eliminate humiliation and imbue honor and self-respect among all children and youth; it should, after all, inspire. In my view, the first responsibility of the school as an institution must be to avoid humiliation" (2002, p. 21).

Two final reminders. From Willis-Rivera and Mecken: "[I]t is very possible that children born today will interact with people from different cultures much more than previous generations . . . it is important that children are taught about other cultures starting at a young age . . . through books"(2002, p. 269). From Davenport: "It is not possible to understand other cultures without understanding one's own; it is also not possible to understand fully one's own culture until the encounter with another culture has put it in perspective" (2003, p. 18).

There are problems and pitfalls, however, when dealing with the literature from "other" cultures, "an important component of the multicultural education movement and a tool that can be used to achieve its goal: diversity and equity in education" as Perini quotes Cai (2002, p. 428). As she discusses the potential of such books, she notes that the "social, cultural, and political value of culturally conscious children's books makes them both appealing and potentially controversial." For as Cai notes, "multicultural education" is a political rather than a literary movement, with all the difficulties that implies.

Before covering some possible areas of difficulty, we should first remember what is clearly described by Roxburgh, the "insular mind-set visible everywhere in our American culture, but nowhere more detrimentally than in our attitude toward other cultures" (2004, p. 48). As a publisher, he decries the lack of translations of books from abroad. Despite the development of "multiculturalism" in education, he finds the books published to support this too often display a cultural bias. Because they are written by Americans, they too often look in a mirror, and not through a window, a distinction noted years back by Rudine Sims Bishop. "We look for the familiar and when we see something we recognize, we think we've had an insight into that culture" (Mendoza 2001, p. 6). But despite the fact that books from another country may be hard to understand, his hope is that we will keep trying. For "they offer a way of seeing that is otherwise unavailable to most of us" (Mendoza 2001, p. 6).

This leads us directly to the problem of what has been called "cultural copyright." Does the book in question have to be written and/or illustrated by a person from the culture it concerns? The question is under constant debate. The answers range all the way from "Of course not. How could we ever have any historical fiction if this were necessary?" and "What's wrong with Flaubert's view of a woman's world in *Madame Bovary*?" to "Only an African American can understand how it feels to be stopped by a white police officer." We have tried to be as sensitive to this as possible, reading comments when available from members of a culture if the book is by nonmembers. But sometimes two of them will not agree. On top of this, Rudine Sims Bishop has formulated widely adopted criteria that state that multicultural literature should offer a positive picture. Reality is not always positive, however. So it is necessary to try to be certain that any materials used in teaching not be offensive, if possible. Reading reviews and asking members of that culture who may be in your community are the best defenses to avoid utilizing disturbing stereotypes. Mendoza gives examples of books that have problems or pitfalls that are not obvious to the "outsider" emphasizing again the fallacy of using just one book to exemplify a group or culture.

A related question is that of the importance of "authenticity." Most authors and/or illustrators currently list their sources. The educator can decide how important it is that a tale is from traditional sources. But the differences between stories, be they original or traditional, and factual information should be made clear to students. Cai offers illuminating discussions of all these problems, summarizing the current trends, including cross-cultural books and "culturally neutral" books; that is, those that have characters from culturally diverse backgrounds but in which these backgrounds have nothing to do with the story. These have become much more evident in the past few years, a positive sign "to rectify the serious underrepresentation of parallel cultures in children's literature." We have not included culturally neutral books in our listing, because we feel that they will not add to cultural understanding, in fact, Cai fears that they may "dissolve cultural identities." He feels that the "melting pot" theory is detrimental to a culturally diverse society; he is concerned that these books may create an illusion that "all Americans, regardless of cultural background, share the same experiences and values." While we do not think that sharing values is a negative, we are trying to point out the distinctions rather than similarities in our selections.

Note should be made here of the problem of the so-called backlash against multicultural education that has arisen over the years, both in the media and in the schools. Some teachers have told us that they are tired of the constant pressure to add materials from many cultures to their already overcrowded curriculum. Former chair of the National Endowment for the Humanities Lynne Cheney was only one voice of many deploring what she felt was a subversion of the curriculum in universities as they diversified the classical canon by adding materials by women, African Americans, and Hispanics. The claim has been that "Western values" are under attack. As Cai notes "Proponents of multiculturalism in education and literature are not only caricatured as 'politically correct' bullies but also blamed for creating a PC crisis, as if they had taken over university campuses" (p. 94). He calls this a ludicrous exaggeration and fears that it is this kind of "attack on political correctness that is actually creating a backlash in the movement of multicultural literature." Indeed, as already noted, this is a political rather than a literary or educational controversy, and the debate goes on.

Despite the difficulties faced in dealing with such materials, the goals of "multicultural education" are certainly worth the effort, and "multicultural literature" is a vital path to help reach them. These are, after all, stories told in words and pictures about people who may be unfamiliar to the readers. Science fiction takes us into other worlds, and fairy tales stretch our imaginations even further. A story about a young kite flyer in 19th-century China also demands a stretch to match our experiences enough with that youngster to understand, to feel, and to see what is happening in that tale. And, in the process, to add a bit of information about our world from that of the child.

USEFUL RESOURCES

Banks, J. A. *Cultural Diversity and Education: Foundations, Curriculum and Teaching.* 4th ed. Boston: Allyn & Bacon, 2001.

Banks, J. A. "Diversity within Unity: Essential Principles for Teaching and Learning in a Multicultural Society." *Phi Delta Kappan* 83, no. 3 (November 2001): 196–203.

Banks, James A. *An Introduction to Multicultural Education.* 2d ed. Boston: Allyn & Bacon, 1999.

Banks, James A., and Cherry A. McGee Banks, eds. *Multicultural Education: Issues and Perspectives.* 4th ed. New York: John Wiley, 2001.

Bishop, Kay. "Making Multicultural Literature Meaningful." *Knowledge Quest* 32, no. 1 (September/October 2003): 27–28.

Blair, Timothy R. *New Teacher's Performance-Based Guide to Culturally Diverse Classrooms.* Boston: Allyn & Bacon, 2003.

Bruchac, Joseph. *Our Stories Remember: American Indian History, Culture, and Values through Storytelling.* Golden, CO: Fulcrum, 2003.

Cai, Mingshui. *Multicultural Literature for Children and Young Adults: Reflections on Critical Issues.* Westport, CT: Greenwood, 2002.

Carpenter, L. M. "Multiethnic Children's Literature: Its Need for a Permanent Place in the Literary Canon." M.A. thesis, Biola University, 2000.

Clark, Leon E. "Other-Wise: The Case for Understanding Foreign Cultures in a Unipolar World." *Social Education* 64, no. 7 (November/December 2000): 448–53.

Copenhaver, Jeane F. "The Intersections of Response and Ethnicity: Elementary School Students Respond to Multicultural Children's Literature." Paper presented at the annual meeting of the South Central Modern Language Association, Memphis, TN, October 1999.

Cotton, Penni. *Picture Books Sans Frontières.* Staffordshire, England: Tretham Books, 2000.

Davenport, Melanie. "Using Simulations to Ground Intercultural Inquiry in the Art Classroom." *Art Education* 56, no. 5 (September 2003): 13–18.

Dirda, Michael. "Classrooms and Their Discontents." *Washington Post Magazine,* November 9, 1997.

Dunn, Ross. "Growing Good Citizens with a World Centered Curriculum." *Educational Leadership* 60, no. 2 (October 2002).

Finazzo, Denise Ann. *All for the Children: Multicultural Essentials of Literature.* Albany, NY: Delmar/ITP, 1997.

Foner, Nancy. "The Transnationals." *Natural History* 107, no. 2 (March 1998): 34–35.

Freeman, Evelyn, and Barbara A. Lehman. *Global Perspectives in Children's Literature.* Needham Heights, MA: Allyn & Bacon, 2001.

Gollnick, Donna M., and Philip C. Chin. *Multicultural Education in a Pluralistic Society.* 6th ed. Upper Saddle River, NJ: Merrill/Prentice Hall, 2002.

Green, Martha, et al., eds. *Resources for a Multicultural Classroom (The Multicultural Resource Series).* Annapolis Junction, MD: NEA Human and Civil Rights Division, 2000.

Jaynes, Gregory. "Coming to America." *Smithsonian* 34, no. 10 (January 2004): 52–60.

Lindsay, Nina. "I Still Isn't for Indian." *School Library Journal* (November 2003): 42–43.

Lindsey, Randall B., Kikanza Nuri Robins, and Raymond D. Terrell. *Cultural Proficiency: A Manual for School Leaders.* 2d ed. Thousand Oaks, CA: Corwin Press, 2003.

Marantz, Sylvia, and Kenneth Marantz. "Picture Books Peek behind Cultural Curtains." *Book Links* (January 2000): 13–18.

Mathis, Janelle B. "Respond to Stories with Stories: Teachers Discuss Multicultural Children's Literature." *The Social Studies* 92, no. 4 (July/August 2001): 155–60.

McAllister, Gretchen, and Jacqueline Jordan Irvine. "'Cultural Competency' and Multicultural Teacher Education." *Review of Educational Research* 399 (spring 2000): 3–24.

Mendoza, Jean. "Examining Multicultural Picture Books for the Early Childhood Classroom: Possibilities and Pitfalls." *Early Childhood Research and Practice* 3, no. 2 (fall 2001): 2–32.

New Press Guide to Multicultural Resources for Young Readers. New York: New Press/Norton, 1997.

Nieto, Sonia. "Profoundly Multicultural Questions." *Educational Leadership* 60, no. 4 (December 2002/January 2003): 6–7.

Perini, Rebecca L. "The Pearl in the Shell: Author's Notes in Multicultural Literature." *The Reading Teacher* 55, no. 5 (February 2002): 428–35.

Phillion, Joann. "Classroom Stories of Multicultural Teaching and Learning." *Journal of Curriculum Studies* 34, no. 3 (2002): 281–300.

Pilger, Mary Anne. *Multicultural Projects Index.* Englewood, CO: Libraries Unlimited, 2002.

Rader, Debra, and Linda Harris Sittig. *New Kid in School: Using Literature to Help Children in Transition.* New York: Teachers College Press, 2003.

Ramsey, Patricia G., and Leslie R. Williams. *Multicultural Education: A Source Book.* 2d ed. New York: Routledgefalmer, 2003.

Rao, Sandhya. "Multiculturalism and Political Correctness in Children's Books: A View from India." *Bookbird* 39, no. 4 (2001): 39–42.

Reddish, Barbara Smith. "What Is Good Multicultural Children's Literature and How Do We Critique It? Distinguishing between Image and Value." *Viewpoints* 120 (August 2000).

Reese, Renford. "Building Cultural Bridges in Schools: The Colorful Flags Model." *Ethnicity and Education* 4, no. 3 (September 2001): 181–82.

Roxburgh, Stephen. "The Myopic American." *School Library Journal* (January 2004): 48–50.

Rubinowitz, Janina. "Thoughts on Authenticity." Unpublished paper. 1983.

Schecter, Sandra R., and Jim Cummins, eds. *Multilingual Education in Practice: Using Diversity as a Resource.* Portsmouth, NH: Heinemann, 2003.

Slapin, Beverly, and Doris Seale, eds. *Through Indian Eyes: The Native Experience in Books for Children.* Los Angeles: American Indian Study Center UCLA, 1998.

Stan, Susan, ed. *The World through Children's Books.* Lanham, MD: Scarecrow, 2002.

Steiner, Stanley F. *Promoting a Global Community through Multicultural Children's Literature.* Englewood, CO: Libraries Unlimited, 2001.

Téllez, Kip. "Multicultural Education as Subtext." *Multicultural Perspectives* 4, no. 2 (2002): 21.

Tiedt, Pamela L., and Iris M. Tiedt. *Multicultural Teaching: A Handbook of Activities, Information, and Resources.* 6th ed. Boston: Allyn & Bacon, 2002.

Willis-Rivera, Jennifer L., and Melissa Mecken. "*De Que Colores:* A Critical Examination of Multicultural Children's Books." *Communication Education* 51, no. 3 (July 2002): 269–79.

ONE

ASIA AND THE PACIFIC

JAPAN AND JAPANESE AMERICANS

ORIGINAL TALES AND FOLKTALES EVOKING THE PAST

Baker, Keith. *The Magic Fan.* San Diego, CA: Harcourt, 1989. 32pp. Grades 1–4.

    This original story in folk-tale style incorporates in both words and pictures many elements of life in the Japan of long ago. Yoshi, a young builder, builds what he sees on a magic fan: a boat, a kite, and a bridge. When an earthquake and a *tsunami*, or tidal wave, come, the bridge saves the people of the village. Then Yoshi realizes he does not need the fan any longer. A modulated gray double page acts as a background for an intensely red, fan-shaped frame that houses the illustrations, with exposed bamboo struts in the center. The small print text on the left side raises a question that is answered in the right-side text. Visually the answer is illustrated by flipping the cut, fan-shaped frame over to disclose another picture as seen on the "magic fan." Acrylic paint is applied thinly enough to show the texture of the rough board on which it is painted. Stylized reality and dreamy vision are combined along with modeled forms and three-dimensional objects in this imaginative use of the fan-shaped cutout and frame for the incorporation of traditional decorative forms in a curvilinear space.

Bodkin, Odds. *The Crane Wife.* Illustrated by Gennady Spirin. San Diego, CA: Gulliver/Harcourt, 1998. 32pp. Also paper. Grades 1–5.

    This classic Japanese folktale concerns a poor sail maker named Osamu who has longed for a wife. One stormy night, he rescues a wounded crane, then sees it fly away. When another storm arrives, a beautiful young woman takes refuge with him and becomes his wife. She offers to weave a magic sail for him, but he must not look at her at work. The sail sells for a lot of money. When they are out of funds again, she makes another. But each time she seems more exhausted. When he asks for one more, she reluctantly agrees. But when he tries to learn her secret, he sees that she is really a crane weaving her feathers into the sail. Discovered, she flies away. Spirin's double-page watercolor and gouache scenes clearly disclose the influence of historic Japanese paintings. The details of costume, buildings, and even ships are stunning. There is a grand lyrical quality to the several scenes of flying cranes. For another very different but worthy version of the story for comparison, see Sumiko Yagawa's *Crane Wife*, translated by Katherine Paterson, illustrated by Suekichi Akaba (Morrow and Mulberry, 1981), unfortunately out of print but available at libraries and online.

Galouchka, Annouchka Gravel. *Sho and the Demons of the Deep*. Willowdale, Ontario: Annick, 1995. 32pp. Grades 2–4.

"It is said" gives a folktale introduction to this original story set in ancient Japan, where the people used to cast their nightmares into the sea. After a while, the nightmares disturb the sea and keep fishermen from their catch. Wise young Sho has the people stop the practice and calms the waters, but the problem of nightmare disposal remains. Sho teaches the children to draw pictures of their dreams. Soon everyone is drawing and painting dreams and sending them up into the air on strings, thus kites are born and perhaps art therapy as well. The details of interaction enhance the strong emotions of the tale. The complex gouache paintings incorporate Japanese clothing, artifacts, and facial features, but these are organized in a florid style redolent with decorative textures and frenetic layouts.

Gollub, Matthew. *Ten Oni Drummers*. Illustrated by Kazuko G. Stone. New York: Lee & Low, 2000. 32pp. Grades PreS–2.

A young boy dreams that he is on a Japanese beach in the moonlight. In rhymed couplets, he describes the company he finds there. First one *oni*, a creature from Japanese folklore, joins him. Then others appear, one by one, running, raising flags, playing "nasty goblin games," until finally there are ten. They "pound their giant drums of wood, / drum because it feels so good," with appropriate noises added. They are friendly to him rather than menacing, chasing spooky dreams away. Although the story is not Japanese, it introduces, with added notes, the *oni*, the *taiko* drums, and additional information about the written Japanese *kanji* characters for the numbers included in the text. These multicolored, red-eyed characters with odd hairpieces and wearing Japanese "happy coats" are designed to make us giggle. While they provide information about the drums and drumming techniques, their antics, illustrated with watercolor and colored pencil, make it easy to learn the numbers.

Hamanaka, Sheila. *Screen of Frogs: An Old Tale Retold.* New York: Orchard/Scholastic, 1993. 32pp. Grades 2–5.

Rich but lazy Koji has to sell off his property to buy what he pleases until he has only his house, a lake, and a mountain left. Dreaming by the mountain, he is approached by a frog who begs him not to sell the mountain for the sake of the creatures living there. So Koji sells the furnishings of his house instead, leaving only a blank screen. That night he hears frog noises, sees frog footprints, and finds the screen full of painted frogs. Everyone wants to buy the beautiful screen, but Koji refuses to sell. Instead, he acquires some perspective; he begins to work and soon has a family and a happy life. The night he dies, the frogs disappear from his screen. His family keeps the land, understanding its importance. Boldly conceived, Hamanaka's illustrations exploit collage and opaque paint to create double-page spreads able to integrate the simple, large-print text while maintaining an appealing narrative flow. Brush strokes are vigorous, more delicate when defining a striding horse's legs and wildly expressionistic when painting the screen. Costumes, landscapes, and objects are all historically Japanese; faces tend to caricature, similar to the comic story line adapted from a Japanese text, a story ending in a dreamy landscape.

Hamilton, Morse, reteller. *Belching Hill.* Illustrated by Forest Rogers. New York: Greenwillow, 1997. 32pp. Grades 1–4.

A poor woman and her pig live on top of Belching Hill. One day a dumpling she has made rolls down the hill. She chases after it even after it is taken inside the hill by an ogre. When the other ogres find out that she makes good dumplings, they put her to work making more with a magic spoon and pot that can produce more and more from a few grains of rice. Finally she runs away with the pot and spoon, tricking the ogres so they can't catch her. The double-page, image-packed scenes are played for slapstick laughs that go along with the title. Many-eyed ogres come in various colors; all have teeth and claws that mean business. But the frenetically designed pages are stabilized by the gray-haired, wrinkled heroine in her orange kimono.

Harik, Elsa. *The Fox Maiden*. Illustrated by Tatsuro Kiuchi. New York: Simon & Schuster, 1996. 32pp. Grades 1–4.

The lengthy text tells an original story inspired by Japanese folklore. A fox decides, despite warnings, to assume human form. As a young woman, she is taken by Haruo, a manservant, to his rich master's house and hired. After a while at hard work, she decides to become a fox again but cannot forget her human home. When the humans plan to hunt the foxes, she warns them so they can move to safety. She is cautioned about trying to change herself a third time. When she tries, her tail remains, and she is chased away. Haruo helps her escape and tells her that he loves her. She realizes that she loves him too, leads him to safety, then resumes her fox form and leaves. Kiuchi's full- and double-page Western-style acrylic paintings emphasize mood rather than detail, although these naturalistic figures, appropriately costumed, are distinct personalities. The thickly packed tree trunks of the end-papers set the tone for the somber tale.

Hodges, Margaret, adapter. *The Boy Who Drew Cats*. Illustrated by Aki Sogabe. New York: Holiday House, 2002. 32pp. Grades K–3.

The story, adapted from Lafcadio Hearn's version of a Japanese legend, has echoes of the supernatural. A boy who draws cats constantly begins to paint many on the wall of a temple. Having been warned to avoid large places at night, he is in a cabinet when the resident goblin arrives. Dreadful noises are heard outside. When he emerges, he finds a dead goblin; the cats on the wall have bloody mouths. A 15th-century artist, Sesshu Toyo, may have inspired this tale. His drawings were said to be so realistic that they could come to life. Created with cut paper, watercolor, and airbrush, Sogabe's double-page scenes reflect an old Japanese art style. The houses, rice fields, and pictures of cats are all organized in very appealing and moving designs. The violent but happy ending is forecast by the blood-red end-papers and words on the title page.

Kajikawa, Kimiko. *Yoshi's Feast*. Illustrated by Yumi Heo. New York: Melanie Kroupa/Dorling Kindersley, 2000. 32pp. Grades K–4.

In this folk tale, which has parallels in other cultures, Yoshi the fan maker enjoys the smell of the eels his neighbor Sabu cooks but never buys any. Sabu sends him a bill for the smells. Then Yoshi dances to the sound of the money in his money box and says he has paid for the smells with the sound of the money. Angry, Sabu cooks bad-smelling fish, which makes Yoshi ill. Yoshi finally finds a solution that makes them happy, prosperous friends. The stylized colored illustrations that use oils, pencil, and collage cut from patterned papers incorporated as clothing, need only a few objects and screens as settings. Very lively actions are fundamentally comic in character, the scenes of Yoshi dancing across the pages are particularly engaging. The clothing and settings are Japanese in flavor.

Kimmel, Eric A., reteller. *The Greatest of All: A Japanese Folktale.* Illustrated by Giora Carmi. New York: Holiday House, 1991. 32pp. Grades 1–5.

With sly humor, Kimmel recounts the classic tale of the mouse who insists that his daughter cannot marry the humble field mouse of her choice but only "the greatest of all." His search for the greatest leads to the sun, which the emperor says is greater, to the cloud that hides the sun, to the wind that scatters the clouds, to the wall that blocks the wind, and finally to the field mouse who tunnels within the wall. Other versions that may still be available include Junko Morimoto's *Mouse's Marriage* (Viking, 1986, 1988) and Gerald McDermott's *The Stonecutter* (Viking, 1975; Puffin paper, 1978.) For a version from Korea, with no Korean visual references, see Julia Gukova's *The Mole's Daughter* (Annick, 1998). The thinly bordered illustrations are set on a flecked background suggestive of the fabrics used to mount paintings in the Far East. They vary from double-page scenes to vignettes. The text is set in framed, cream-colored panels. The paintings include bits of architecture and costumes hinting at a historic period. There is a roughness to the style, almost a crude quality to some of the representations of the personified natural phenomena that seem at odds with our perceptions of Japanese restraint. The page of haiku is particularly out of character. The illustrations should be compared with those more traditional to see the contrast.

Kimmel, Eric A., reteller. *Three Samurai Cats: A Story from Japan.* Illustrated by Mordicai Gerstein. New York: Holiday House, 2003. 32pp. Grades K–4.

The story comes from Japanese mythology; the philosophical meaning is based in Zen Buddhism. But the tale is both intriguing and humorous. The canine *daimyo,* or lord of a castle, begs for help from the head monk of a shrine which has fighting samurai cats, because a ferocious rat has taken over his castle. The first two cats who come fail to oust the rat. When Neko Roshi, "the greatest living master of the martial arts" finally arrives, he is a great disappointment at first. But he finally succeeds, using the principles of Zen. The visual narrative begins on the half-title page; we get a close-up of the villain rat on the title page as he enters the castle. A series of boxes follows with a sequence of the rat's initial conquests. Lively pen and ink drawings with oil paint using translucent hues suggest some of the artistic Japanese heritage, particularly on early scrolls. This is delicious illustration filled with character, action, and humor.

Mayer, Mercer. *Shibumi and the Kitemaker.* New York: Marshall Cavendish, 1999. Also paper. 48pp. Grades 1–4.

Although the story is an original one, not a folktale, it is imbued with the appreciation of things Japanese declared by the author in his note at the end. To protect his daughter Shibumi from the evils of the world, the emperor keeps her within the palace walls. One day, when she climbs the wall, she is shocked to see the ugly city and the poor ragged people. Wanting to see more, she has the royal kite maker fashion a very large kite. Shibumi flies up on it and refuses to come down until the city is as beautiful as the palace. When the nobles send an archer to shoot her down, because they do not care to help the suffering, the gods of the sky have Shibumi and the kitemaker flown far away. Years later, a young samurai seeks her out to return her to her repentant father. Dramatic settings in architecture of some historic Japanese period combine with clothing and even plants to produce full-page Adobe Photoshop-created illustrations brimming with the emotions that drive the narrative. The actors are delineated forcefully; the kitemaker's mature strength contrasts effectively with Shibumi's more gentle determination.

Melmed, Laura Krauss. *Little Oh.* Illustrated by Jim LaMarche. New York: Lothrop/Morrow, 1997. 32pp. Grades 1–4.

This charming original story with folktale overtones concerns an origami doll that comes to life. She has many adventures out in the world. Befriended by a crane, she tries to have him fly her home. Instead, she lands by the home of a man and his son. Remembering the lonely woman who had made her, Little Oh brings her and the man together. Then she magically becomes a real little girl. The story is not essentially Japanese, but it is an excuse for the illustrator to include some of that country's interior architecture, dress, origami, and landscape, giving the reader a sense of place. The portrait of the mother is particularly sensitively created, as is that of the crane; all are done naturalistically in acrylics and colored pencils.

Merrill, Jean, adapter. *The Girl Who Loved Caterpillars: A Twelfth-Century Tale from Japan.* Illustrated by Floyd Cooper. New York: Philomel/Putnam, 1992. Also paper. 32pp. Grades 2–5.

This is an unfinished story from an 800-year-old scroll, retold in small print with lengthy text from three English translations. Its feisty, independent heroine Izumi, the clever, attractive daughter of an official in the emperor's court in Kyoto, is fascinated by insects, worms, toads, and especially caterpillars, an interest no one can understand. Her parents wish she would be more conventional, but she has a mind of her own. Her encounters with a Captain who is curious to meet the odd girl he has heard about ends inconclusively, an invitation to create an ending involving silkworms and her future. Cooper paints portraits, costumes, and settings with opaque pigments in a slightly fuzzy manner, accentuating the romantic qualities of events. Details are few but chosen both to inform and to complement the design of the pages. This is a Westerner observing historical Japan and interpreting its social structure through careful study. His characters are real people we can care about as we bridge time and cultures.

Namioka, Lensey. *The Hungriest Boy in the World.* Illustrated by Aki Sogabe. New York: Holiday House, 2001. 32pp. Grades K–3.

This amusing original cautionary tale reflects the Japanese background much more in its illustrations than in the text. Young Jiro, who puts everything in his mouth, one day swallows the Hunger Monster, which keeps demanding more to eat. When neither doctor nor priest nor medium can help, the monster is finally lured out. Clothing, architecture, and landscape are all Japanese. Cut paper, watercolors, and airbrush create strong black outlines filled with colors to add a greater naturalistic sense to this comic drama that may help persuade youngsters not to put things in their mouths.

Partridge, Elizabeth, adapter. *Kogi's Mysterious Journey.* Illustrated by Aki Sogabe. New York: Dutton, 2003. 40pp. Grades K–4.

The legend-like tale, rich in imagery and love of nature, tells of a 9th-century Buddhist priest-painter. Yearning to capture the essence of a fish he has caught and set free, Kogi finds himself turned into a fish, experiencing life in the water. He also feels the pain of being caught and cut up for cooking. After waking in his bed, he begins to paint fish that magically swim off the scrolls when he takes them to the water. Kogi himself follows them. Sogabe's choice of cut colored paper creates pictures that seem to exude the stillness of the water's rippling surface and the pine trees' stately stature. The heavy outlines that delineate the humans also add to the seriousness of their activities. The many fish with hundreds of scales forming decorative patterns become the clear life force that so entrances Kogi. These illustrations suggest rather than imitate some historic Japanese art. Notes add information on the source.

Paterson, Katherine. *The Tale of the Mandarin Ducks.* Illustrated by Leo and Diane Dillon. New York: Dutton/Lodestar/Penguin, 1990. 40pp. Also paper. Grades 2–6.

A greedy lord captures and cages a beautiful wild duck in this folk tale retold in a lengthy text by the award-winning author. The duck grieves for his mate, but the lord will not let him go. Yasuko, a kitchen maid, pities and releases the duck, but the steward Shozo is blamed and demoted. The two fall in love. The angry lord wants them put to death, but instead he is ordered to send them to the Imperial Court. On the long journey, they have a strange encounter in the woods, which puts a happy ending to their story. This is a deliciously designed, visually elegant book, from jacket and cover through end-papers, half-title pages, all the way to the end. Using an 18th-century Japanese woodcut style for illustration, the text is integrated into the two-page spreads, each side designed as one of a pair of prints separated by white borders. Patterns of costumes, flowers, trees, or feathers demonstrate the values placed on such controlled design by this culture.

San Souci, Robert D. *The Samurai's Daughter.* Illustrated by Stephen T. Johnson. New York: Dial/Penguin, 1992. Also Penguin paper. Grades 2–6.

Based on a legend, this tale of Medieval Japan has a young heroine, Tokoyo, trained by her samurai father in the warrior's duties as well as those of a lady. She is also schooled by the women divers who harvest shellfish. When her father is arrested and exiled by order of a ruler with a disturbed mind, Tokoyo sets out on a difficult journey to join him in exile, becoming his rescuer after battling a sea serpent. This visual costume drama emphasizes the large gestures associated with Japanese theatrical performances, moody in its exploitation of colors, like the yellow greens of a forest or the purple reds of a moonlit seascape. Pastel paintings of costumes, boats, and bits of architecture suggest Japan of long ago. The visual sequence frequently juxtaposes pages full of text with pages of illustrations of only a part of the narrative, making this a borderline picturebook. Notes detail the time setting and the primary sources.

San Souci, Robert D. *The Silver Charm: A Folktale from Japan*. Illustrated by Yoriko Ito. New York: Doubleday/Random, 2002. 32pp. Grades K–3.

Young Satsu's parents have warned him not to go near the woods where there is a wicked ogre and also not to lose the family's good-luck charm, a tiny silver ship. But one day he gets too close to the woods and is snatched by the ogre. Satsu offers the ogre his charm so he will not be eaten; then he falls ill. Guarded by his friend the fox, Satsu lies on the beach until his puppy friend brings his parents. But since he has lost the charm, they all despair. With the help of a mouse, however, his friends bring it back and all ends well. Ito's watercolors create double-page scenes that define the coastal landscape and the animal and human characters with animated sensitivity, while at the same time enveloping the scenes in mists that enhance the magic in the telling. The young dog and fox are particularly expressive, while the ogre is effectively frightening. The tale is from the Ainu culture, but only the clothing specifically suggests Japan.

Sierra, Judy. *Tasty Baby Belly Buttons*. Illustrated by Meilo So. New York: Alfred A. Knopf, 1999. 32pp. Also paper. Grades K–4

The villains of this traditional tale are the *oni*, large, ugly monsters who live on an island, but travel around kidnapping children for "their favorite treat—belly buttons." A baby girl is found in a melon by a childless couple. Uriko, as she is called, is grown enough at five to study sword fighting as well as cooking. When the *oni* come to her village and steal the little babies, furious Uriko determines to rescue them. Soon a dog, a pheasant, and a monkey join her. At the *oni's* castle, the challengers defeat the *oni* and bring the babies and some treasure back to the village. The light-hearted tone and the use of repetitious Japanese story-telling words make the violence in the story have no sting. So's equally light-hearted watercolors convey much of the qualities found in some Japanese scrolls. There's a looseness to the depictions created without outlines and with a respect for the white of the page, along with a sense of everything in motion. The author adds a note on other versions of the tale.

Snyder, Dianne. *The Boy of the Three-Year Nap*. Illustrated by Allen Say. Boston: Houghton Mifflin, 1988. 32pp. Grades 1–5.

In this traditional folk tale from the author's childhood, a lazy but clever boy named Taro is the despair of his poor, hard-working mother. Disguised as the *ujigami*, or village god, he tricks a wealthy merchant into giving him his daughter in marriage but is in turn tricked by his mother. There is a crispness of the black outlines, an evenness of the watercolors that neatly flood them, that recall the work of 19th-century Japanese woodcut masters. Many details of costume and architecture are from that period. The contemporary approach to facial and body gestures, however, helps create the comic adventures. The scenes are framed in thick black borders; the text appears in the white spaces below. This formal setting, however, doesn't detract from the lively flow of the humorous visual narrative.

Spivak, Dawnine. *Grass Sandals: The Travels of Basho.* Illustrated by Demi. New York: Atheneum/Simon & Schuster, 1997. 40pp. Grades 4–8.

This is three books in one: the story of the 17th-century Japanese poet Basho's travels around his country; a key to some Japanese written characters, beautifully brushed; and Basho's spare, evocative haiku relating to each part of his journey. The steps of his wandering are described in simple language, with details such as the food people give him, the creatures and folks he encounters, even the pillow he sleeps on. A map shows us where he traveled, with notes on what he saw in each place. The quiet simplicity of the story and poetry evokes the spirit of the poet and his time. The delicate illustrations on rice paper provide an appropriate visual setting. Fine lines create characters and landscape, white subtly applied colors are naturalistic but also evoke emotions only hinted at in text and poems.

Wisniewski, David. *The Warrior and the Wise Man.* New York: Lothrop/HarperCollins, 1989. 32pp. Also paper. Grades 2–6.

This original story set in long-ago Japan has a familiar theme: a father sets twin sons a task to prove who should succeed him as emperor. Tozaemon is a brave, fierce warrior, while Toemon is clever but gentle. The test is to bring back the five eternal elements from the demons who guard them. As Tozaemon steals the Earth That Is Ever Bountiful, the Water That Constantly Quenches, the Fire That Burns Forever, the Wind That Always Blows, and the Cloud That Eternally Covers, Toemon follows after him, helping to repair the damage his brother has caused in the thefts. When he finally saves the castle, Toemon's wisdom is acknowledged by his father, who appoints him emperor. The story is told simply but with a lengthy text. The intricacy of cut, solid-color papers that overlap conveys some of the potent visual force found in the scroll paintings of the samurai warriors. Costumes, weapons, decorations are all drawn from 12th-century Japan. Black silhouettes are especially effective in creating scenes that integrate these artifacts and the personified forces of nature. Although the cut-paper medium is not associated with Japanese art, the thoughtful use of traditional symbols caries a flavor of

Japan. The extensive Author's Note describes, along with his artistic technique, the time period, the society, the religion, and the arts upon which he has drawn, plus the instances when he has used artistic license.

JAPAN TODAY AND IN RECENT HISTORY

Akio, Terumasa. *Me and Alves: A Japanese Journey.* Illustrated by Yukio Oido. Translated by Susan Matsui. North York, Ontario: Annick, 1993. 32pp. paper. Grades K–4.

A young boy living on a farm on Japan's north island of Hokkaido tells in simple language how a visitor from Brazil comes to stay with his family, despite his grandfather's objections. Alves pitches right in helping with the farm work, makes Grandpa happy by listening to his stories, wins the Sumo wrestling tournament at the village festival, talks to the students at school with the other foreign visitors, and is sadly missed when he has to leave. The young narrator is inspired to hope he can visit Alves some day and also make friends in many countries. The story is based on an actual program to help acquaint the very insular Japanese with outsiders. The author's note explains the program. Beginning with etchings that produce black lines of infinite variety, the artist uses mostly transparent paints to infuse the illustrations with emotional content to enhance the narrative flow. The technique allows for details of everyday objects and events as well as realistic portraits of the characters. The illustrations occupy two-thirds of each double-page spread, with the few lines of text on a cream-colored background. Words and pictures unite to create the sense of real people and emotions in a part of Japan.

Brenner, Barbara, and Julia Takaya. *Chibi: A True Story from Japan.* Illustrated by June Otani. New York: Clarion, 1996. 64pp. Also paper. Grades 1–4.

This lengthy but simply told true story of a duck raising a family in the middle of a busy city is reminiscent of Robert McCloskey's classic *Make Way for Ducklings.* When a wild duck nests in an office park in Tokyo and hatches ten ducklings, the crowds gather, and TV news broadcasts "Duck Watch." Photographer Sato-San names the smallest duckling Chibi. Sato-San is there the day when the duck family crosses a busy street to take up residence in the Imperial Gardens. After a big storm and flood, Chibi and two other ducklings are missing, but Chibi and one other are found. The emperor then builds a duck house to which the family returns each year. Many scenes of people in Tokyo today, plus Japanese words with translation and pronunciation included, give flavor to the engrossing story. Otani's detailed ink and watercolor pictures of varying sizes create character as people, ducks, and the settings fill the pages. Although most illustrations are conservative and informative, storm scenes are both inventive and esthetically provocative.

Carle, Eric, and Kazuo Iwamura. *Where Are You Going? To See My Friend!* New York: Orchard/Scholastic, 2001. 32pp. Grades PreS–3.

The very simple cumulative story of friendship is told from front to back in English and from back to front in Japanese. In the English version, a dog is joined by a series of other animals on his way to meet his young boy friend. The Japanese tale has a dog finally meeting a young girl. A double fold-out has them all singing a song together when they meet in the middle. Carle's rough and ready collages contrast with Iwamura's more constrained watercolor drawings, although both produce clearly happy pictures. The Japanese words are set vertically with the English pronunciation next to each character. Picture symbols of each animal are placed alongside the letters to inform us of who is speaking. A description of how the book came to be is inside the jacket.

Hidaka, Masako. *Girl from the Snow Country.* Translated by Amanda Mayer Stinchecum. La Jolla, CA: Kane/Miller, 1986. 32pp. Grades K–3.

Mi-chan lives in the part of northern Japan where the snow piles up in the cold winters. The small girl uses the pointed leaves of the camellia to make ears for the clumps of snow that look like bunnies to her. Bundled against the cold, she walks to market with her mother, stopping to brush the snow from the statue of Jizo, the protector of children. Perhaps he helps her find the perfect berries to make eyes for the snow bunnies she has made. The end-papers set the stage depicting in thin gray watercolor a waterwheel in a mountainous landscape buried in snow. Color is used mainly for clothing, heavy wrappings that expose only faces. The few details like the toys and flowers in the market are used as much for visual attractiveness as for information. And the snow keeps falling.

Iijima, Geneva Cobb. *The Way We Do It in Japan.* Illustrated by Paige Billin-Frye. Morton Grove, IL: Albert Whitman, 2002. 32pp.

When young Gregory's father's company sends him to Japan, Gregory and his mother go as well. Gregory explores his new life there, learning many things that are different, with the title a repeated refrain. From the money system and where they sleep to school and lunch, he discovers much to enjoy. Japanese words and their pronunciation are salted throughout, with more serious factual information in notes following the story. Cartoon-like watercolor, gouache, acrylic and colored pencil illustrations describe contexts and the details necessary for the text. These are clearly produced to provide useful information. In the main, Gregory finds that clothes, furniture, school rooms, etc. are not that different from home and that fish and rice make a fine lunch, even with chopsticks.

Little, Mimi Otey. *Yoshiko and the Foreigner.* New York: Farrar, Straus, 1996. 34pp. Grades 2–4.

In this true story of how her parents met and married, Otey introduces us to the life of a young woman in Japan at the time when American soldiers occupied the country. The woman, Yoshiko, cannot tell her family that she is meeting with a foreigner. When the soldier returns home to America and writes to ask her to marry him, her family is shocked. She finally wins her father's consent. The last illustration is a photograph of the 1960 wedding. Large, double-page watercolors are filled with the story's lively characters in appropriate dress and in settings typical of daily life at the time.

Mannis, Celeste Davidson. *One Leaf Rides the Wind: Counting in a Japanese Garden.* Illustrated by Susan Kathleen Hartung. New York: Viking/Penguin, 2002. 26pp. Grades PreS–3.

This counting book from one to ten introduces a haiku for each number as it describes the pleasures of a garden seen by a young, kimono-clad girl. Notes on each page add information on the subject pictured, including some Japanese words. Full-page paintings created with oil paint glazes on sealed paper show a young Japanese girl interacting with lotus blossoms, pagoda roofs, stone lanterns, etc. Page layouts vary for added visual appeal.

Nomura, Takaaki. *Grandpa's Town.* Translated by Amanda Mayer Stinchecum. La Jolla, CA: Kane/Miller, 1991. 32pp. Text in Japanese and English. Grades K–4.

A young boy who has worried about his grandfather's loneliness spends time with him, stopping at the fish store and the greengrocer's on their way to the public baths. There they meet the grandfather's friends. The boy realizes why his grandfather wants to keep his life in the town instead of moving to live with his family. The life of the town is depicted in detailed woodcuts reminiscent of the traditional Japanese art. Diluted watercolors define the variety of produce at the grocer's and the naked bodies of the men in the steam bath. Both the English and Japanese text fit comfortably on pages facing the boldly expressive illustrations. Note that at least one librarian was affronted by the small "squiggle" of frontal nudity in the baths (*School Library Journal*, April 1993, p. 86) that is part of the realism.

Ray, Deborah Kogan. *Hokusai: The Man Who Painted a Mountain*. New York: Frances Foster/Farrar, Straus, 2001. 34pp. Grades 1–4.

In lively, appealing prose, Ray offers the life story of this famous artist, along with a wealth of information on life at the time, on the art world, and on the techniques he used. Some Japanese characters are included. The watercolor and colored pencil illustrations depict scenes from the artist's life through the eyes of an American. Like the text, they offer considerable information in lively, crowded scenes. A reproduction of "The Great Wave" woodcut and end-papers from the artist's sketchbooks add important insights into Hokusai's masterful skills. A chronology of his life is included.

Say, Allen. *The Bicycle Man*. Boston: Houghton Mifflin, 1982; paper 1989. 40pp. Grades 1–4.

A young boy remembers with affection his life in school in southern Japan after World War II, in particular one sports day when two American soldiers arrived. One did fantastic tricks on a bicycle and won the prize. The illustrations, in black outline and watercolor washes, depict the people and the life he recalls from time past, which may have been colored by the passing years.

Takabayashi, Mari. *I Live in Tokyo*. Boston: Houghton Mifflin, 2001. 32pp. Grades PreS–2.

A seven-year-old girl describes her life in the busy city, month by month through the year. Each double-page spread is filled with family activities for that month and salted with Japanese words and phrases. There is a New Year celebration in January, a traditional spring welcome along with Valentine's Day in February, and so on until Christmas and New Year's Eve in December. They have their own traditional "Christmas" although they don't celebrate it as we do. Time in school and the tea ceremony are included subjects, along with helpful word lists. The watercolor illustrations are convenient for browsing, for getting an overview of living as well as the details of "ten favorite meals" or the ten steps in putting on a kimono. The illustrations provide considerable information by painting the objects in easy-to-access page layout.

Takeshita, Fumiko. *The Park Bench*. Illustrated by Mamoru Suzuki. Translated by Ruth A. Kanagy. La Jolla, CA: Kane/Miller, 1988. 32pp. Text in Japanese and English. Grades K–3.

The bench in the park could be anywhere, but the people are Japanese and the scenes are from Japan in 1988. The story follows the bench from morning to night, showing all the people, young and old, who pass it or sit on it or maintain it. The tale is printed in small type. The Western look of modern Japan is represented here. Vignettes, double-page spreads, even a couple of pages of comic-strip sequences are rendered in realistic line drawings and dilute watercolors. The changing colors from dawn to night make a circle that encloses a lively collection of minidramas.

JAPANESE AMERICANS AND THE IMMIGRANT EXPERIENCE

Bunting, Eve. *So Far from the Sea*. Illustrated by Chris K. Soentpiet. New York: Clarion/Houghton, 1998. 32pp. Grades 1–4.

A young girl describes the journey her Japanese American family takes back to the site of the Manzanar War Relocation Center, where her father and his family were interned during World War II. It is their last visit, for they are moving far away to the East Coast. Her father tells again for her younger brother the story of why they were there and what it was like. Their mother tells about the camp she was kept in, where it was even colder than Manzanar. The atmosphere is icy and almost ghostly as they bring flowers for her grandfather's grave. He missed the sea out in the desert, for he was a fisherman and found life in the camp without dignity. Laura has brought a symbol to place on the grave as they try to move on in their lives without bitterness. The historic scenes are created with black watercolors, while the contemporary parts of the story are depicted in color. All the illustrations are double page and detailed, almost photographic. We are moved by the depictions of desolation, the regimentation of the displacement, and the sadness of the modern family's farewell. The sense of unfairness expressed by the narrator is effectively communicated. Notes fill in details of the history.

Falwell, Cathryn. *Butterflies for Kiri*. New York: Lee & Low, 2003. 32pp. Grades 1–3.

For her birthday, Kiri's Auntie Lu sends the art-loving girl a box of origami paper and an instruction booklet. But she finds it discouragingly difficult not to ruin the beautiful papers as she tries in vain to follow the directions. One lovely day she goes home to try to paint the sky, grass, and flowers she has experienced. Disappointed with her effort, she finds she can cut the origami papers to make a satisfying collage and can top it with an origami butterfly at last. Here is an introduction and encouragement for both aspiring artist and origami makers. The pictures of Kiri's adventures with picture-making combine cut papers and paint in ways to clearly show us what she is about. The early frustrations with origami will be familiar to many readers. The fifteen-step instructions on the last page will work out best if some knowledgeable adult supervises. Youngsters will learn that patience seems to be necessary for origami mastery.

Kroll, Virginia. *Pink Paper Swans.* Illustrated by Nancy L. Clouse. Grand Rapids, MI: Eerdmans, 1994. 32pp. Grades 1–4.

Janetta's mother has warned her not to "be botherin' folks," but she is fascinated by old Mrs. Tsujimoto, who makes things from paper with no glue or tape. When given a folded frog, Janetta tries to unfold and refold it, but can't. All summer she watches, until she finally asks how it is done. Mrs. Tsujimoto explains that it is origami and that she sells her creations at gift shops. Janetta thinks about it all through the school year as she treasures the folded pink swan Mrs. Tsujimoto has given her. By the summertime, when Mrs. Tsujimoto isn't folding outside, Janetta goes to find out why. The older woman tells her that arthritis makes it impossible for her to do origami any more. Janetta asks her to teach her how. It is very difficult, but together they manage to make enough to sell. Then Janetta is ready to learn bonsai. The non-detailed, flat paint and cut paper illustrations seem appropriate for the theme of origami. Page designs vary, but most include some origami examples. A concluding twelve-step set of instructions demonstrate how to make a swan. Again some adult help will probably be needed.

Mochizuki, Ken. *Baseball Saved Us.* Illustrated by Dom Lee. New York: Lee & Low, 1993. 32pp. Grades 2–6.

After a note on the U.S. government's internment of all people of Japanese descent in camps in 1942, the author takes us to a desert camp with a young boy who tells his story. In the boredom of the camp, baseball gives his life some focus; he even helps win a game. When the war is over and the family returns home, the boy is shunned and called names when he tries to play on the school team. But through baseball he finally gains acceptance. The story is a satisfying one, told with much information about both the history and the character of the people. The artist tells this story of prejudice and oppression without melodramatic clichés. The mixed media produce a light source that permeates all scenes, a light drenched with the many browns of the "endless desert" of the internment camps. Blue appears in the sky only in the final hopeful scenes. People in groups and close-ups are the focus of these illustrations, which have a modified photographic look, in mostly full-page but occasional smaller pictures.

Mochizuki, Ken. *Heroes.* Illustrated by Dom Lee. New York: Lee & Low, 1995. 32pp. Also paper. Grades 2–6.

Donnie, a Japanese American, is tired of playing war games in which he is always the enemy, even though his father and uncle fought with the U.S. Army in World War II. His father and uncle don't want to talk about it with him, and his friends don't believe him. One day his friends chase him, "shooting" all the way to his father's gas station, teasing him. He begs his father to prove them wrong. The next day his father and uncle, wearing their army medals, meet the boys outside school. Donnie is chased no more. Lee's full-page paintings done in a form of encaustic illustrate the action mostly in tones of browns and greens, suggesting the darker emotions of prejudice. The characters are drawn like portraits, with Donnie being particularly appealing.

Noguchi, Rick, and Deneen Jenks. *Flowers from Mariko.* Illustrated by Michelle Reiko Kumata. New York: Lee & Low, 2001. 32pp. Grades 2–4.

Mariko's family's story begins when they are finally allowed to leave the internment camp where they were confined with other Japanese Americans during World War II. Her father, who had to leave a gardening business behind, is looking forward to returning to it. But his truck and his land have been sold. The family must stay in a depressing trailer park while her father unsuccessfully looks for work. Mariko hopefully plants some seeds. When the flowers bloom, they augur better times ahead for them all. The illustrations, first rendered in ink and gouache to create black and white drawings, then scanned into a computer, with colored fabric and textured papers also scanned for patterns, have a flat, bleak look. The images show the sterile living conditions, while the color of the flowered patterns offer symbols of hope. A note fills in the history of the Japanese American internment.

Say, Allen. *Grandfather's Journey.* Boston: Houghton Mifflin, 1993. 32pp. Grades 1–5.

Say tells, in simple, brief sentences, the story of his grandfather's trip "to see the world" when he was a young man. He explored America's deserts, prairies, cities, rivers, and mountains, meeting people along the way. He married his childhood sweetheart in Japan and brought her back to live in San Francisco, his favorite American place. Later he is drawn back to Japan, and although he remembers California fondly, the Second World War makes return impossible. Say tells of his own birth and subsequent trip to see the California his grandfather had so fondly described. Succinctly here he summarizes the complex emotions of an immigrant torn between the old country and the new. Each illustrated page has a thinly framed picture and caption-like text below. The illustrations are portraits and landscapes. The watercolors are exploited to emphasize their transparencies, allowing the white paper to unify the shapes to make it seem as if all is seen through memory. Frozen poses seem like a collection of photographs lovingly reproduced. The painting of Say's mother as a child holding a blonde-haired doll is perhaps most symbolic of the two cultures.

Say, Allen. *Home of the Brave.* Boston: Houghton Mifflin, 2002. 32pp. Grades 2–6.
A man has a kayak accident that brings him, perhaps in his imagination or a dream, to the desert, where he meets two children with whom he goes to a World War II Japanese internment camp. It seems empty, but there he finds his name, the same as his mother's father, on a tag. Outside are many children, with name tags, who soon disappear. Another tag has his mother's name. The strange, mystical experience continues when he awakes amid a group of children. Pieces of paper and name tags are scattered by a gust of wind, then turn into birds, who can finally go "home." The mystery of this allegory is made no clearer in the sequence of full-page paintings, each of which faces a page of text. Gray-greens dominate the barren landscapes and even tint the sky. The scene showing the long line of empty wooden barracks in the camp is particularly depressing. Say invites us to create our own meaning from his tantalizing script, although Japanese Americans may well find a special one. He notes that it was at an exhibition about the camps that the facts became human beings to him.

Say, Allen. *Tea with Milk.* Boston: Houghton Mifflin, 1999. 32pp. Grades 1–4.
This story of being caught between cultures is based on the experiences of the author's mother. Brought up near San Francisco, she is used to speaking both English and Japanese and drinking both green tea and tea with milk and sugar. But when she finishes high school, her parents take her back to Japan with them. She is unhappy and uncomfortable there. She has to return to high school "to learn her own language" and take lessons to be "a

proper Japanese lady." They even hire a matchmaker for her. She leaves home for Osaka and becomes a guide for foreign businessmen. This is how she fortunately meets the like-minded man who becomes the author's father. Say's almost photographic full-page watercolors produce the narrative sequence that shows us the evolution of the mother's bicultural life. We see her resistance to the rules of Japanese society, her determination to follow her own desires, and her eventual pairing with a man with a similar history. Details such as her clothing, the tea ceremony, an Osaka department store, and street scenes are effective parts of the visual narrative.

Terasaki, Stanley Todd. *Ghosts for Breakfast.* Illustrated by Shelly Shinjo. New York: Lee & Low, 2002. 32pp. Grades 1–4.

The author takes us to a Japanese American farming community in the 1920s where her father grew up for this tale of strange happenings in a farmer's field. His apprehensive son accompanies the father through the foggy night to investigate the report of ghosts in the field. The ghostly white shapes are only white radishes hung to dry. A good laugh is followed by crunchy *daikon* pickles for breakfast in this slice of life in an immigrant community. Shinjo's double-page acrylic painted scenes are designed for chuckles. Stylized swirls of colors emphasize the spooky superstitions of the farmers, while the use of shades of blue enhance the emotional responses. The simplified depictions of the characters barely hint at their ancestry.

Trottier, Maxine. *Flags.* Illustrated by Paul Morin. Toronto: Stoddart, 1999. 32pp. Grades K–4.

A young girl recalls a visit to her grandmother's house by the Pacific after the U.S. entered World War II. Next door lives Mr. Hiroshi, who has a different, wonderful garden, without flower beds but with gravel and stepping stones and a fish pond in the center. Mary's grandmother is concerned about Mr. Hiroshi because of the relocation of Japanese; he is indeed taken away. Mary tells him that she will care for his garden and the fish, but when his house is sold, all she and her grandmother can do is set the fish free. Mary also saves two iris bulbs and a stone. Back home on the prairie, Mary plants the bulbs and sets the stone nearby. She remembers Mr. Hiroshi's words, "a garden must begin somewhere." The author's note adds facts about the Japanese relocation, adding the hope that such a thing can never happen again. There is a grainy quality to the double-page scenes, but the images of people and places are created with a clarity of personality, mostly in intimate close-ups. Both sadness and hopefulness are embodied in the visual sequences.

Uegaki, Chieri. *Suki's Kimono*. Illustrated by Stéphane Jorisch. Tonawanda, NY: Kids Can, 2003. 32pp. Grades K–3.

Suki's decision to wear her kimono on the first day of school is frowned on by her sisters. But she loves it; it reminds her of the happy day at a festival when her grandmother bought it for her. At first the other children don't accept her choice. But Suki manages to convey the excitement of the festival and imitate the dance she saw there, a touch of Japanese culture finally appreciated by all. Lightly crafted watercolor drawings, set mostly against the white page, depict a charming Suki involved with the paper kites of the street festival and later with her young classmates. The animated sequence of her dance is particularly endearing. The kimono represents a lingering tradition in a changing world. The few Japanese words included are explained with a pronunciation guide.

Wells, Rosemary. *Yoko's Paper Cranes*. New York: Hyperion, 2001. 32pp. Grades PreS–2.

Yoko, the appealing Japanese American heroine of *Yoko*, misses the grandmother and grandfather she had to leave when she came to America. For her *Obaasan's* birthday, Yoko has no money for a present. Knowing that her grandmother missed the cranes from her garden in the winter, Yoko makes origami paper cranes the way her grandfather taught her and sends them across the sea to cheer her grandmother. Wells incorporates a variety of Japanese-style decorated papers in her collages, with added gold paint. They create an impression of the exotic. A few icons like the snow-covered mountain peaks and gardens, an echo of Hokusai's Great Wave, a dozen or more origami animals, decorated borders and background pages all add to Yoko's sense of her grandparents' home. A map shows the distance that the love has to travel.

CHINA AND CHINESE AMERICANS

ORIGINAL TALES AND FOLKTALES EVOKING THE PAST

Andersen, Hans Christian. *The Nightingale*. Illustrated by Lisbeth Zwerger. Translated from the Danish by Anthea Bell. New York: Picture Book/ North-South, 1984. 24pp. Paper. Grades 2–5.

The classic tale of the power of the real nightingale over that of the bejeweled artificial bird is a lengthy one but retold often enough to have become legendary in Western culture, although it is set in ancient China.

Zwerger's subtle approach in understated watercolors suits the restrained sensibilities, using a lot of empty space with a hint of gray or tan. The costumes, architecture, and furniture drawn in fine lines are period Chinese; the people are convincing in their actions and facial expressions.

Armstrong, Jennifer. *Chin Yu Min and the Ginger Cat.* Illustrated by Mary Grandpré. New York: Crown, 1993. 32pp. Also paper. Grades 1–4.

Set "many years ago in a village near Kunming," this original story rich in description is concerned with the haughty wife of a prosperous man and how she finds what is really important in life. When her husband dies, Chin Yu Min wants no help from anyone, until her money is all spent and her possessions are sold. A cat comes to her rescue, catching fish for her to eat and sell, bringing back a good life. When the cat is suddenly gone, Chin Yu Min first just misses his help but then realizes that it is the cat himself that matters. The search for him humbles her; she appreciates both the cat and her helpful neighbors. Each village scene is a stage set with light sources creating shadows that accentuate the unfolding drama. The human characters tend toward caricature; Chin Yu Min's long fingers almost have a life of their own as they shoo off neighbors or hold a teacup or stroke the cat. Her face seems carved from wood like some Oriental theatrical mask. There are many touches of China in utensils, coins, and parts of buildings. Full-page illustrations face white pages of text, often with story-enhancing vignettes.

Bouchard, David. *Buddha in the Garden.* Illustrated by Zhong-Yang Huang. Vancouver, British Columbia: Raincoast, 2001. 32pp. Grades 1–5.

The original story is set in a Buddhist monastery that could be anywhere, at any time. It draws on the four Buddhist signs of enlightenment: hunger, illness, death, and the search for enlightenment. While the monks seek enlightenment everywhere, the young boy who was left abandoned in the monastery as a baby works in the garden. One day he hears an old blind monk tell him, "Buddha is in the garden." Two more times he is told this. Each time he goes to the garden he finds no Buddha but something related to the signs. As promised by the monk, after his actions in the three trials, he finds enlightenment, in this mystic example of the Buddhist faith. There is a gentle spirituality to the large watercolor scenes that set the tale in an architecture and landscape conducive to contemplation. The characters are appropriately clothed and are presented in postures and gestures that convey the emotional content. At the end of the book, the illustrator writes about his own experiences in the monastery used as a model.

Casanova, Mary, reteller. *The Hunter: A Chinese Folktale.* Illustrated by Ed Young. New York: Atheneum/Simon & Schuster, 2001. 32pp. Grades K–3.

Out hunting one day, Hai Li Bu saves a snake's life. She turns out to be the Daughter of the Dragon King of the Sea, who offers him his choice of reward. He wishes to understand animals so that he can be a better hunter in time of drought. But he must never reveal his secret, or he will turn to stone. So when the animals warn him of a terrible flood, the only way he can convince the villagers to save themselves is to tell them his secret and die. They later raise his stone body on the mountain as a reminder to listen to what everyone says. Young uses dark brown pastel and gouache to create brushed drawings on toned backgrounds, images that are charged with energy. Touches of chalky color produce sweeping tones of sky and landscape, drawing us into the exotic story. Some Chinese characters are included.

Chang, Margaret, and Raymond Chang. *Da Wei's Treasure: A Chinese Tale.* Illustrated by Lori McElrath-Eslick. New York: Margaret K. McElderry/Simon & Schuster, 1999. 32pp. Grades 2–4.

When Da Wei's father dies, the only thing he has to leave him is a rock that looks like a mountain. One day, he is told, a light will shine there to lead to treasure. And indeed, one night it does, and a cart rolls out of it. The next day it waits for him in the garden. When Da Wei decides to use it to visit the old fisherman who gave the rock to his father, the cart rolls into the sea, making a path for him to follow. After a strange experience in the sea, he returns home with a kitten that seems to have strange powers. She turns out to have been an enchanted woman named Lian Di, who consents to marry him. Her fine embroidery earns them enough money to make the jealous Magistrate arrest him. But Lian Di's magic saves him for the happy ending. The expressionistically oil painted full-page scenes are a bit fuzzy but just detailed enough as to furniture and costume to set the story in some once-upon-a-time place in China. The visual narrative offers a sequence of scenes that make the tale easy to follow. The sources of the story are noted.

Chen, Kerstin. *Lord of the Cranes: A Chinese Tale.* Illustrated by Jian Jiang Chen. Translated by J. Alison James. New York: Michael Neugebauer/North-South, 2000. 30pp. Also paper. Grades 1–4.

A wise old man, friend of the cranes, decides to come down from his mountain to see whether people in the city remember to be kind and generous. Having exchanged clothes with a beggar, he finds that no one will even notice him. But at a small inn, the owner welcomes him and feeds him every day. Old Tian, to repay the kind man, paints a magical picture of three cranes on the inn wall. They dance when Tian sings and claps. The inn becomes popular and the owner prospers, but always helps those in need. When the old man returns and flies away with the cranes, he is recognized as the Lord of the Cranes. Large paintings retain a magical romantic reality as they emphasize atmosphere rather than define characters and settings with specific details. But there is enough representation of objects, clothing, and architecture to identify this as "China" and sufficient lyrical brush strokes for us to find spiritual enjoyment in the dancing cranes. Chinese characters appear on the end-papers, but no source is given for the story, which contains elements of other tales of cranes.

Compestine, Ying Chang. *The Story of Chopsticks* (2001); *The Story of Kites* (2003); *The Story of Noodles* (2002); *The Story of Paper* (2003). All illustrated by Yongsheng Xuan. New York: Holiday House. 32pp. Grades K–3.

Each of these stories is fictionalized history. The three mischievous Kang brothers "invent" the subjects of each of the books to solve a problem in a humorous way. Each tale offers added actual information on the inventions; then ends with factual historical background notes, along with instructions for creating one of the items. Xuan's use of a traditional Chinese cut paper method of illustration adds strong visual appeal to double-page scenes with considerable amount of text. Thick black outlines filled with solid colors produce static images. A decorative series of scenes describes the actions in a light-hearted, attractive fashion. The costumes, architecture, and household objects refer to their Chinese origins.

Conrad, Pam. *Blue Willow.* Illustrated by S. Saelig Gallagher. New York: Philomel, 1999. 32pp. Grades 2–5.

This lengthy, dramatically told love story of long-ago China is loosely based on the legends that arose following the creation of the well-known Blue Willow plates in 18th-century England, inspired by Chinese culture. The daughter of a rich man falls in love with a poor fisherman. Her father refuses to let her marry him, setting one condition after another. After their tragic deaths, the father has a plate made so the story will "never be forgotten" and parents will listen to what is in their children's hearts. The full-page acrylic, pastel, and mixed media illustrations are like stage sets for a theatrical performance complete with props, scenery, and costumed actors. A few vignettes are used to bridge the action between scenes. They may be as authentically "Chinese" as the plates. The appealingly realistic visual narrative brings us into the exotic environment as we experience the varied emotions, while Chinese calligraphy adds a note of authenticity.

Davol, Marguerite W. *The Paper Dragon*. Illustrated by Robert Sabuda. New York: Atheneum/Simon & Schuster, 1997. 32pp., including 12 fold-outs. Grades K–4.

This original folktale has a Chinese background, with the Chinese characters for courage, loyalty, love, and sincerity on each text page. Mi Fei, a humble artist, must confront the frightful dragon Sui Jen and persuade it to go back to sleep. The dragon says it will continue destroying the countryside until someone performs three tasks. Clever Mi Fei figures out how, using his scroll paintings, to bring the dragon fire wrapped in paper, wind captured in paper, and finally the strongest thing in the world caught in paper. This, the dragon agrees, is the love in Mi Fei's painting of his village, so he disappears. Sabuda's use of cut precolored art tissue papers reflects a traditional Chinese art form. He chooses to tell the visual tale in a series of fold-out pages. The text's simple actions are illuminated effectively with suitable emotions of anxiety and fear. Of course, the appearances of the gloriously frightening dragon with orange eyes and long, scaly, sinuous green tail are the most impressive. The dragon's demands create mounting tension and ultimately a peaceful resolution.

Demi. *The Dragon's Tale and Other Fables of the Chinese Zodiac*. New York: Henry Holt, 1996. 26pp. Grades 1–4.

Demi retells a traditional tale about each of the twelve animals of the zodiac. The text is framed by a wide circular border of varying colors filled with appropriate symbols. The facing pages also use a circle, often broken, with deliciously delicate and softly humorous animal pictures. Her description of her paints and brushes used is not to be missed. For example, "A brush of one mouse whisker was used for extremely delicate work."

Demi. *The Emperor's New Clothes: A Tale Set in China*. New York: Margaret K. McElderry/Simon & Schuster, 2000. 28pp. 5 fold-outs. Grades 1–4.

Demi's lively retelling of the Andersen fairy tale is an excuse for a riotous display of costumes, some scenery, and other decorations, including a set of traditional symbols and their meanings. This all surrounds the story of the vain, proud king through the seasons of the year as the bogus tailor and weaver promise "clothes . . . so magical only clever people can see them." Demi's unique style of tiny colored paint and ink drawings fills the pages with dozens of active figures busy at symbolic tasks as well as with the larger characters richly costumed and acting out their roles. Even the birds and animals are naturalistically depicted in this appealing version of the classic. A lengthy Author's Note offers an analysis of the painters of early China, of the use of color and symbols, and of her aim "to capture the magic that is China by including elements of Chinese culture in each picture. . . ."

Granfield, Linda, reteller. *The Legend of the Panda.* Illustrated by Song Nan Zhang. Toronto: Tundra/McClelland & Stewart, 1998. 24pp. Grades K–4.

Deep in the Sichuan mountains, a young shepherdess named Dolma tends her sheep and gathers flowers and medicinal herbs. A young white cub or *Beishung* joins the flock to play. One day a snow leopard attacks the cub. When Dolma defends it, she is killed. All the people of the valley turn out to mourn her. The *Beishung* smear themselves with ashes and wipe their weeping eyes in sympathy. The soot has stained them black there for the distinctive panda markings ever since. And where Dolma's four mourning sisters were received into the earth now rise the mountains where the giant pandas now live. The lush paintings that fill the double pages and bleed off the sides describe the pastoral environment and the lovely Dolma. The two scenes of horror when the leopard attacks are followed by further quiet forest scenes, enlivened by the pandas. No source for the legend is given, but many facts on pandas are included.

Hong, Lily Toy. *The Empress and the Silkworm.* Morton Grove, IL: Albert Whitman, 1995. 32pp. Grades 1–4.

According to legend, nearly 5,000 years ago a cocoon from a mulberry tree fell into Empress Si Ling-Chi's cup of tea. In this telling, the empress notices the strands of thread on the cocoon and has them spun into a cloth she has seen in her dreams. The result was silk, and the Chinese kept its making a secret for over 2,000 years. Details on the discovery and manufacture of silk are added on a final page. Airbrushed pigments and multicolored outlines create a decorative setting for the stylized compositions that suggest ancient China.

Kimmel, Eric A. *The Rooster's Antlers: A Story of the Chinese Zodiac.* Illustrated by Yongsheng Xuan. New York: Holiday House, 1999. 32pp. Grades K–3.

There are many tales of how the animals of the Chinese zodiac were selected. Here the action moves past the choice by the Jade Emperor to the once generous Rooster. He gives his beautiful antlers to Dragon at Centipede's request to help him win. But when Dragon is picked before him, he is sorry and wants them back. Dragon feels she still needs them, and refuses. Rooster is angry with Centipede for arranging the deal. Ever since, roosters have blamed centipedes for the lost antlers and gobbled them up. Blue pages house the powerful images that tell this mythic story. Heavy black outlined cut paper creates the animals and such landscapes as are needed to help give context to the story. Colors are added to inject personality, particularly to the multihued Rooster, the star of the show, and the flamboyant Dragon. There are added notes on the Chinese calendar, the source of the tale, the animals and what their meanings are.

Kimmel, Eric A. *Ten Suns: A Chinese Legend*. Illustrated by Yongsheng Xuan. New York: Holiday House, 1998. 32pp. Grades K–3.

Kimmel's version of the traditional tale makes for an interesting contrast with Lawson's *Too Many Sons* below. He begins in the jade palace of the eastern emperor Di Jun. His ten sons, who are the alternating suns in the sky at that time, tire of taking turns going alone across the sky and decide to go together. Of course the heat is terrible. The great emperor of the world demands that Di Jun stop his sons, but they won't listen to him. So he calls Hu Yi, the Archer of Heaven, to save the earth, although he must kill the sons to do it. One by one they are shot and turned into crows. Luckily the last arrow is taken away, so one son/sun is left to shine. Expressionistic paintings enliven the text, combining naturalistic representations of the major characters with symbolic pictures of clouds, suns, and parched earth. The visual narrative exudes strong emotion as we feel the tension of Hu Yi's bow and ride with the emperor's messenger to save the earth. Notes on the source are included.

Kraus, Robert, and Debby Chen. *The Making of the Monkey King: Adventures of Monkey King 1*. Illustrated by Wenhai Ma. Union City, CA: Pan Asian, 1999. 36pp. Grades 1–4.

This is only one part of the adventures of this traditional hero of Chinese literature from the 16th-century classic *Journey to the West*, which was inspired by the pilgrimage of a real seventh century Buddhist priest and his mythical monkey attendant. The stone monkey magically born from a rock becomes king by jumping through a waterfall and finding a safe cave for the monkeys to inhabit. Monkey King then sets out to find the secret of eternal life. He studies with a master to learn Immortal Secrets and the Seventy-Two Transformations. But he is such a show-off that the angry master sends him home. There he must defeat the Demon of Chaos and save his monkey friends.

These adventures are set in a landscape of mountains and trees like those often seen in Chinese paintings. Animated line drawings with watercolor washes describe the Monkey King in his many activities along with the other characters, with attention to the magic of the story, along with the added appeal of the anthropomorphic monkeys. A detailed history and background of possible sources of the epic are included.

Lawson, Julie, reteller. *The Dragon's Pearl*. Illustrated by Paul Morin. New York: Clarion/Houghton, 1993. 32pp. Grades 2–5.

In a time long ago a boy named Xiao Sheng works at cutting grass and selling it to support himself and his mother. During a terrible drought, he finds a strange patch of green grass that seems to grow back each day for him to cut. While digging up the grass to transplant it nearer his home, he finds a beautiful pearl. The transplanted grass dies, but the pearl brings rice to the rice jar and money to the money box. When robbers threaten, Xiao Sheng pops the pearl into his mouth and accidentally swallows it. Seized by a terrible thirst, he drinks the river dry and turns into a dragon. Clouds from his mouth finally bring rain. His mother cries and misses him, but the people honor him and tell his story. Although there is no source specified for this tale, the author's note gives a great deal of information about the significance of dragons in Chinese iconography and belief, their powers, their qualities, and their difference from dragons in European mythology. In the mixed-media illustrations, objects like coins and fabrics are integrated into a cement-like surface that exploits golds and browns with streaks of red. The pearl is found on the end-papers photographed on a similar mixed-media background. Inside, pages are bordered with a thick, decorated strip across the bottom and thin strips on the other sides of white pages, with the straightforward text usually set below the paintings. If the style does not, the landscapes, interiors, and clothing help define the place as long-ago China.

Lawson, Julie. *Too Many Suns*. Illustrated by Martin Springett. Toronto: Stoddart, 1996. 32pp. Grades 1–4.

The author has researched many versions of the traditional story of the Ten Suns. She begins her tale "[i]n a time when dragons were still young" and there are ten suns. In a farm family of ten brothers, the youngest is a sun lover. Instead of taking their usual turns, all ten suns decide to make him happy and shine together. The smallest of the ten tries to stop them, because the heat is causing drought and suffering, but they will not listen to him or to the Jade Emperor. So the emperor calls Yi the Immortal Archer to shoot them down. One by one they fall, until only the smallest remains. Youngest Brother reminds Yi that he must leave one, and so he does. Black lines are used to suggest woodcut illustrations, in full-page scenes and small bands at the bottom of facing text pages. Costumes, mountains, and dragon all relate to traditional Chinese paintings. A note discusses the many versions of Yi the Archer, such as that in Kimmel's *Ten Suns* above.

Louie, Ai-Ling. *Yeh-Shen: A Cinderella Story from China.* Illustrated by Ed Young. New York: Philomel/Penguin, 1982. 31pp. Also Puffin paper. Grades K–4.

This mistreated Cinderella has help from a fish. Young divides each page into two vertical panels with thin red borders, some housing the text while others try to contain the illustrations. Mixed media, mostly pastels, create the characters in proper period dress. There are no detailed scenes, rather there are swirls of color across boxes that on close inspection take on a fish shape.

Mahy, Margaret. *The Seven Chinese Brothers.* Illustrated by Jean and Mou-sien Tsien Tseng. New York: Scholastic, 1990. 40pp. Grades 1–5.

Mahy tells her brisk, humorous version of this traditional tale using a real person as a character: Emperor Ch'in Shih Huang, 259–210 B.C., who unified China, planned the Great Wall, and may have exploited the workers building it. His end in the story is fiction, however. Each of the brothers has a special power: super hearing, super seeing, extraordinary strength, bones of iron, legs that can grow and grow, the ability never to be too hot, and for the baby brother, the gift of weeping tears big enough to drown a village. Since all the brothers look alike, each time the emperor sentences one brother to death, the one who can survive that method of execution replaces him. A variety of layouts are employed for the naturalistic watercolor illustrations, including vignettes of some of the brothers preparing, full scenes of adventures, multiple panels showing action, parts of objects breaking the thin line borders to emphasize three dimensions, double-page spreads to capture the sweep of a powerful piece of magic. Ornate costumes of royalty, armed soldiers, banners, throne, even the Great Wall, all create the make-believe of ancient China in a dramatic but light-hearted way.

McCully, Emily Arnold. *Beautiful Warrior: The Legend of the Nun's Kung Fu.* New York: Scholastic, 1998. 40pp. Grades 1–5.

Jingyong, or "Quiet Courage," was not raised as a girl in long-ago China but studied as a boy, including the martial arts, in which she excelled. This exciting version of the story of this legendary character traces her life from her childhood to her becoming a Buddhist nun, renamed Wu Mei, or "Beautiful Warrior." Here she teaches the principles of meditation and kung fu to a young girl, enabling her to overcome a bully. In a note, the author further explains the history and styles of kung fu, adding that the characters may be historic or legendary. Historic Chinese settings incorporate village scenes with action episodes, visualizing aspects of kung fu in detailed watercolor, tempera and pastel illustrations. These are not delicately painted, but rather the paints have been applied with an energy that relates to the practice of kung fu.

Muth, Jon J., reteller and illustrator. *Stone Soup.* New York: Scholastic, 2003. 32pp. Grades 1–4.

This version of the traditional folk tale told in many cultures is set in a Chinese village. Here three monks, wandering in search of "what makes one happy" come to poor, hostile village. With the help of a young girl, they find the stones for the soup they are preparing. Gradually, people come to add to the pot, and from this sharing comes a celebration and knowledge villagers and monks, all in a Buddhist tradition. The ink and watercolor scenes combine a Western sense of representation and design with a more spiritual Asian sensibility. Part of this comes from the costumes and architecture as well as the subtle range of colors in this gentle visual telling with philosophical underpinning. The double-page banquet with blazing red lanterns and multiple smiling faces shows the result of the final magic. Notes fill in information on the Zen Buddhist background.

Poole, Amy Lowry. *How the Rooster Got His Crown.* New York: Holiday House, 1999. 32pp. Grades K–4.

In this retelling of a Miao folktale from Western China, the ten suns of other Chinese folktales are only six. One year no rains come and the crops are withering. Emperor Yao and his advisors have their best archers try to shoot the suns down, in vain. Then they send for a master archer, who realizes he can never reach the suns. Instead he shoots the reflections of five of them in a pond. The sixth sun is so frightened that he hides in a cave. Only the sound of a rooster can persuade him to return. The "red crown" the rooster wears was given to him by the appreciative sun. The double-page scenes employ abstract figures painted in ink and gouache set on textured rice papers to tell the visual story. There are next to no contextual details. But objects like arrowheads, clothing, the suns, are all decorated with mysterious designs to enhance this magical tale. There is nothing overtly Chinese in the imagery except for the symbols inside the six suns, which are explained in a note.

Rappaport, Doreen, reteller. *The Long-Haired Girl: A Chinese Legend.* Illustrated by Yang Ming-Yi. New York: Dial/Penguin, 1995. 32pp. Grades 1–4.

During a terrible drought, Ah-Mei discovers the secret spring of Lei-Gong, the God of Thunder, who threatens to kill her if she tells about it. Seeing the despair around her, she decides to sacrifice herself to save her village. Before the Thunder God puts her to slow death in a waterfall, he allows her to go home to say goodbye. An old man tells her to substitute a statue he has made of her, to which he adds her hair, turned white in the drought. She places the statue in the waterfall to fool the Thunder God. Ah-Mei's hair soon grows back, black as before, and the village has the waterfall in dry times. There are no notes of the source of the story. Woodcuts of varying sizes make the lively retelling even stronger. They depict the characters and settings with appropriate costumes.

Rumford, James. *The Cloudmakers.* Boston: Houghton Mifflin, 1996. 32pp. Grades 2–6.

The facts are stated at the end of this story: in 751 the Chinese lost a battle with the Arabs. Captured paper makers taught the Arabs the Chinese secret of making paper. On this information Rumford has built a moving story of Wu and his grandfather, taken prisoner by the Arabs during the battle. Wu tells his captors that his grandfather can "make clouds." They are given seven days to do so. Each day they take another step in papermaking, finally producing the "cloud" that the Sultan recognizes as paper. Teaching the method earns their freedom. Full-page watercolors, impressionistic but naturalistic, skillfully describe the action with necessary details, in colors and compositions that convey the wonder of the process along with the facts.

San Souci, Robert D. *Fa Mulan: The Story of a Woman Warrior.* Illustrated by Jean and Mou-Sien Tseng. New York: Hyperion, 1998. 32pp. Grades 1–4.

This is only one version of the story of the legendary woman warrior that was also a Disney full-length cartoon. When her old father is called to serve in the Khan's army, Mulan disguises herself as a man and takes his place. She fights bravely in many battles, rising in rank to be a general. Her clever tactics defeat the enemy. When the Khan asks her what reward she wishes, she asks only to return home to the life and the family she has missed. Her fellow-soldiers are amazed to see her dressed as a woman. Research has provided the images needed for the sequence of detailed, naturalistic acrylic paintings that create an exciting narrative. We witness the transformation of an energetic young woman into a brave warrior and eventual general, with appropriate battle scenes and royal ceremonies. The jacket's illustration of Mulan in full armor leading flag-carrying troops sets the stage, while the scroll pictured at the beginning and end symbolizes the tradition that the illustrators tell us inspired their design. Background notes are included.

Wang, Rosalind C., reteller. *The Treasure Chest: A Chinese Tale.* Illustrated by Will Hillenbrand. New York: Holiday House, 1995. 32pp. Grades 1–4.

Wang retells a story her parents told her, which she has not found in print elsewhere. Laifu, a poor fisherman, is engaged to Pearl, a beautiful orphan. The wicked ruler Funtong, wanting Pearl for himself, challenges Laifu to a contest for her hand. Laifu has previously set free a rainbow fish who turned out to be the son of the Ocean King. In gratitude, the Ocean King has given Laifu a box with three sticks to break for help if he needs it. These enable Laifu to complete the three tasks set by Funtong, win the contest, and thus peace and harmony are restored. Ink and transparent watercolors evoke the delicacy of ancient Chinese scroll paintings. From the characteristically tall, humped mountains to the clumps of distant rooftops, on variously toned pages, the pictures tell the story of good defeating evil with dramatic, upbeat flair. Clothing and architecture show attention to historic references.

Ye, Ting-xing. *Three Monks, No Water.* Illustrated by Harvey Chan. Toronto: Annick, 1997. 32pp. Grades 1–4.

The author has created his own story from an old saying heard from his mother: "One monk has two buckets of water; two monks have one bucket of water; three monks have no water." A young monk lives in a temple up a mountain far from water. He is tired of carrying the water by himself. But when another monk arrives, they cannot work together. A third monk joins them. Each thinks the others should fetch the water, but no one does. When a fire breaks out, the emergency makes them all work. They finally realize they must work together. The pages have been prepared with a grainy yellow/tan textured background; the acrylic and colored pencil illustrations of the monks tend to blend to create a tone of a contemplative life style. Only a few buckets and household objects and a hint of architecture are needed to set the Chinese stage, although some Chinese seals and characters are introduced. Touches of humor first, then near hysteria as the crisis arises, come in contrast to the calm exposition.

Ye, Ting-xing. *Weighing the Elephant.* Illustrated by Suzane Langlois. Toronto: Annick, 1998. 32pp. Grades K–3.

This original tale begins "long ago, in the green mountains of China," where a cruel and clever emperor ruled far away. The hard-working village farmers have the help of good climate and soil and an elephant family. Hei-dou, the keeper of the elephants, takes special care of the baby elephant, Huan-huan, who performs many tricks. Hearing of this, the emperor sends for Huan-huan. Hei-dou reluctantly lets him go. When Huan-huan refuses to perform, the emperor wants to send him far away, despite the pleas of the farmers for his return. So instead he sets them an impossible task. They must tell him how heavy the elephant is. Clever Hei-dou figures out a solution so that Huan-huan can return to the village. The first double page shows a birds-eye view of the mountain terrain surrounding the village, a peaceful, attractive place. Detailed watercolor paintings of the villagers, the emperor and his court, and of course the elephants include costumes and objects that mark it as historically Chinese.

Young, Ed. *The Lost Horse: A Chinese Folktale.* San Diego, CA: Silver Whistle/Harcourt, 1998. 26pp. Also paper, 2004. Grades K–2.

During a thunderstorm, the fine horse of a wise man named Sai is frightened and runs away. But Sai says that it may not be such a bad thing. In a few days, the horse returns with an equally fine mare. But Sai says it may not be such a good thing. When the mare tosses Sai's son and breaks his leg, Sai figures that's not so bad. Sure enough, when army recruiters arrive to pick up soldiers, his son can't be taken. So Sai's son learns "to trust in the ever changing fortunes of life." The subtle tale starts on the cover with a violent image of a rider's fall from a horse. But the delicately suggestive end-papers, whose surfaces seem barely touched by Young's pastels and watercolors, set a different tone. The visual story itself is told with figures cut out and set into appropriate contexts, most of which are bare of all but the most basic information. The clothing, however, is traditional. A source note is included. A bonus is a set of articulated cardboard puppets of the characters, which probably will not survive many circulations, however.

Young, Ed. *Monkey King.* New York: HarperCollins, 2001. 32pp. Grades 1–4.

This tale is only an introduction to the Chinese classic epic *Journey to the West,* in which the journey of Monkey and his fellow-travelers reflects the spiritual Buddhist journey toward enlightenment. After studying for many years, Monkey arrives home at Flower Fruit Mountain to defeat the invasion of Red Beard Bandit. His mischievous activities bring Jade Emperor and his army after him, but he defeats them. Buddha finally traps Monkey. After 500 years, he becomes the disciple of a holy monk and is released. He then has further adventures and begins to learn humility. Flamboyant use of cut papers combined with a large typeface create a stunning visual narrative. The fold-out of Buddha's black hand is particularly commanding, contrasting with floral patterned papers. A note offers a list of the characters involved.

Zhang, Song Nan. *Five Heavenly Emperors: Chinese Myths of Creation*. Toronto: Tundra, 1994. 36pp. Grades 3–6.

Some traditional Chinese legends relating to creation, including the creation of the Chinese alphabet and the acquisition of fire, are retold here. Although the text is lengthy, the volume itself is in picturebook format. The full-page illustrations sometimes use ancient Chinese icons and conventions, but the overall style is Western, reminiscent of the murals of the 1920s and '30s.

CHINA AND TAIWAN TODAY AND IN RECENT HISTORY

Brett, Jan. *Daisy Comes Home*. New York: G. P. Putnam's Sons, 2002. 32pp. Grades PreS–3.

Young Mei Mei takes good care of her chickens, but the other chickens pick on poor Daisy all the time. When Daisy moves into a basket to get away from them, the rising river carries her away. She is found by a fisherman who wants to take her to the market to sell. Meanwhile, Mei Mei, sad because she cannot find Daisy, takes her eggs to the market. When she sees Daisy for sale, she calls to her and they run back home. Daisy, emboldened by her adventure, finally asserts herself among the other chickens. Perhaps a bit hard to believe but still a good story. What a glorious way Brett has to employ watercolor and gouache with airbrush back to depict both landscapes and animals! Here she treats us to a flock of pushy hens in their rural henhouse and a busy village market, to say nothing of Daisy's grand adventures along the river and her eventual rescue by her appealing owner. Fully detailed double-page scenes plus clever vignettes that extend the story in the corners provide cultural information in a very attractive package. The scenes of life along the river show that Brett has done her homework.

Bridges, Shirin Yim. *Ruby's Wish*. Illustrated by Sophie Blackall. San Francisco: Chronicle, 2002. 30pp. Grades K–4.

This story of China in days past is about the author's grandmother. It depicts a time when men could have many wives and large families. Ruby studies with the many other children, although girls didn't usually learn to read and write then. She still has to learn to do all her female household chores as well. When her grandfather questions her assertion that boys are treated much better than girls, in particular that they can go to university, Ruby tells him how much she wants to go. She is thrilled when she gets her wish, a step forward for gender equality. The text is low key in tone, and Blackall's colored gouache illustrations are equally almost devoid of strong emotion, although Ruby's determination comes through clearly. Architecture, clothing, and the few artifacts such as vases are all properly of the time and place. A photograph of the author's triumphant grandmother closes the story.

Butler, John. *Pi-shu the Little Panda*. Atlanta: Peachtree Publishers, 2001. 32pp. Grades PreS–1.

The tiny baby panda, born on the slopes of Misty Mountain, is cared for by his loving mother. He learns to walk, to eat bamboo shoots, to explore and play with other animals. But one day men come to begin cutting down the trees. Pi-shu and his mother must travel through the snow to another valley where they can live safely. The brief, simple text brings us close to the endangered creatures, while facts added at the end emphasize the threat to their survival. Affectionately created very realistic paintings of the pandas are set in a Chinese landscape. Pi-shu's growth is documented within the esthetics of the settings. The sequences of the visual story help show the appeal these rare animals have all over the world.

Chen, Chih-Yuan. *On My Way to Buy Eggs*. La Jolla, CA: Kane/Miller, 2001. 40pp. Grades PreS–1.

The lively little girl sent to the store by her father to buy eggs could be in any urban area where there are still small convenience stores. Only her name, Shau-yu, places her in this award-winning import from Taiwan. Her actions along the way, from looking at the world through a blue glass marble she finds to donning a pair of glasses and imagining herself someone else, are universal. In this briefest of texts youngsters can find a bond with a child far away. The scenes created in tones of tans and grays from cut paper collage with line drawings are minimal stage sets which use bits of fences, misty tops of buildings, shadows on sidewalks, to let us focus on our heroine, a real charmer.

Czernecki, Stefan. *Paper Lanterns.* Watertown, MA: Talewinds/Charlesbridge, 2001. 32pp. Also paper. Grades 1–4.

Old Chin, maker of the most beautiful paper lanterns, is getting old. A young boy, Little Mouse, wants to learn how to make the lanterns, but Chen already has two apprentices. Little Mouse is left with only the sweeping. He also watches the others work and practices, until he finally produces a lantern that proves to Old Chen that he can do it. Months later, as they prepare for the annual lantern festival, Old Chen's hands are too cold to make any. Little Mouse puts the apprentices to work with him on a fantastic dragon. Old Chen is happy to have found a worthy successor. Examples of real cut-paper lanterns hang in the margins of the text pages. The facing pages depict the story's events and many more lanterns in bright gouache paintings. The heads of the characters are perhaps symbolically round like many of the lanterns; they have an exaggerated cartoon-like style. Chinese characters are included.

Lee, Huy Voun. *1, 2, 3, Go!* New York: Henry Holt, 2000. 28pp. Grades K–3.

We count from one to ten in English and in Chinese characters. For each double page, there are pictures of the number of actors indicated. They are energetically involved in the action verb that is the only other word of text. So we have "two stomp" in puddles, "three hit" drums, "four push" big balls of snow, etc. Cut paper creates simplified forms of children, while bits of color fill in some of the empty spaces to add eye appeal. There is nothing particularly Chinese about the activities; just energetic fun. Notes on dialects, characters, and numbers also have a word list with Mandarin pronunciation guide.

Lee, Huy Voun. *In the Snow.* New York: Henry Holt, 1995. 28pp. Also paper. Grades K–3.

A young boy and his mother go for a walk in the snow. There is nothing particularly Chinese about the people, the setting, or the story. But as they walk, Xiao Ming's mother points out objects and writes the Chinese character for each of them in the snow. She also draws comparisons between the characters and what they designate and shows the relationship of the combined characters in words. The ten words and their characters, with pronunciation in Mandarin Chinese, are repeated on the end-papers. Very simple cut-paper shapes portray the activities in the snow with children, a few animals, and lots of the trees. The brief text makes it easy to perceive the logic of the pictures in the words. There are added notes on the Chinese language and characters. The author-illustrator's similar *At the Beach* (Holt,

1994) had Xiao Ming's mother draw him Chinese characters in the sand as the people on the beach enjoy the sun, sand, and water.

Reddix, Valerie. *Dragon Kite of the Autumn Moon*. Illustrated by Jean and Mousien Tseng. New York: Lothrop/HarperCollins, 1992. 32pp. Grades 1–4.

The tradition of celebrating Kite's Day, the author's note suggests, came from China to Formosa (Taiwan) with early settlers. Tad-Tin is accustomed to flying the special kite his grandfather makes him every year for the holiday. Tradition says that if the string is cut, the kite will carry misfortunes away. But this year, Tad-Tin's grandfather is sick, and the kite is unfinished. The only kite Tad-Tin has to fly is the magnificent dragon kite that grandfather made for his birth, which he is reluctant to part with. But he feels he must try to fly the heavy kite, and perhaps have grandfather's sickness fly away with it. Does Tad-Tin really see a live dragon when he succeeds? Perhaps, for grandfather is better when Tad-Tin returns. Double-page scenes that completely fill the pages are painted naturalistically with an eye for the furniture and clothing of modern rural Taiwan. Rather restrained illustrations of earthbound family life are juxtaposed with five action-packed, visually inventive scenes of the flight of the dragon kite.

Tsubakiyama, Margaret Holloway. *Mei-Mei Loves the Morning*. Illustrated by Cornelius Van Wright and Ying-Hwa Hu. Morton Grove, IL: Albert Whitman, 1999. 32pp. Grades K–3.

Mei-Mei enjoys her time in the morning with her grandfather. They eat breakfast, then taking their bird in its cage, they ride a bicycle through the busy city traffic. They stop in the park to hang the cage on a tree with those of their friends. They practice tai chi and have some tea. They stop for pancakes on the way home. The double-page watercolor and pencil illustrations offer detailed pictures of this simple sequence of events in what we would call a typical morning in scenes that picture urban China. Of note are the few utensils in the kitchen, including chop sticks and a wok, some typical buildings, and the mass of cyclists thronging the streets.

CHINESE AMERICANS AND THE IMMIGRANT EXPERIENCE

Cheng, Andrea. *Goldfish and Chrysanthemums*. Illustrated by Michelle Chang. New York: Lee & Low, 2003. 32pp. Grades K–3.

Nancy's grandmother Ni Ni, who lives with her family, is distressed to hear from her brother back in China that their old house will be torn down. She tells Nancy how she loved the fish pond and the chrysanthemums in the courtyard. With a lot of help, Nancy manages to build a pond and plant flowers to bring joy to her grandmother; photos can be sent to her brother back in China to cheer him as well. Chang uses a subdued palette for her naturalistic oil painted illustrations depicting the steps Nancy takes toward her goal. Some scenes from China are also included.

Cheng, Andrea. *Grandfather Counts.* Illustrated by Ange Zhang. New York: Lee & Low, 2000. 32pp. Also paper. Grades 1–4.

A young girl relates what happens when her Gong Gong, or grandfather, arrives from China. She has had to move in with her sister to give him her room, where she has always liked to watch the trains go by. At first she resents him and can't understand him. He doesn't seem to want to do anything. But she notices that he does wave to the train engineers when they pass, as she does from the nearby wall. One day he joins her there and counts the passing train cars in Chinese. She practices saying them, then teaches him the English. Communication builds as they teach each other. Acrylic paints describe each family member along with their home and the passing trains without too much detail. However, we all understand and respond to grandfather's thumbs-up and the happy faces of the family. There is a word list with Chinese characters and pronunciation.

D'Antonio, Nancy. *Our Baby from China: An Adoption Story.* Morton Grove, IL: Albert Whitman, 1997. 24pp. Grades K–4.

Told as if by the little girl herself, the story begins with an orphan in China and a couple in the United States who want a child. It takes us to China with the couple, with quick stops at three tourist attractions. Then we meet Ariela Xiangwei and other babies with the parents who have come to adopt them. We follow this new family as they do a bit more sightseeing, then return to America so that Ariela can meet all of her new family. The clear color photographs are placed as if in a keepsake album for Ariela. The facts match those observed in a trip to China. No mention is made that these babies are all girls or the harsh reason why.

Demi. *Happy, Happy Chinese New Year!* New York: Crown, 2003. 20pp. Grades K–4.

Demi describes various facets of the New Year celebration in this hand-sized version of an earlier edition. Each double page covers another aspect, from cleaning up, preparing and cooking, to fireworks, lanterns, and the lion and dragon dances. The explanations are clear and very brief, with some facts in tiny type added. Demi's tiny colored drawings of characters in action and costume illustrate the various activities with accuracy, verve, and humor. The end-papers and front and back are used to house more informative pictures of this jolly holiday.

Hodge, Deborah. *Emma's Story.* Illustrated by Song Nan Zhang. Toronto: Tundra, 2003. 24pp. Grades K–3.

Adopted children can't hear their story too often, it seems. The reassurance for those who look very different from the rest of their family is particularly important; it is also of interest to other children. Here it is her grandmother who tells Emma how her parents prepared for her and went to China to bring her back to the welcoming family. "It's not how we look that makes us a family. . . . It's how we love each other," says Grandma. Large, naturalistic paintings convey the joy of each of the family members, indeed of all those involved in Emma's life. Local details provide contexts for this personal story with a happy ending.

Hoyt-Goldsmith, Diane. *Celebrating Chinese New Year.* Illustrated by Lawrence Migdale. New York: Holiday House, 1998. 32pp. Grades 3–6.

We follow Ryan and his Chinese American family through the celebration of their most important holiday of the year. The history of the Chinese New Year is followed by some information on the arrival of Chinese immigrants to the U.S. Ryan and his father shop for what is needed for the holiday, then pay their respects to the ancestors in the cemetery. We learn about Ryan's special Chinese school, the Chinese zodiac, the food preparations, the events of New Year's Day, and of course the spectacular parade. Clear color photographs show Ryan involved in all the activities. Others inform us of details behind events. A glossary is included.

Lee, Milly. *Nim and the War Effort.* Illustrated by Yangsook Choi. New York: Frances Foster/Farrar, Straus, 1997. 40pp. Also paper. Grades 2–4.

The lengthy text takes us back to San Francisco's Chinatown during World War II. Nim is hoping to win her school's contest for collecting the most newspapers for the paper drive. Nasty Garland Stephenson is not only catching up to her but is making remarks about her not being "American." Nim goes beyond Chinatown after school to find more papers. She has been told to call the police when she needs help, so when she finds huge stacks of papers, she calls the police to help her get them to her school. She has promised her grandfather not to miss her Chinese school that afternoon. Although she wins the drive, she fears she has disgraced him. Fortunately Grandfather seems to understand his American grandchild. Full-page paintings include only the most necessary objects to give specificity to the narrative. There is a stillness to even the active scenes that show emotional restraint. The respect for her elders expected of Nim is emphasized, along with the atmosphere of the time of war.

Lewin, Ted. *Big Jimmy's Kum Kau Chinese Take Out.* New York: HarperCollins, 2002. 32pp. Grades K–4.

The actual menus on the end-papers introduce Chinese American take-out food to anyone who doesn't know about it and make the mouth water of anyone who does. Through the eyes of the young son of the owner, we go through a Saturday from early morning food delivery through meticulous preparation, cooking, and serving to final closing and a humorous end. The food may not be "authentic" Chinese, but the workers in these restaurants frequently are Chinese Americans. The watercolor scenes are lively, detailed, and convincing in their depiction of the restaurant operations. We can almost feel the heat of the cooking wok and the outpouring of energy as plates are filled and orders taken in this appetite-stimulating introduction to Chinese American food.

Lin, Grace. *Dim Sum for Everyone!* New York: Alfred A. Knopf, 2001. 26pp. Grades PreS–2.

This very simple, brief introduction to the dishes available at a dim sum restaurant in Chinatown is printed in large type. A family is at a table, selecting different dishes from the rolling trolleys. Everyone eats "a little bit of everything." A note at the end gives the history of the dim sum tradition and its customs, including the counting of the dirty dishes to figure the bill. Equally simple, almost cartoon-like pictures of the family give human scale to the variety of dishes which arrive on the carts. The front end-papers display the ingredients and utensils necessary for making the twenty dim sum laid out on the back pages. Allover patterns add visual interest.

Lin, Grace. *Kite Flying.* New York: Alfred A. Knopf, 2002. 26pp. Grades PreS–2.

On a windy day, a Chinese American family makes a dragon kite to fly. Only a few words per page are needed to describe the construction. Background notes fill in information on kites and their history from two thousand years ago in China. The double-page scenes are dominated by the family members in varied patterned clothes. Their black hair and eyes may hint at their ancestry, but they are depicted simply as Americans who join others in kite flying. Some readers may try to make kites from the pictures provided, but all can admire the fanciful decorative examples displayed. The front end-papers show the materials needed to make a kite; the back end-papers depict beautiful kite designs with names like "repels bad magic," "love," "joy," and "peace."

Look, Lenore. *Henry's First-Moon Birthday.* Illustrated by Yumi Heo. New York: Anne Schwartz/Atheneum/Simon & Schuster, 2001. 32pp. Grades K–3.

Jen, or Jenny, introduces herself as Older Sister. She and her *GninGnin*, or grandmother, are preparing for her baby brother's one-month birthday, or his first-moon, as it is called in Chinese culture. Grandmother bustles about cooking chicken, pigs' feet, ginger soup, and writing "good luck" words on red cloth with Chinese ink. There are eggs to boil and dye, and cleaning to do, and then dressing before the guests arrive. The party is a big success; Jen-Jen is proud when her grandmother says she "was in charge of everything." She is sad to see her grandmother leave and is finally reconciled to her new brother. In keeping with the youngster's recitation of events, the illustrations have a child-like quality, with rounded heads, no perspective, simplified objects. Collage is used for dresses, but pencil and oils produce backgrounds and assorted objects scattered around the double-page scenes. A glossary is included.

Look, Lenore. *Love as Strong as Ginger.* Illustrated by Stephen T. Johnson. New York: Anne Schwartz/Atheneum/Simon & Schuster, 1999. 32pp. Grades 1–4.

The author has based the story on her *GninGnin* or grandmother, who worked in a Seattle cannery in the 1960s and 1970s. The narrator recalls her time with her grandmother, enjoying the good food she cooks. She has heavy rubber gloves to protect her hands from the crab shells at her job cracking crabs for canning, the only job she could find without good English. In answer to her request, her grandmother takes her to the factory where she works. The job is unbelievably difficult; there is not even a place to sit down. Our narrator finds that she can't crack a crab herself even with a mallet. But her grandmother assures her that she can become whatever she dreams. Together they enjoy a special crab dish "made with love as strong as ginger and dreams as thick as black-bean paste." Small, evocative drawings with added pastels and watercolors offer genuine character studies of grandmother and child along with some shrimp and crabs. We learn something of the work the immigrants did while we experience the warm affection between the fellow-workers and the grandmother and of course between grandmother and child. There is a glossary of unfamiliar Chinese words.

Low, William. *Chinatown.* New York: Henry Holt, 1997. 32pp. Grades PreS–2.

A young boy takes us on a walking tour to introduce New York's China-town. He and his grandmother pass a tai chi class in the park, a street cob-bler, restaurants, an herbal shop, the crowded outdoor market. He talks about his kung fu lessons on Saturdays and his favorite holiday. On the Chi-nese New Year, he stands with the crowds watching the parade, firecrackers and all, hoping to march next year himself. Double-page paintings supply impressions of the brief text's tour. The naturalistic visuals depict the work-ers, shoppers, and lookers, ducks hanging in a restaurant window, cooks working with flaming woks, etc. for a sense of place and community.

Mak, Kam. *My Chinatown: One Year in Poems.* New York: HarperCollins, 2002. 32pp. Grades K–3.

Lyrical free verses take us through the seasons as a young boy describes his life in New York's Chinatown, far from the home he has left and really misses in Hong Kong. Here "the English words / taste like metal in my mouth." We meet his family and the people in the neighborhood, watch the Dragon Boats and the lanterns of the Moon Festival, and finally, as the New Year comes again, celebrate it with him Remarkably realistic full-page paintings project the spirit of each poem while depicting concrete objects like exotic kites and the New Year parade. The images have concentrated impact as we view the Chinatown of our narrator along with his words.

Nunes, Susan Miho. *The Last Dragon.* Illustrated by Chris K. Soentpiet. New York: Clarion/Houghton, 1995. 32pp. Also paper. Grades 1–4.

Peter has been sent to spend the summer in Chinatown with his great-aunt, and he is not happy about it until he spots an old parade dragon in a shop. He buys the bedraggled, dirty dragon, made to be held by ten men, and begins the task of restoring it. He is helped by members of the China-town community as he does errands for them, learning all the time about dragons, and about his heritage. Just before he has to leave at the end of the summer, Peter gets to see the finished dragon at its magnificent best. There is room enough in the double-page, naturalistic watercolor scenes for the somewhat lengthy text. The illustrations are crowded with the sights of Chi-natown along with portraits of Peter's many relatives and friends.

Partridge, Elizabeth. *Oranges on Golden Mountain.* Illustrated by Aki Sogabe. New York: Dutton/Penguin, 2001. 40pp. Also paper. Grades 2–4.

It is a time of drought and hardship for Jo Lee's family and village in late-19th-century China. Despite his protests, his mother sends him to join his Fourth Uncle on "Golden Mountain," California. With him she sends cuttings from her orange trees to plant and assures him that his dream spirit will go also with him. Through the hardship of the journey and the work of fishing with his uncle, Jo Lee's thoughts are with his mother and sister as he carefully saves the money to bring them across the ocean. Meanwhile, the tree shoots he has planted take root and grow. And his dream spirit sends hope across the sea to his mother and sister. Traditional cut paper pictures provide the settings with objects and clothing that inform us about life in both China and California for a poor family at that time. Watercolor is airbrushed to create coastal mists and interior scenes, producing pictures which effectively tell of Jo Lee's labors and of the magic dream spirit and wonderful Dragon King in his dream. An afterword gives many details of the history of the Chinese immigration and also a bit of Chinese philosophy.

Roth, Susan L. *Happy Birthday Mr. Kang*. Washington, DC: National Geographic Society, 2001. 32pp. Grades 1–4.

On his seventieth birthday, Mr. Kang gets his wishes: to read the *New York Times* and paint poems every day, and to have a bird, a *hua mei*, of his own. As the author notes, many Chinese American men take their caged birds to the park just as their Chinese grandfathers did. One Sunday, his grandson Sam goes with Mr. Kang and his bird to the park. Sam suggests that his bird might prefer to be free, so Mr. Kang releases him. Sam and Mrs. Kang fear that his grandfather will be sorry or that the bird may get lost or die. To their surprise, *hua mei* is waiting for them at home. Mr. Kang writes and paints (in Chinese characters) a poem celebrating that "We are Americans by choice." The author has based Mr. Kang on her Chinese American uncle and used his poems for those by Mr. Kang. Collage illustrations and a few photographs offer insights into community values along with the main characters of the story. A full-page portrait of the bird against a blood-red wall is stunning. Notes describe the facts about the birds in a New York park, as well as how the collages were made.

Sun, Chyng Feng. *Mama Bear*. Illustrated by Lolly Robinson. Boston: Houghton Mifflin, 1994. 32pp. Grades K–4.

Mei Mei and her mother are Chinese Americans, struggling to survive in contemporary Boston's Chinatown, but their theme is a universal one. Mei Mei wants the cuddly teddy bear she sees in the toy store window for Christmas. She tries to help earn enough to buy it, working with her mother in a Chinese restaurant. But she settles for the warmth of her own "mama bear" instead. Pale watercolor illustrations do little more than echo the emotions of the elaborate text.

Vaughan, Marcia. *The Dancing Dragon.* Illustrated by Stanley Wong Hoo Foon. New York: Mondo, 1996. 20pp. Fold-out. Also paper. Grades K–2.

Rhymed couplets briefly describe the preparation for the New Year in Chinatown and detail the parade with its noise, dancing, and especially the dragon. Watercolor paintings, exuberantly and rather innocently drawn, depict the people gathering for the parade and watching the dragon as it goes by. The fold-out is meant to open into a single scene, front and back. The heavy paper stock should take repeated opening and closing.

Wang, Janet S. *This Next New Year.* Illustrated by Yangsook Choi. New York: Frances Foster/Farrar, Straus, 2000. 32pp. Grades K–3.

A young boy describes his family preparation for the Chinese New Year. His friends, whose parents are from many other countries, enjoy it too. After the family cleans the house and themselves thoroughly, he prepares himself to be brave when the firecrackers go off to scare away bad luck. He "will not say one awful thing," because this is his fresh start, his time for good luck to make his dreams come true. In a style that simplifies, avoiding realistic clutter, the double-page illustrations visualize the events of the text, including a spectacular dragon in the parade, with gentle humor. The author adds notes on the Chinese New Year, including symbols, and childhood memories.

Waters, Kate, and Madeline Slovenz-Low, *Lion Dancer: Ernie Wan's Chinese New Year.* Illustrated by Martha Cooper. New York: Scholastic, 1990. 32pp. Also paper. Grades K–3.

Young Ernie tells about his excited preparation to perform his first Lion Dance. Being part of the undulating lion in the Chinese New Year celebration in New York City's Chinatown is the culmination of his tale. He also gives factual information about his life as a Chinese American, attending both American and Chinese schools, maintaining some ancient customs, and cooking a traditional festival feast in a modern kitchen. The clear photographs as illustrations are in full color. A Chinese lunar calendar and horoscope are included.

Ye, Ting-xing. *Share the Sky.* Illustrated by Suzane Langlois. Toronto: Annick, 1999. 32pp. Also paper. Grades 1–4.

Fei-Fei loves kites, especially those she makes with her grandfather, although she is too small to fly one herself. Her mother and father are far away in North America which, her grandfather says, "doesn't even share the same sky with us." She is apprehensive when they send for her to join them but soon gets used to being with them. Then she worries about school. But when she arrives there, she is greeted by a teacher who speaks some Chinese and, best of all, by a beautiful kite. Her class will make kites, and Fei-Fei will hold one all by herself. The watercolors tell a fact-filled story of both a Chinese home with grandparents living in a small town and an American home and school. Where kites appear, they are elaborate and shaped like a variety of creatures from insects to animals.

Yee, Paul. *The Boy in the Attic.* Illustrated by Gu Xiong. Vancouver, British Columbia: Groundwood/Douglas & McIntyre, 1998. 34pp. Grades 1–4.

The lengthy text tells a kind of ghost story as it reveals the emotions of a young immigrant boy from China. After a sad farewell to the ancestors, Kai-ming Wong and his parents have come to America. He is left in an old rented house while his parents seek work. Everything seems strange. One day he notices a face in the attic window of the house next door that is supposed to be vacant. When he goes to investigate, he finds an oddly dressed boy. At first they cannot understand each other, but when a black butterfly similar to one at his ancestor's grave sits on Kai-ming's shoulder, magically they can. After a wonderful summer playing together, Kai-ming's parents are ready to move on. Reluctantly he says goodbye to his friend, leaving him the butterfly but now ready to meet new buddies. Colored pencils create full-page scenes that tell the visual story with quiet emotion. The details of the houses and the two boys at play are secondary to the unreality of the situation. The final illustration of them shaking hands is the visual symbol of Kai-ming's cultural adaptation.

Yee, Paul. *Ghost Train.* Illustrated by Harvey Chan. Toronto: Groundwood/Douglas & McIntyre, 1996. 32pp. Grades 2–5.

Choon-yi's father has left South China to work on building a railroad line in the American mountains. Although she has only one arm, Choon-yi is a fine painter. One day a letter from her father tells her to bring paper, brushes, and colors to him. When she arrives, she finds that her father has been killed. In a dream, he tells her to paint the train for which he died. She studies the trains, rides them, and finally paints the train in the mountains. In another dream, her father tells her to spread the painting, with incense, on the tracks. Magically, a train rises there and her father appears, telling her that the souls of all who died can now ride to their rest when she takes the painting back to China and burns it. And on the painting appear faces at every window, with her father as train engineer. This strange and mystic tale is based on the conditions and fate of the Chinese workers on the railroads. Somber full-page oil paintings done in shades of warm browns supply information about the trains and the story while enhancing the mysterious feeling of the text.

Yee, Paul. *The Jade Necklace*. Illustrated by Grace Lin. Brooklyn, NY: Crocodile/Interlink, 2002. 32pp. Grades K–4.

After her father is lost at sea, Yenyee is sent to the New World to help care for May-jen. One day at the shore, as Yenyee thinks about her family across the sea, May-jen falls into the water. When Yenyee jumps in to save her, she comes out of the water with a jade necklace tangled in her hair. It is the same one that her father had given her and that she had tossed into the sea to ask it to bring back her lost father. It rekindles her faith and her hope that her family can join her. The story is long and perhaps surreal, but it gives a picture of the immigrant experience of the time. Lin's illustrations suggest some Asian art styles with their heavy black outlines and solid color areas. The emphasis is on design rather than action. Some hand lettering and Chinese seals add to the atmosphere.

Yee, Paul. *Roses Sing on New Snow*. Illustrated by Harvey Chan. New York: Macmillan, 1991. 32pp. Also paper. Grades 1–4.

The story of a Chinatown restaurant at the turn of the nineteenth century draws on the Chinese immigrant experience. The restaurant's reputation for fine food comes from Maylin's hard work in the kitchen. But she never hears the compliments because her father tells everyone that his two lazy sons do the cooking. When the governor of South China visits, each restaurant prepares a specialty. Maylin creates the title dish. The governor wants to learn how it is made so he can take it back for the emperor. Maylin is finally credited with the cooking, but she shows that food creation, like a painting, can never be completely duplicated. The illustrations tell a story even more complex than the words, replete with details of Chinese cooking and life in Chinatown. A variety of page layouts encompasses the seriocomic tale of a heroic but obedient daughter and her piggish brothers. Watercolors depict the street life as well as the tables bearing the variety of Chinese foods, which we can almost smell.

Yin. *Coolies*. Illustrated by Chris Soentpiet. New York: Philomel/Penguin, 2001. 40pp. Grades 2–5.

The story, based on historic events, is introduced as a tale told at the Ching Ming Festival honoring ancestors by a grandmother to her grandson about her great-grandfather and his brother. In a time of troubles in China in the mid-1800s, Shek and his younger brother Wong take the long voyage to America hoping to find work. Although they were considered weak and strange, disparagingly called "Coolies," the Chinese laborers hired to build the transcontinental railroad running east worked incredibly hard under terrible conditions. Shek tries to take care of his brother and to write to their mother regularly though the heat, cold, and danger. When the railroad is finished, the brothers settle in San Francisco and bring the rest of the family over. The young boy hearing the story understands more about why the ancestors deserve respect. Large, very detailed, naturalistic watercolor scenes emphasize the hardships involved in the labor. Light is used to produce melodramatic effects and to enhance the attachment between the brothers as we are drawn into their lives. Notes are added on the history of Chinese Americans and on those who labored on the railroad.

Zhang, Song Nan, and Hao Yu Zhang. *A Time of Golden Dragons*. Illustrated by Song Nan Zhang. Toronto: Tundra, 2000. 24pp. Grades 2–6.

In celebration of a Dragon Year in the millennium year of 2000 comes not a story as such but a compendium of information about dragons in Chinese history, legends, and culture. Notes on the origin and symbolism of dragons up to today are followed by the place of dragons in the counting of hours and years. Zhang's finely wrought detailed watercolor paintings vary in size from the double-page dragon boat races to quite small details of individual objects. Their extreme naturalism adds to the effectiveness of scenes crowded with the specifics of each event, from an action episode of "The Monkey King" to St. George driving his lance into a fire-breathing dragon.

KOREA AND KOREAN AMERICANS

ORIGINAL TALES AND FOLKTALES EVOKING THE PAST

Farley, Carol. *The King's Secret: The Legend of King Sejong*. Illustrated by Robert Jew. New York: HarperCollins, 2001. 32pp. Grades 1–4.

"Long ago when tigers smoked long pipes and rabbits talked to dragons, a rich king ruled . . . Korea." The king knows he is rich in his mind as well because he can read and write. But a poor boy reminds him how difficult reading can be, because Koreans must learn thousands of Chinese characters to read; there is no written Korean. The king decides to find an easier way to write the sounds. Determining that there are twenty-eight sounds in the language, he and his wise men design the signs for them. But the people believe that the Chinese characters must be used, because they come from the gods. So he causes the new signs to appear on the leaves of trees for the elders and teachers, by drawing them on the leaves with honey for insects to eat. He thus makes "the gods" speak for the change. The large paintings set a lush, somewhat exotic stage for this intellectual drama. Flowers, birds, a few people, and bits of architecture create a positive and attractive setting. A lengthy note tries to separate legend from the historic facts as we know them. Modern Hageul symbols are included.

Han, Suzanne Crowder. *The Rabbit's Tail: A Story from Korea*. Illustrated by Richard Wehrman. New York: Henry Holt, 1999. 32pp. Grades K–3.

This is another version of *The Tiger and the Dried Persimmon* by Park (below). Here the tiger, afraid of the unknown persimmon, is seized and mounted by the thief. Both are terrified, but after he shakes off the thief, the happy tiger here encounters a rabbit. The rabbit is caught by the thief with a rope around his tail, the explanation for rabbit's stumpy tail. Double-page acrylic and gouache paintings create a series of melodramatic scenes, with a realism that compels us to be afraid of this toothy tiger as well as the imagined persona of his "dried persimmon." Nighttime deep purples and skimpy moonlight enhance the mystery. There are only hints of the settings. Notes are added on background and sources.

Heo, Yumi, reteller and illustrator. *The Green Frogs: A Korean Folktale*. Boston: Houghton Mifflin, 1996. 32pp. Grades K–3.

Two green frogs constantly disobey their mother. They even croak backwards. When their mother becomes old and sick, she wants to be buried on the sunny side of the hill, but knowing her contrary children, she asks them to put her in the shade by the stream. The now contrite children actually obey her wishes. Whenever it rains, the green frogs croak to beg the stream not to wash away their mother. Now we know why green frogs croak in the rain and why disobedient Korean children are called green frogs. This simple story is really funny, despite the death of the mother frog. Heo's helter-skelter design and personal abstraction of natural objects, like the bandy-legged anthropomorphic frogs, are suitable to this fantasy.

O'Brien, Anne Sibley, adapter and illustrator. *The Princess and the Beggar: A Korean Folktale.* New York: Scholastic, 1993. 32pp. Also paper. Grades 1–4.

Many years ago, says this traditional tale, the king grew so tired of the incessant weeping of his sensitive youngest daughter that he threatens to marry her off to the wild beggar who lives in a cave. When she becomes sixteen, she refuses an arranged marriage, saying she would just as soon marry the beggar. Surprisingly, the two learn from and to care for each other. Later, the princess sends the beggar, Ondal, to compete in the Festival of the Hunt, where he does surprisingly well but hides his identity. Finally, he writes a prize-winning poem in the Festival of the Scholars, when he is supposed to be illiterate. His identity is revealed. The king then offers his favor, but the couple asks only to serve him; they are content. Several visual devices produce a sense of an ancient Korean place. The end-papers are decorated with symbolic roundels. An opening double-page aerial view lays out a meandering river and a walled village below craggy mountains. The story unfolds on horizontal and vertical panels with text on white panels. Pastels create naturalistic scenes more to evoke emotion than to provide details. Costumes and architecture provide visual cultural context. In a note, the author explains the setting and time period she has selected, plus additional information about the culture.

Park, Janie Jaehyun, adapter. *The Tiger and the Dried Persimmon.* Toronto: Douglas & McIntyre, 2002. 32pp. Grades K–3.

A fierce, hungry tiger misinterprets what he hears as a mother tries to quiet a crying child. The tiger is surprised that the baby doesn't seem to be afraid of anything, even a tiger, but a persimmon makes him stop crying. This unknown object connects in the tiger's mind with a nearby thief; both of them flee in fear from what they don't understand. Employing a style adapted from some Korean traditional paintings, Park gives the gesso and acrylic illustrations both vigor and an exotic quality. The characters, including the emotional tiger, are primarily set against textured backgrounds with hints of settings such as a decorative mountain landscape. There is humor in the tale as well.

San Souci, Daniel. *In the Moonlight Mist: A Korean Tale.* Illustrated by Eujin Kim Neilan. Honesdale, PA: Boyds Mills, 1999. 32pp. Grades 1–4.

When a poor young woodcutter saves a deer from a hunter, the deer promises to grant him his wish: that he could have a wife and children. But he must follow certain rules. He must steal the clothes of a heavenly maiden as she bathes in a lake, so she cannot return to heaven and will marry him. He cannot return the clothes to her, however, before she has her second child. All goes well and happily for him as foretold. But when his wife persuades him to return her clothes, she and their child rise up into the sky. When the miserable woodcutter meets the deer again, he is offered the chance to join his wife but sacrifices himself for his mother. For this he is rewarded by a reunion in heaven. Neilan's large, sometimes double-page acrylic paintings are designed to create a romantic visual narrative that exploits gestures and colors to emphasize the emotional content. Details of landscape like bonsai trees and the architecture of the rustic hut plus the clothing help fix the location.

San Souci, Daniel, reteller. *The Rabbit and the Dragon King: Based on a Korean Tale.* Illustrated by Eujin Kim Neilan. Honesdale, PA: Boyds Mills, 2002. 32pp. Grades 1–4.

The Dragon King is told that eating a rabbit's heart will cure his illness. Turtle sets out from the ocean kingdom to bring back a rabbit. The clever rabbit, however, manages to escape, while simple belief is enough to cure the king. The imaginative retelling is based on "one of the most beloved folk tales of Korea." Neilan's imaginative renderings of both fantastic and natural creatures are set in complex theatrical settings with melodramatic lighting. The Dragon King has a look we associate with Asian dragons, but there are no other visual connections with Korea.

KOREA TODAY AND IN RECENT HISTORY

Balgassi, Haemi. *Peacebound Trains.* Illustrated by Chris K. Soentpiet. New York: Clarion/Houghton, 1996. 48pp. Also paper, 2000. Grades 3–6.

Sumi is staying with her grandmother while her mother is away. She loves to watch the trains go by. One day her grandmother tells her the story of riding on the top of a train with two small children to escape the invading North Korean and Chinese armies in 1950. Sumi's mother was only a baby at the time. The story, although fiction, is based on the experiences of the author's grandmother. It fills in a poignant piece of Korean history. The watercolor illustrations are realistic, creating genuine characters and settings to reinforce the biographical basis of the story. They are frequently melodramatically lit and alive with tension.

Park, Frances, and Ginger Park. *My Freedom Trip*. Illustrated by Debra Reid Jenkins. Honesdale, PA: Boyds Mills, 1998. 32pp. Grades 1–4.

This story of a young girl's escape from North Korea is based on the experiences of the authors' mother. After all her friends have crossed to South Korea and freedom, Soo cries when her father leaves as well. Only one person can go at a time, but he promises that she, and then her mother, will join him. One day Mr. Han comes to tell them that her father is safe, and he will guide her next. Soo cries again when she leaves her mother, who tells her to be brave. The journey is difficult and frightening. A soldier stops them at the river but finally lets her go to her waiting father. Then more soldiers are posted along the border and the Korean War breaks out. Soo never sees her mother again. Jenkins's oil paintings are heavy with emotional content, from the narrator's lonely walk through the father's leave taking to the ultimate escape. The focus is on the characters, with suggestions of architecture. There is a list of Korean words and characters.

Wong, Janet S. *The Trip Back Home*. Illustrated by Bo Jia. San Diego, CA: Harcourt, 2000. 32pp. Grades K–3.

In brief, poetic prose, the narrator tells of the trip back to "the village where Mother grew up." After the long flight to Korea, they give the gifts they have brought for *haraboji*, grandfather, *halmoni*, grandmother, and *imo*, aunt. The grandfather uses charcoal to warm the house; our narrator feeds the pigs; she goes to market with grandmother. They cook and eat the traditional foods, talk and play cards together, cement warm family ties. She and her family had brought gifts with them to Korea. The family there gives them gifts to take back. The hugs are also given and returned. The simple story is based on a trip the author and her mother took to rural Korea. Large watercolors detail the architecture, market, fields, home in which the family activities take place. Although not photographic, the scenes offer insights into a way of life quite different from our own.

KOREAN AMERICANS AND THE IMMIGRANT EXPERIENCE

Bercaw, Edna Coe. *Halmoni's Day*. Illustrated by Robert Hunt. New York: Dial/Penguin, 2000. 32pp. Grades K–3.

Jennifer's grandmother arrives from Korea just in time for Grandparents' Day. Jennifer worries that she will be embarrassed by her *halmoni*, who speaks no English and is dressed in the traditional costume. But when called upon, her grandmother tells of her five-year wait for her father while he was fighting in the Korean War and of her joy at his return. Then she notes her pleasure in the reminder of her father that she sees in Jennifer. After translating, in tears, Jennifer thanks her for making the day belong to them both. The author has based the story on some personal family experiences. Hunt's full-page, sensitively rendered oil paintings of the family, particularly the grandmother, give distinctive visual identities to the characters. The joy in the reunion is clearly portrayed in a palpable hug. There is a list of the few Korean words with pronunciation and meaning.

Bunting, Eve. *Jin Woo.* Illustrated by Chris Soentpiet. New York: Clarion/ Houghton, 2001. 32pp. Grades PreS–3.

There are bits of information about Korean customs, but basically this is a story of adoption told from the point of view of the prospective older brother. David is not sure how happy he will be with the baby brother his parents are adopting from Korea. But of course he accepts Jin Woo, as his parents had welcomed him into their family earlier. They assure him that their love for him is still there. They are also determined to keep Jin Woo aware of his cultural heritage. The large, realistic watercolor paintings are loaded with appropriate contextual details of the air trip and the American home. The artist also creates a full cast of believable people, including the appealing narrator and the adorable Jin Woo.

Choi, Sook Nyul. *Halmoni and the Picnic.* Illustrated by Karen M. Dugan. Boston: Houghton Mifflin, 1993. 32pp. Grades K–3.

The simple but lengthy text describes young Yunmi's concern when her grandmother, who has just arrived from Korea, agrees to chaperone her class picnic. Yunmi fears the others will not accept the grandmother's traditional Korean dress or cooking. Of course, all goes well. The illustrations, in Korean-inspired borders, portray both the children of today and the traditional costume of the grandmother.

Paek, Min. *Aekyung's Dream.* San Francisco: Children's Book Press, 1988. 24pp. Text in English and Korean. Grades 1–4.

Drawing upon her own experiences and those of other newcomers, the author tells of Aekyung's feelings as a stranger in school, teased by other students, thinking even the birds are singing in English. Inspired by her aunt's return from a visit to Korea and a dream about 15th-century King Sejong, Aekyung gains the strength to learn English and help others as well. Thin black lines define highly simplified shapes, a very few of which represent traditional Korean costumes and a building. Stylized figures stiffly posed in either empty spaces or sterile settings show Aekyung's efforts to adapt to her new life in the United States.

Pak, Soyung. *Sumi's First Day of School Ever.* Illustrated by Joung Un Kim. New York: Viking/Penguin, 2003. 32pp. Grades PreS–1.

Sumi's mother has taught her what people would say when they asked her name and how she should reply. Otherwise, Sumi goes off to school understanding no English. At first she is apprehensive, finding school scary and the students mean. But as her teacher smiles at her and hangs her drawing on display, and as another girl becomes friendly, Sumi decides that school is not so bad. No specific nationality is given for Sumi, although the author is from Korea. The experience of a non-English-speaking newcomer here is benign and we hope universal. There's a childlike quality to the illustrations, a focus on Sumi and her emotions as she enters the strange world. There are few contextual details, but her emotions are easy to read.

Park, Frances, and Ginger Park. *Good-bye, 382 Shin Dang Dong.* Illustrated by Yangsook Choi. Washington, DC: National Geographic, 2002. 32pp. Grades K–3.

Jangmi describes what it is like to have to leave home to go on an airplane halfway around the world. After a traditional Korean farewell, her parents try to prepare her for the differences she will find in America. But Jangmi just wants to go back, until friendly neighbors finally make her feel welcome. Perhaps one day she may get to like her new home. The authors have based the story on the experience of their sister. Choi's low-key oil paintings help reinforce the sense of anxiety. Making the leave taking happen on a rainy day adds further to the depression. Depicted in a simplified style are the particulars of Korean life that she is leaving behind. The final scenes in America are painted in brighter colors pointing to a happy resolution.

Recorvits, Helen. *My Name Is Yoon.* Illustrated by Gabi Swiatkowska. New York: Frances Foster/Farrar, Straus, 2003. 32pp. Grades PreS–3.

Yoon and her family come to the U.S. from Korea. She very emphatically declines to write her name in English letters. She prefers the happy way the Korean symbols for it seem to dance together. Her parents try to prepare her for school, but everything is too strange. Each new English word suggests something she would rather be, from cat to cupcake, and that is the name she chooses to use. It is only with the help of a sympathetic teacher and a friend that she can allow herself to be an American named "Yoon." The visual version of this story is told in full and double-page scenes, some naturalistic and some surreal, excluding all but the most salient details. Yoon is an appealing child whose wishes produce dream-like scenes to help her deal with her new life. Interior spaces open up through doors and windows on distant landscapes, inviting us to join her in her early desire to move back to Korea.

THE PHILIPPINES

ORIGINAL FOLKTALE

De la Paz, Myrna J. *Abadeha: The Philippine Cinderella.* Illustrated by Youshan Tang. Auburn, CA: Shen's Books, 2001. 32pp. Grades K–3.

The stepmother of this motherless girl gives her impossible tasks. Weeping, Abadeha asks for help from the Spirit of the Forest, who does aid her. At her mother's grave, an enchanted tree grows, laden with jewels. The son of a chieftain, seeing the tree, takes a ring from it but cannot remove it. The chief declares that whoever can take the ring off will be his bride. Of course, Abadeha manages to do it, for the happy ending. The full-page pastel scenes focus on the appealing characters in presumed "native" attire of the precolonial period. A very few objects and plants provide context in the minimal visual narrative. The author describes how she researched religious beliefs, practices, native landscape, and traditional Filipino family behavior. The writing on the title page is in *Alibata,* a writing system now forgotten.

THE PHILIPPINES TODAY OR IN THE RECENT PAST

Arcellana, Francisco. *The Mats.* Illustrated by Hermès Alègrè. Brooklyn, NY: Kane/Miller, 1999. 24pp. Grades 1–4.

The narrator recalls a time when his father returned from an inspection trip with some special new mats made by a weaver he calls an artist. The family already has a mat used only on special occasions, given to their mother when she was married. They all eagerly anticipate the new ones. Each has the owner's name and a special symbol related to that person. There are three extra mats. Each is for a child who has died—for they are a part of the family also, always in their hearts. Full-page paintings depict the little action. Figures are treated more symbolically than with an effort to instill individual personalities. Attention is directed to the mats and their special patterns. Traditional patterns decorate the end-papers as well.

FILIPINO AMERICANS

Gilles, Almira Astudillo. *Willie Wins.* Illustrated by Carl Angel. New York: Lee & Low, 2001. 32pp. Grades K–3.

After a disappointing baseball game, Willie realizes he must have a bank for school the next day. The play money each student earns in class will go into the bank, and the student with the most will get circus tickets. His father gives him an *alkansiya,* a hollow coconut shell from his childhood in the Philippines. He tells Willie that there is something special inside; the shell must be broken to open it. Willie is dubious, especially when a classmate derides the "dusty shell." But when the time is up and Willie cracks open his bank, not only does he have the most money, but also there is a real baseball treasure inside. The focus of the double-page acrylic scenes is on the actions and emotions of the characters. Although the illustrations tend to simplify, there are sufficient details for the story. The center of attention is the unusual bank, its reception, and its surprise.

HAWAII

ORIGINAL TALES AND FOLKTALES EVOKING THE PAST

Martin, Rafe. *The Shark God.* Illustrated by David Shannon. New York: Arthur A. Levine/Scholastic, 2001. 32pp. Grades K–4.

After having freed an entangled shark, a brother and sister dare defy the king's order and touch the drum that is forbidden to any but the king. They are sentenced to die. Their distraught parents go bravely into the Shark God's cave to seek his help. He tells them to prepare a canoe for a journey. On the day of the execution, a storm arises, and a terrible wave sweeps the children out to where the shark can take them to their parents' canoe. From there, with the drum, they can proceed to a new home. Drama dominates the double-page scenes, with paints applied to create sculptured, appropriately clothed characters, some in powerful close-ups. Tropical foliage and surf-washed shoreline make a proper setting; the shark's cave is a frightening place. The author notes his sources and the changes he made.

Schields, Gretchen. *The Water Shell.* San Diego, CA: Gulliver/Harcourt, 1995. 32pp. Grades 2–5.

To restore her island home destroyed by the Fire Queen, Keiki is told by the Great Shark of the Sea that she must take back the magic water shell stolen by the Queen. The shark gives Keiki a magic tooth to help her. On her way she meets characters who give her advice and more help. Finally she confronts the Queen and takes the shell back by force. The shell then splits like an egg, and its magic restores the land. The lengthy tale includes elements from Hawaii and Polynesia as noted in the listed sources. The illustrations are stylized, brightly colored, but full of fantasy rather than realism.

Takayama, Sandi. *The Musubi Man: Hawai'i's Gingerbread Man*. Iillustrated by Pat Hall. Honolulu: Bess Press, 1996. 24pp. Grades K–3.

The author uses the framework of the original tale, but the "man" is made of Hawaiian ingredients, explained in the glossary. He runs away from Hawaiian creatures. His final adventure is with a surfer in the waves. The language of the Musubi Man may reflect local patois: "You no can catch me," "I wen' run away." But it is not explained. Rather heavy-handed black outlines define most characters in double-page watercolor scenes. A few palm trees and waves and several cartoon-y characters keep the action going.

Wardlaw, Lee. *Punia and the King of Sharks: A Hawaiian Folktale*. Illustrated by Felipe Davalos. New York: Dial/Penguin, 1997. 32pp. Grades K–4.

Since Punia's fisherman father was eaten by sharks, he and his mother have only yams and poi to eat. Ten sharks and their king guard the tasty lobsters in a nearby cave for themselves. Clever Punia devises one trick after another to obtain lobsters. When the angry shark king is left alone, a final ruse gets him to swim away for good. The villagers can all feast on lobsters and cheer Punia as the new King of Sharks. Full-page ink and watercolor paintings offer portraits of the toothy sharks and young Punia as well as landscapes and village life, creating the tone and place of the story. Particulars of the sharks' activities in the sea emphasize the society's reliance on the ocean for their food. A glossary and pronunciation guide to Hawaiian terms is included.

HAWAII TODAY AND IN THE RECENT PAST

Guback, Georgia. *Luka's Quilt*. New York: Greenwillow/HarperCollins, 1994. 32pp. Grades 1–4.

Luka's grandmother, who takes care of her while her parents work, decides to make her a quilt. Instead of the many colors Luka envisioned, the quilt turns out to be only the traditional two colors, green and white in this case. Luka is disappointed and feels alienated from her grandmother. On traditional Lei Day, Luka makes a flower lei using all the colors she misses in her quilt, and grandmother quilts a multicolor lei for Luka, who happily begins to see beauty in both kinds of quilts. The story is an introduction to a part of Hawaiian culture and to the unique style of Hawaiian quilts. Naturalistic watercolors leave no space free of details, filled with all manner of plants, Luka's stuffed animal collection, a much-used kitchen, a page of Japanese lunch boxes, and of course the quilts.

INDONESIA

FOLKTALES

Sierra, Judy. *The Dancing Pig.* Illustrated by Jesse Sweetwater. San Diego, CA: Gulliver/Harcourt, 1999. 32pp. Grades K–3.

This variation on the traditional story of children left alone who are menaced but triumph, similar to Ed Young's *Lon Po Po* (Philomel, 1989), is based on a Balinese folktale. Twin girls, Klodan and Klonching, live with their mother on the edge of the forest. Watching them as they dance for their pig is the ogress Rangsasa. When their mother goes to the market, she warns them to open the door only for her. But the ogress finally fools them and carries them away. It is the pig, with other animal friends the girls have cared for, that lures Rangsasa into dancing the traditional Legong dance with her while the girls escape. The painted acrylic, watercolor, and gouache scenes convey the tropical climate with palm trees and lush landscapes as well as the typical houses and gardens of Bali. Children and mother have characteristic features and wear appropriate wraps. Of course, the star of the show is the Rangsasa, with her grotesque face mask typical of Bali and long red nails, although the dressed-up pig makes the most of her seductive dance, dressed in the patterned fabric of the area. There are notes on the music and dance and a pronunciation guide.

Weitzman, David. *Rama and Sita: A Tale from Ancient Java.* Boston: David R. Godine, 2002. 32pp. Grades K–5.

The traditional tale is told in the context of the traditional *dalang,* or storyteller, and his shadow puppets. It begins when Prince Rama is declared king by his father. But the king has promised his son Barata's mother to grant her wishes, and she insists that he banish Rama to the forest and make Barata king. So Rama leaves, accompanied by his wife Sita and his brother Lesmana. By trickery, wicked Ravana steals Sita away. The monkey king

Hanuman leads the monkeys to battle to rescue Sita. In the fierce fight Lesmana kills a mighty giant, Rama kills Ravana, and with Sita they return so that Rama can rule the kingdom. "Harmony is restored," and the puppets are put away. Shadow puppets painted with extensive use of gold in the ornate patterns of Java create impressions of the major characters. These are not illustrations in the sense of depicting specific actions. But they definitely convey the intense emotions of the mythical beings. Page designs integrate the text blocks with the stunning visuals to produce an appealing work informing us of the different stories other countries tell and of the unusual puppets they use to tell them.

AUSTRALIA

ORIGINAL TALES AND FOLKTALES EVOKING THE PAST

Berndt, Catherine. *Pheasant and Kingfisher.* Illustrated by Arone Raymond Meeks. New York: Mondo, 1987, 1994. 22pp. Paper. Grades 1–6.

A simple telling of the traditional story of two men, Bookbook the Pheasant and Bered-bered the Kingfisher, who "came from the Northwest" and settled in a campground where they hunted and cut bamboo. One day a visitor comes to warn them that the people to whom their campground belongs are returning, angry with them. The men prepare for battle. When the armed men arrive, they overwhelm Bookbook and Bered-bered, who magically become the pheasant and kingfisher we know today, with calls that sound like their original names. The illustrations are based on Aboriginal motifs, distinctly abstract painted human figures and animals produced with what we call x-ray patterning. Four pages of illustrated explanation add considerable information to the visual narrative. The tale was originally told by Nganalgindja in the Gunwinggu language.

Czernecki, Stefan, and Timothy Rhodes. *The Singing Snake.* Illustrated by Stefan Czernecki. New York: Hyperion, 1993. 40pp. Grades K–4.

Long ago, says the legend, Old Man became tired of all the noise the animals on his island made. He decided to make a musical instrument to honor whoever developed the most beautiful voice, the winner to be decided in a contest. Snake decides that Lark has the most beautiful voice, so he swallows her. When he smiles, the sun strikes her, and she begins to sing through his mouth. All the other animals agree that what they think is snake's voice is the best. When asked to sing again, Snake is scratched by Lark until he coughs her up. Meanwhile, Old Man has already begun to make his instrument in the shape of a snake. This becomes the traditional didgeridoo, further described in a note. But snake is thereafter shunned by the other animals. The style of painting of some Australian Aboriginals exploits dots; they make outlines and fill them with dots of color applied methodically. The end-papers show dotted snakes of different colors. The broad border that encloses text and pictures alike houses snakes and decorative areas of dotted color. Scenes are stylized in the fashion of some Aboriginal paintings using simplified forms, many shown with the characteristic x-ray bodies. The brick-red color of the Australian desert predominates.

Germein, Katrina. *Big Rain Coming.* Illustrated by Bronwyn Bancroft. New York: Clarion/Harcourt, 1999. 34pp. Grades PreS–3.

Old Stephen sees dark clouds and forecasts the big rain. But from Monday to Friday the days pass, and all the creatures wait impatiently. Finally, on Saturday, there is "wonderful, cool, wet RAIN." The language is spare, only a few words per page, but it vividly describes the anxious anticipation. The large double pages resonate with patterns painted in gouache and acrylic and shaped by black outlines filled with flat color. The symbolic Rainbow Serpent described in a note meanders along the page bottoms with its traditional dots; earth, sun, and moon are given delightful symbolic treatment, all recalling Australian Aboriginal art. The gray clouds are blown in by one with a face, lips pursed. The eventual rains appear in circular bands of green and white brush strokes surrounding a few dancing figures.

Kipling, Rudyard. *The Sing-Song of Old Man Kangaroo.* Illustrated by John Rowe. New York: Picture Book Studio/Simon & Schuster, 1990. 28pp. Also paper. Grades 2–6.

Kipling's classic tale from *Just So Stories* about Kangaroo, who got his wish to be different from all the other animals by being chased all day by Yellow-Dog Dingo, is presented here in its original distinctive language. The few Australian and Aboriginal terms used are described in notes at the end of the story. The twelve full-page paintings, with broad white bands that blend with the facing text pages, are in no way reproductions or recreations in Aboriginal style. But the choice of colors conveys the feeling of the Australian outback. Nqong, the Little God, is depicted a bit like some of the pictographs seen in the outback on walls. The animal characters are Rowe's own inventions.

Meeks, Arone Raymond. *Enora and the Black Crane: An Aboriginal Story*. New York: Scholastic, 1993. 32pp. Also paper. Grades 1–4.

Enora and his people live in a beautiful rain forest by a river. All the birds are black and white. One day Enora follows a "splash of color" deep into the forest, where it colors the feathers of birds. Since no one will believe his story, he kills a crane for proof. This evil deed causes him to be covered with black feathers. As a bird, he returns to the others but remains black. The simply told tale is from the author's cultural heritage. An unexpected red background delivers a punch behind the stylized white-outlined figures and black-and-white birds. There are the traditional dots, chiefly yellow, but other colors are used in many ways. Forms suggest combinations found in Aboriginal paintings. The final double-page scene of birds makes a stunning climax.

Morin, Paul. *Animal Dreaming: An Aboriginal Dreamtime Story*. San Diego, CA: Silver Whistle/Harcourt, 1998. 32pp. Grades 1–4.

A young boy named Mirri is taken by his friend and elder Gadurra into the outback to learn about when the earth was shaped, the day of Animal Dreaming. When they camp by rock paintings, Gadurra tells him of the beginning. The birds want to take over and attack the land. The animals gather to fight back. But the Ancestral Kangaroo, the Ancestral Long-necked Turtle, and the Ancestral Emu want to bring peace. They dream, then the Kangaroo acts on her dream, making a channel with a digging bone. After a wave washes over the land, it settles and there is peace. And the mystical story is passed on. Some of the paintings are textured like rough rock surfaces, others are "influenced by traditional Dreamtime images" from Aboriginal art, such as the x-ray-like animals and the dots which move in pulsating bands across the page. The few scenes of landscapes and the two protagonists are naturalistic, if dramatically lit, providing a contrast with the other illustrations.

AUSTRALIA TODAY AND IN RECENT HISTORY

Baker, Jeannie. *Where the Forest Meets the Sea*. New York: Greenwillow/HarperCollins, 1987. 32pp. Grades K–6.

In simple language and few words, Baker tells of a boy's visit with his father to a tropical rainforest in North Queensland, Australia. He explores, speculates on the history of the area and wonders how long it will last unsullied. The forest is recreated by photographing a collage of a variety of materials assembled into low relief scenes. A sandy beach, clear creek, interlaced treetops, and intricately convoluted root systems are all represented inventively by natural objects and clay. Then, to enhance the illusion, Baker includes ghost-like images of what the father and son discuss, like the crocodiles and dinosaurs of long ago and the original Aboriginal inhabitants. The final scene is of a projected resort development despoiling a deserted cove.

VIETNAM

VIETNAM TODAY

Shea, Pegi Deitz, and Cynthia Weill. *Ten Mice for Tet.* Illustrated by To Ngoc Trang and Pham Viet Dinh. San Francisco: Chronicle, 2003. 30pp. Grades PreS–3.

"It's time for Tet" say the parading mice. In brief, simple sentences we count with them from one to ten the preparations for the Vietnamese holiday. The plan is designed, the marketing done, the house made ready, and we proceed through the cooking and feasting to dancing and fireworks. Full details on the holiday and on each of the steps of preparation follow at the end, for older interested readers and adults, as does more information on how the illustrations are made, on the jacket flap. Anthropomorphic mice act out the steps conceived in a style suggestive of some traditional drawings. But these are created by embroidery, black outlines with solid colors filled in. Settings are very simple, with stylized trees, landscape, clouds, even a sinuous dragon. The medium appears only as a subtle texture in the very attractive double-page scenes.

VIETNAMESE AMERICANS AND THE IMMIGRANT EXPERIENCE

Garland, Sherry. *The Lotus Seed.* Illustrated by Tatsuro Kiuchi. San Diego, CA: Harcourt Brace, 1993. 32pp. Grades 2–5.

The story is written as if told by a Vietnamese-American girl recounting her grandmother's tale. It concerns a lotus seed she saved from a pod in the Imperial garden the day she, as a young girl, saw the emperor cry when he gave up his throne. The grandmother hid the seed through the years as she married, saw war come, fled in a small boat, and arrived in this strange new country. The girl tells how her grandmother weeps when her little brother steals the precious seed. But a lotus grows where he planted it, with a seed pod so that the grandmother and each grandchild can have a seed to remember. Subtly framed oil paintings on cream-colored pages supply detailed information about the adventures that the words leave out, including the family in the American kitchen and the objects on the altar where the lotus seed is hidden. The text is simple, the print large, but the history and issues raised are complex. The author adds a helpful note on Vietnamese history.

Hoyt-Goldsmith, Diane. *Hoang Anh: A Vietnamese American Boy.* Illustrated by Lawrence Migdale. New York: Holiday House, 1992. 32pp. Grades 2–6.

A young boy describes his new life in America, including the customs and rituals his family have brought with them from Vietnam. Clear photographs, a glossary, and a map all help bring the culture to life.

Tran, Truong. *Going Home, Coming Home: Ve Nha, Tham Que Huong.* Illustrated by Ann Phong. San Francisco: Children's Book Press, 2003. 32pp. Grades 1–4.

At first Amy Chi does not want to travel to Vietnam with her parents. They have not been back since they left as children, but to them it is still "home." Many things are strange to Amy Chi when she gets there, but she finally begins to feel closer to her uncle and grandmother. Meeting friendly children in the market also helps. By the time they leave to return to America, she is sorry to go. She realizes that "I am from the East and I am from the West." She is both American and Vietnamese. Phong's somewhat impressionistic acrylic paintings cover the pages where the text is printed in both English and Vietnamese. The technique helps unify the bilingual story, providing space for many details of the living conditions, the crowded market, the busy streets, and the quiet village.

Tran-Khanh-Tuyet. *The Little Weaver of Thai-Yen Village.* Illustrated by Nancy Hom. San Francisco: Children's Book Press, 1987. 24pp. Text in English and Vietnamese. Grades 2–5.

The war in which her father has been fighting for eight years comes to Hien's village in the rice fields, killing her mother and grandmother and sending her to the hospital. In her depression, she is comforted by a dream of the spirit bird Me-Linh, who has traditionally inspired her people in time of war. She needs an operation for which she must go to the United States, a place she fears because its people brought war to her village. Although the operation is a success, Hien misses her country. Until she can return, she weaves the spirit bird into blankets to be sent back to her people. The author's note further explains her experiences with children like Hien in 1969 and 1970 and since. Historic background is necessary to understand this sad story. There is also a harshness to the unmodulated saturated enamel-like colors used to fill in the black lines that outline all the shapes of the illustrations. Borders of solid colors contain the bilingual texts and scenes of both village life during the war and Hien's life in this country. Shapes are simplified, while gestures are linear embellishments.

Trottier, Maxine. *The Walking Stick*. Illustrated by Annouchka Gravel Galouchko. Toronto: Stoddart, 1999. 24pp. Grades K–3.

The story begins in the Vietnam forest, where young Van finds a branch from an old teak tree outside a Buddhist temple. His uncle helps him fashion it into a walking stick that he hopes means that Buddha will watch over him. Van marries and has a child. When war comes, the family escapes over the sea. There Van's daughter marries and has a daughter. Van tells Lynn, his granddaughter, about the stick and its history. When she is grown, she decides she must travel back to Vietnam. Van gives her the stick, which she lays at the feet of the Buddha at the temple with thanks for his help in the family's long journey. The full-page pictures are created with decorative patterning. Plants, clothing, and landscapes all are covered with textile-like patterns. The effect gives the tale symbolic expression while integrating such scenes as busy American streets into the visual story. References to Buddhist beliefs are introduced throughout.

LAOS

ORIGINAL TALES AND FOLKTALES EVOKING THE PAST

Day, Nancy Raines, adapter. *Piecing the Earth and Sky Together: A Creation Story from the Mien Tribe of Laos*. Illustrated by Genna Panzarella. Fremont, CA: Shen's Books, 2001. 32pp. 2 fold-outs. Grades K–4.

As Mei Yoon works at learning how to embroider "in the Mien way," her grandmother tells her the traditional creation story. From the heaven comes Faam Koh to make the sky and his sister Faam Toh to make the earth. Their disagreement on method makes for a contest. Working in secret, Koh quickly finishes stars, moon, and sun. Toh works more slowly on rock and soil. When they are both finished, they admire each other's work. But the sky is too small for the earth. Toh uses her needle to make the necessary adjustments for the fit. And meanwhile Mei Yoon has made a fine beginning herself with her needle. The visual narrative is produced by depicting the supernatural creators as humans seriously involved in their tasks. Pastels illuminate portraits and are used to totally fill the pages. The double fold-out is needed to give ample room for the final creation scene of earth, sky, and animal-filled jungle. Playing minor roles, grandmother and child are sympathetically pictured. A lengthy author's note describes the distinctive embroidery of the Mien tribe and the Laotian Handcraft Project in Berkeley, California that is working to preserve the traditions and culture. A sampling of the traditional stitches is clearly shown on a separate page and across the end-papers.

Xiong, Blia. *Nine-in-One Grr! Grr!: A Folktale from the Hmong People of Laos.* Adapted by Cathy Spagnoli. Illustrated by Nancy Hom. Fremont, CA: Children's Book Press, 1989. 32pp. Also paper. Grades K–4.

In this simply told tale heard during the author's childhood in Laos, Tiger goes to visit the great god Shao in the sky to find out how many cubs she will have. Shao tells her "nine each year" but only if she can remember the words. Tiger, whose memory is bad, makes up the song of the title to sing all the way home so she won't forget. Bird, unhappy at the thought of all those tigers, distracts tiger long enough to substitute "one in nine." This keeps the tiger population down.

Silk screen has been used to translate the needlework of the story cloths that have emerged as a new form of traditional Hmong craft. Each illustration is a scene with a distinctive and multiframed border, thin bands of color, and a thicker band with geometric patterns. The scenes use symbols, stylized animal and floral shapes, set onto colored backgrounds, mostly without horizon or ground line. Costumes and a building derive from the culture. The palette of saturated blues, reds, and greens is consistent with both the needlework and the land. Similar work comes from the Chung Mai area of Thailand.

LAOS TODAY AND IN THE RECENT PAST

Cha, Dia. *Dia's Story Cloth.* "Stitched by" Chue and Nhia Thao Cha. New York: Lee & Low, with Denver Museum of Natural History, 1996. 24pp. Also paper. Grades 2–5.

The author, a refugee herself, received a story cloth from her aunt and uncle in a refugee camp in Thailand. Using parts of the cloth for illustration, she tells the story of her people, from their original flight from China to Burma, then Thailand, and in her family's case, Laos. She describes their rural agricultural life. The war arrives, with tragic consequences. She and her mother escape to a refugee camp and eventually to the United States. But many, including her aunt and uncle, remain in the camps. The white story cloth, as shown on a textless double page, is about five feet high and ten feet long. Each of the sections used to illustrate the text is crowded with black-robed people, trees, buildings, and all the other elements of their saga. The interwoven scenes are pure visual storytelling. Joyce Herold, curator at the Denver Museum, adds several pages of information on the Hmong and their arts.

CAMBODIA

CAMBODIA TODAY

Lipp, Frederick. *The Caged Birds of Phnom Penh.* Illustrated by Ronald Himler. New York: Holiday House, 2001. 32pp. Grades K–4.

Young Ari lives in the grimy city. She has only heard that outside there are blue skies and birds flying free. She takes her hard-earned money to the bird lady, where you can buy a bird that you can set free to fly away and make your wishes come true. But the bird she buys comes back to its cage, and Ari feels that she and her family will never get away from their deprived life. From her grandfather, she learns that only a "blessed" bird can grant her wishes. So she chooses another bird very carefully. This time the bird flies away, giving Ari hope for a better life. Himler's detailed watercolor and gouache over pencil illustrations of field and city bring us directly into Cambodia. Ari's adventure dealing with the bird vendor is depicted with naturalistic conviction; her wish for the bird's freedom is really for her own as well. The use of color in the final pages effectively symbolizes that hope.

THAILAND

FOLKTALE

MacDonald, Margaret Read. *The Girl Who Wore Too Much: A Folktale from Thailand.* Illustrated by Yvonne Lebrun Davis, with Thai text by Supaporn Vathanaprida. Little Rock, AR: August House, 1998. 32pp. Grades K–3.

Invited to a dance, spoiled, vain Aree cannot decide which of her many beautiful dresses to wear. So she puts them all on. She can't leave any of her jewelry off either. She displays it all to her friends but finds she cannot climb up the hill to the dance so laden. She refuses to take anything off, so the friends go to the dance without her. She is still struggling along when they return. Exhausted, she admits she has too much and has learned her lesson. Stylized gouache, watercolor, and colored pencil illustrations with a variety of borders focus on the story's details of clothing and jewelry but also supply background landscapes. The Thai text runs along the bottom of the pages; the English text is incorporated into the scenes. The many versions of the tale are noted. Although the story is old, it has been set in the present "so the illustrator could use beautiful contemporary Pu-Thai silk colors in the pictures."

THAILAND TODAY

Ho, Minfong. *Hush! A Thai Lullaby.* Illustrated by Holly Meade. New York: Orchard/Scholastic, 1996. 32pp. Also paper. Grades K–2.

In repetitive rhyming verse, a mother asks creatures like the mosquito, lizard, and buffalo to hush so her baby can sleep. Of course, when everyone else is asleep, the baby is awake. Each double-page scene is complete with animal and setting. Cut papers depict specifics of a rural life style with clarity and considerable esthetic impact. Although unconcerned with most naturalistic details, these illustrations create a sense of being there, sensing the hot silence.

BUDDHIST TALES FROM THE AREA
(ADDITIONAL REFERENCES IN THE INDEX UNDER "BUDDHISM")

Demi. *Buddha.* New York: Henry Holt, 1996. 42pp. Grades 3–8.

A Buddhist herself, Demi retells the story of the young prince Siddhartha who became the Enlightened One and established a religion with millions of followers today. According to predictions, the prince was to become a poor beggar and seeker of truth. The king tried to keep this from happening, but the compassionate prince left the palace riches to become a monk. Demi tells of the lessons he learned, his battles with the forces of evil, and his Enlightenment. His wisdom and parables have lasted to this day. Although the story of his life and teaching is simply told, the underlying meanings may require some thought and maturity. Based on careful study of the art of many Asian cultures, the stunning pictures and page designs add significantly to the emotional impact. The gold and red cover illustration and fine calligraphy-like line drawing on the end-papers prepare us for a detailed presentation of costumes and artifacts arranged in settings reminiscent of Buddhist painting.

Lee, Jeanne M. *I Once Was a Monkey: Stories Buddha Told.* New York: Farrar, Straus, 1999. 40pp. Grades 2–5.

Six animals taking shelter during a monsoon storm end their bickering when a statue with a glowing halo offers to tell a story. It concerns the need for harmony, because "all creatures depend on one another for their existence." For the statue is Gautama Buddha, who tells of his past lives in five more stories, each with a lesson for those in the shelter. When they leave, wiser, they wonder if it was all a dream. In the afterword, Lee adds more information on Buddha, Buddhism, and on the Jatakas, or "birth stories," in Buddhist literature. Black-and-white linoleum cuts depict the Buddha and animals in the cave; color is added for the illustrations of the tales. These show just a piece of the action. The Buddha looks like the conventional statues. The portraits are thoughtfully positioned in esthetically designed contents. Collectively, they help the Buddha point out what all creatures have in common—their interdependency.

Rockwell, Anne. *The Prince Who Ran Away: The Story of Gautama Buddha.* Illustrated by Fahimeh Amiri. New York: Alfred A. Knopf, 2001. 38pp. Grades 2–5.

The lengthy text relates the basic facts about the life of Prince Siddhartha who became Gautama Buddha, along with a few of the incidents that have come to be part of his story, as related in Demi's *Buddha* above. Rockwell details how, even after his marriage, he feels he must go out into the world. Although Mara the Evil One tempts him and sends demons to frighten him, Gautama spends seven weeks in contemplation under a Bo tree and finds enlightenment, then travels throughout the world carrying his message. The author adds additional information in a note to this introduction to the origin of Buddhism. The detailed, full-page paintings describe the events in the Buddha's life in a style based on old Indian miniature painting. These capture the spirit of the tale's intent in spelling out the peaceful message attractively and effectively, including the architecture, the costumes, the demons, and the iconography of Buddhism.

TIBET

ORIGINAL TALES AND FOLKTALES EVOKING THE PAST

Berger, Barbara Helen, reteller and illustrator. *All the Way to Lhasa: A Tale of Tibet.* New York: Philomel/Penguin, 2002. 32pp. Grades K–4.

Briefly and simply told, but full of symbolic mystical meaning, the parable relates the journey of a young boy through danger and difficulty, placing "one foot in front of the other," to his goal, the sacred city of Lhasa. Persistence delivers its reward. A lengthy note explains some of the cultural background and the strenuous physical conditions. There's a fairy-tale look to the double-page acrylic, colored pencil, and gouache narrative illustrations, with their decorative sculptural clouds, softly modeled animals, the mysterious old woman giving the advice, etc. This otherworldly impression has Eastern overtones enhanced by the clothing and the architecture at the journey's end.

Demi. *The Donkey and the Rock*. New York: Henry Holt, 1999. 32pp. Grades PreS–2.

A poor man carrying a jar of oil while walking with his ten children sets the jar on a rock while he rests. Another man comes along with his ten children driving his donkey laden with wool. The donkey knocks over the jar, which breaks, spilling all the oil. The angry jar owner blames the man with the donkey, who promptly blames the donkey. The two men go to the wise king to settle the argument. Since both are good men, the king reasons, they can't be at fault. He has the donkey and the rock arrested. The case sounds crazy, so everyone comes to the trial. The king fines each spectator ten coins for their silly curiosity, gives the money to the poor man, and settles the problem. Demi's very small, finely wrought gouache, ink, and watercolor drawings portray scenes with robed priests, peasants in traditional dress, yaks and tents, and the king's palace. All are set with lots of space around them except for the crowded courtyard. This is a particularly attractive, lighthearted visualization of a story also told in India and China.

TIBET AND THE HIMALAYAS TODAY AND IN RECENT HISTORY

Lama, Tenzing Norbu. *Himalaya*. Toronto: Groundwood/Douglas & McIntyre, 2002. 34pp. Grades 1–4.

The lengthy story is fiction, but it is based on the lives of the Dolpo people of the Himalayas, who make the difficult trek to the plains of Nepal regularly to trade salt for the grain they need to survive. Conflict erupts between old Tinle and young Karma over who should lead the caravan after the death of Tinle's son, the chief. Tinle's other son and grandson become involved in the arduous journey, where tragedy strikes before the people end their struggle and a new chief can emerge. The nearly double-page illustrations combine compelling detailed drawing with smoothly applied paints, naturalistic, in colors that emphasize the cold desolation, effectively engaging us in the heroic struggles. The story, a powerful look into human character, was originally a film. Note: *Secret of the Snow Leopard* by Lama with Stéphane Frattini, a follow-up adventure, is scheduled for 2004 publication.

Sís, Peter. *Tibet: Through the Red Box.* New York: Frances Foster/Farrar, Straus, 1998. 57pp. Grades 2–8.

Enclosed within a memoir Sís writes about his childhood, his relationship with his father, and the stories his father told, is his father's diary, left to him in the red box. The lengthy tale his father pens concerns his journey in the 1950s, when he and a film crew are wandering lost in Tibet. Along with details of the landscape and people he encounters are mystic tales and additions by the author as he reacts to the diary, printed in a form of script. Additional facts about Tibet are added alongside the strange events recounted. Full page, mysteriously detailed pictures and intriguing vignettes challenge us as we turn the pages of this large, square book. The artist's fine line drawings and toned pages draw us into an exotic world. This approach gives a hint of a totally different society's look and way of living.

INDIA

ORIGINAL TALES AND FOLKTALES EVOKING THE PAST

Bash, Barbara. *In the Heart of the Village: The World of the Indian Banyan Tree.* San Francisco: Sierra Club, 1996. 32pp. Paper. Grades 2–4.

The author begins with a Nirantali creation folktale, with sources to "explain" the origin of the banyan tree. After describing the tree and its widespread tropical locations, she focuses on one particular tree in an Indian village, giving a picture of the ebb and flow of animal and village life through day and night. The double pages are conceived with artistic concern for the overall design as well as for the gentle rhythm of the lives around the tree.

Brown, Marcia. *Once a Mouse . . . : From Ancient India, a Fable Cut in Wood.* New York: Scribners/Macmillan. Aladdin paper, 1961. 32pp. Grades K–4.

After saving a mouse from being snatched by a crow, a hermit turns him into a cat to keep him from being eaten by one. He turns the cat into a dog when another dog frightens the cat. Finally he turns the dog into a tiger, who becomes so proud that he threatens the hermit. The hermit then turns him into a mouse again. The very simple story, told in few words, offers room for discussion. The three-color woodcuts exploit the medium in their rough minimal chiseling and near-miss overlapping of the olive, red, and gold inks. The objects that convey a sense of India are the old bearded man in turban and *dhoti* and the tiger. From the end-papers with their leaping deer and other animals and the abstracted forest in which the hermit tends to the animals' needs come a spiritual quality. Conveying concepts from another culture is sometimes possible through such spare esthetic means.

Demi. *One Grain of Rice: A Mathematical Folktale.* New York: Scholastic, 1997. 36pp. Fold-outs. Grades 1–4.

This is Demi's version of the traditional tale of the rajah who kept all the rice in a time of famine. A girl tricks him by asking for only one grain of rice the first day and double that each day thereafter for a month. The rajah agrees, and so the numbers rise. Finally he has no more rice to give and agrees to be fairer in the future. Red and gold, Demi's favorite colors, are used to frame illustrations that resemble Indian miniature paintings. The double fold-out of 256 laden elephants is a masterful example of her patient craftsmanship.

Jendresen, Erik, and Joshua M. Greene, retellers. *Hanuman: Based on Valmiki's Ramayana.* Illustrated by Li Ming. Berkeley, CA: Tricycle Press, 1998. 40pp. Grades 2–6.

Hanuman the monkey tells this lengthy saga, beginning from his youth when he had mystical powers, which he loses. Ravana the beast kidnaps prince Rama's beautiful wife Sita and carries her away in his airship. The monkeys agree to search for her and bring her back to Rama. Hanuman recalls his powers to reach Lanka, where Ravana is keeping Sita. How they win a terrible battle and finally rescue Sita makes an exciting climax to this portion of the traditional legends of Rama. Another version appears in Weitzman' *Rama and Sita* above. Perhaps more Hollywood than traditional in its naturalistic visualization of the mythic tale, the double-page paintings nevertheless supply a moving melodrama with imaginative monsters and chilling battles. Close-ups of men and monkeys keep a measure of humanity in what almost seems science fiction. Further notes on Valmiki's classic *Ramayana* are included.

Martin, Rafe. *The Brave Little Parrot.* Illustrated by Susan Gaber. New York: G. P. Putnam's Sons, 1998. 32pp. Grades K–3.

When lightning starts a terrible forest fire, all the animals run away. Only a small gray parrot thinks that they should try to save the forest. The animals refuse to help her, so all by herself she braves the heat and flames to carry drops of water back onto the fire. The gods and goddesses in the sky laugh at her futile efforts. One god, taking the shape of an eagle, tries to persuade her to save herself, but she perseveres. Ashamed that the gods are doing nothing to help, the eagle begins to weep. Miraculously, not only do his tears put out the flames but also grass, trees, and flowers grow again. And on the brave parrot grow beautifully colored feathers. This traditional *Jataka* tale from India shows the reward for doing what comes from your heart. Naturalistic paintings create the forest, the fire, and the animals on large single and double pages. The scenes including the gods show them as they look in Indian sculptures. The parrot and the eagle involve our emotions, as does the peaceful scene after the lush forest is restored.

Martin, Rafe. *The Monkey Bridge.* Illustrated by Fahimeh Amiri. New Yok: Alfred A. Knopf, 1997. 32pp. Grades 1–4.

According to the traditional Buddhist Jataka tale, a tree with delicious fruit grows in Benares because of the sacrifice of the brave and noble Monkey King, who also appears in Kraus's *The Making of the Monkey King* and Weitzman's *Rama and Sita,* above. High in the Himalayas, a tribe of monkeys enjoys the fruit of a Treasure Tree. The wise Monkey King realizes that if any fruit reaches the village downstream, people will come in search of the tree and the monkeys will be in danger. So he rules that all fruit must be plucked before it falls into the river. Downstream in Benares, one piece of fruit that was not picked is found in the river by the king. He determines to find the tree; then orders his archers to shoot the monkeys. The Monkey King makes a bridge of his own body for the monkeys to escape. The king is so impressed with this selflessness that he promises to leave the tree alone. In return, the Monkey King gives him a seed so that he can grow his own tree. Double-page paintings with borders clearly have been influenced by 17th- and 18th-century Indian illustrations. Both the attractive decorative qualities and the excitement of the actions are conveyed with imagination. Further source notes are included.

Ravishankar, Anushka. *Tiger on a Tree.* Illustrated by Pulak Biswas. New York: Farrar, Straus, 2004. 40pp. Grades PreS–2.

In jaunty rhymes, a few words to a page, we follow a tiger as he crosses the river to explore. Frightened by a charging animal, he decides, "This tree is the only place to be!" But when some men spot him, they decide: "Get him! Net him! Tie him tight! Will he bite? He might!" Fortunately one man suggests that they let him free, a fine preservationist message. Although the story is not traditionally Indian, it was originally written and published there. The costumes and setting, such as they are, are traditional. Visually told in two-color woodcuts, black and orange, and with large typeface, there is a vigor to the design with its simplified figures and bits of landscape against the blank white page.

Rumford, James. *Nine Animals and the Well*. Boston: Houghton Mifflin, 2003. 32pp. Grades K–4.

This original fable/counting book, set "in the long-ago, rose-fragrant, animal-talking days in India," concerns animals bringing gifts to a raja-king. They discover in the end that their friendship is the most prized gift of all. The author note explains the setting as the source of the numbers, falsely called "Arabic," that we use today and that inspired this story. Cut paper collage, brush, pen- and pencil-created animals are basically natura-listic but clearly simplified and in odd colors. They are cleverly organized in frames with other creatures on the text pages adding their bit to the amusing story.

Shepard, Aaron. *Savitri: A Tale of Ancient India*. Illustrated by Vera Rosen-berry. Morton Grove, IL: Albert Whitman, 1992. 40pp. Grades 2–5.

The loyal and clever Princess Savitri's story is part of the Hindu epic *Ma-habharata*. She chooses to wed Satyavan, who has no kingdom, lives with his father in a simple hermitage, and is doomed to die within a year. When Yama, god of death, comes for him, Savitri follows after, gaining concessions from Yama and finally cleverly forcing him to release her husband's spirit. Stylistically the figures, gestures, facial expressions, and surrounding details of landscape and artifacts suggest aspects of illustrated books from Indian history. Gold frames enclose the text and facing page of illustration. These pictures are frequently overpainted, breaking out of confinement. Ink and transparent watercolors create decorative foliage, peaceful-looking animals, and a starkly stylized environment for the simply told story.

Thornhill, Jan. *The Rumor: A Jataka Tale from India*. Toronto: Maple Tree, 2002. 32pp. Grades PreS–3.

In this Indian version of the traditional "sky is falling" story, a young hare, frightened by a falling branch, is followed in her racing away by animal horde after animal horde as she declares: "The world is breaking up! Run for your life!" A wise lion finally makes them all stop and think; then he scolds them for their foolishness. There is a formality to the painted illustrations in their decorated borders that supports the notion of folktale. But the stylized pictures of verdant trees and multiple animals dashing through the forests have a vitality that helps break the confines. Notes discuss the source of the tale and its relationship to Buddhism. Each of the included animals is pictured in miniature with details of their nature at the end.

INDIA TODAY AND IN THE RECENT PAST

Atkins, Jeannine. *Aani and the Tree Huggers.* Illustrated by Venentius J. Pinto. New York: Lee & Low, 1995. 32pp. Grades 1–4.

The story of a brave young woman's fight to save her village's forest is based on an actual event in Northern India in the 1970s. One day when Aani is enjoying a peaceful moment by her favorite tree away from her crowded family hut, she is shocked by a loud noise. It is the sound of men from the city coming in trucks with axes to cut down and take away the trees. The villagers need the wood from the trees, and the roots keep the land from eroding. But the men have their orders. Aani suddenly ignores the axes and saws and hugs her favorite tree. The other women do the same. The men leave, and all is safe. Tree-protecting laws are soon passed, the author informs us. The full and double-page gouache scenes are adapted from some early Indian miniatures, a style that is basically naturalistic but with ornamental patterns for leaves and dresses. The overall effect helps tell the story of the emotions generated by the danger and the women's response. The illustrator has added notes on the sources he has used from Indian art, including line and dot page borders.

Bond, Ruskin. *Cherry Tree.* Illustrated by Allan Eitzen. Honesdale, PA: Caroline House/Boyds Mills, 1991. Also paper, 1996. 32pp. Grades 1–4.

Young Rakhi's grandfather suggests she plant the seed from one of the cherries she has eaten in the soil of the stony Himalayan foothills of northern India. She watches it grow, cares for it through accidents and insect threats, and grows herself as well. As a young woman, she can enjoy the cherry blossoms with her grandfather and imagine telling her own children the story of the tree. The author, who lives in India, has written this original story about his local area. Eitzen's combination of patterned cut paper (mostly for Rakhi's clothes) and paint creates scenes that suggest the peaceful, bucolic life. The few lines of text are given space, while the illustrations fill the pages. While Rakhi and her grandfather are drawn appealingly, the trees, mountains, even the weather are treated somewhat abstractedly.

Kamal, Aleph. *The Bird Who Was an Elephant.* Illustrated by Frane Lessac. New York: HarperCollins, 1989. 32pp. Grades 1–4.

The story describes Bird's progress to the village from the desert, past shops, beggars, a sacred cow, a wise man, a snake charmer, the train station, the temple, and finally to rest at night in a tree. A palmist tells him, incidentally, that he was an elephant in his past life and will be a fish in the next. Nothing happens beyond everyday life in an Indian village. The author's note discusses the Hindu belief in rebirth, and the Indian words he uses. Jaunty opaque painted scenes depict the contemporary Hindu village. Figures and buildings are rendered simply without modeling, as much for their overall decorative effect as for the conveying of information. Each page is bordered with a different band of color containing tiny pictures of objects relating to the subject of the illustration, adding to the sense of place.

Krishnaswami, Uma. *Monsoon.* Illustrated by Jamel Akib. New York: Farrar, Straus, 2003. 32pp. Grades K–3.

The importance of and the experiencing of the arrival of the monsoon rains in India are related by a young girl. As they go about their lives, she and her family feel the hot winds, while she worries about what will happen if it doesn't rain. When it finally does, the excitement and relief are clear. Akib's naturalistic painted double-page scenes depict the urban family going about its daily life while awaiting the rains. The bustling street scenes include a headstrong cow. The final few pages add the darkening clouds followed by a wet joyousness. There is also a summary of detailed information about the monsoon; the few Hindi words are explained.

Lewin, Ted. *Sacred River.* New York: Clarion/Houghton, 1995. 32pp. Also paper. Grades 2–4.

The Ganges River is the most sacred river of all for Hindus; a pilgrimage to Benares on the Ganges is "the highest goal of life." In the simplest of caption-like texts to accompany his double-page illustrations, Lewin describes the arrival of pilgrims and what occurs at the river as they bathe in the water, while the ashes of those cremated in funeral pyres are cast into that same river to flow down to the sea. The very naturalistic watercolors are more effective than photographs in showing the humanistic activities of the men and women crowding the river's edges. We see palatial buildings with windowless walls loom over the shoreline, women in multicolored saris, boats, sun-screens, clouds of gray smoke from the pyres. We can almost smell the mixed odors and hear the masses of voices. There is a brief introduction to the faith that brings the people to Benares.

McDonald, Megan. *Baya, Baya, Lulla-by-a.* Illustrated by Vera Rosenberry. New York: Richard Jackson/Atheneum, 2003. 32pp. Grades PreS–1.

The lullaby text is original but inspired by an Indian lullaby. It is filled with soothing words, some in Hindi explained in a glossary. The images are both universal and specifically Indian. The baya bird weaves its nest as the mother weaves a quilt for the baby. Her scarf makes a cradle in a tree to rock the baby; the bird warns of a cobra. A note tells more about the baya bird and its nest. There is a concern for nature in the rendering of the baya bird and tree. The layouts of landscape and the mother's typically patterned clothing, all in borders with some stylization, are equally attractive. The resulting visual watercolor narrative is both appealing and informative.

Nagda, Ann Whitehead. *Snake Charmer.* New York: Henry Holt, 2002. 32pp. Grades 1–4.

Young Vishnu longs to become a snake charmer like his father and grandfather before him. Through his eyes, we see life today in an Indian village without electricity. We also see him begin to work with the snakes. A note adds much background about this trade and its history. Clear, framed color photographs on colored backgrounds add local details important for understanding living conditions in parts of India. Added patterns and patterned borders are typical decorations.

PAKISTAN

PAKISTAN TODAY AND IN THE RECENT PAST

Khan, Rukhsana. *Ruler of the Courtyard.* Illustrated by R. Gregory Christie. New York: Viking, 2003. 34pp. Grades K–3.

A young Pakistani girl must fight her fear of the nasty, pecking chickens each time she crosses the courtyard to enjoy the relaxing peace of the bath house. One day while there, she spots a snake by the door. She is afraid to scream and have her Nani come to her aid, for she might be bitten by the snake. She faces her fear and traps the snake in her bucket. When she peeks in at it, she is relieved to see that it is only the rope from her Nani's pants.

Her bravery has shown her that she, not the chickens, rules the courtyard. Christie's acrylic paintings emphasize the emotion, using reds and yellows applied roughly in large areas. He focuses in on the girl's face, which seems overly large, with tension obvious in the rest of her body. Her final release from fear is delightfully visualized in a laughing dance, swinging the rope. Background information is added.

PAKISTANI AMERICANS AND THE IMMIGRANT EXPERIENCE

English, Karen. *Nadia's Hands.* Illustrated by Jonathan Weiner. Honesdale, PA: Boyds Mills, 1999. 32pp. Grades K–3.

In her role as flower girl in her Auntie Laila's wedding, Nadia will have the *mehndi,* henna designs traditional at Pakistani weddings, painted on her hands. Nadia is concerned that the orange designs will be hard to explain to her classmates. Amid the excitement of the wedding preparations, Nadia must be patient while her hands are painted and then dry. She manages her part in the ceremony, still worried about her hands but noticing how beautiful the patterns are and how happy they seem to make the whole family. She finally looks forward to showing her hands to the class as part of her heritage. Full-page oil pastel scenes show Nadia's changing moods as the focus in the hand-painting process. Several naturalistic pictures of the hands display the traditional patterns, as well as pictures of the wedding procession. Some Urdu words are used and explained.

AFGHANISTAN AND THE SUFI TRADITION

ORIGINAL TALES AND FOLKTALES EVOKING THE PAST

Shah, Idries. *The Boy without a Name.* Illustrated by Mona Caron. Boston: Hoopoe Books, 2000. 32pp. Grades K–3.

A young boy's parents are told not to give him a name. The unhappy boy offers his friend a dream in exchange for his name. When he and his friend go to a wise man for advice, a name, Hasni, comes to him from a magic box. His friend asks for the promised dream. Hasni puts dreams from his head into a box; then from another, the man allows each boy to choose a wonderful dream that they can have from then on. The story, from the Sufi tradition, is a strange one with the meaning unclear. Caron supplies very detailed double-page paintings filling the visual narrative with the feel of some anonymous Middle Eastern city. Clothing, architecture, shops, artifacts, are interwoven effectively and, in the wise man's house, magically.

Shah, Idries. *The Clever Boy and the Terrible, Dangerous Animal.* Illustrated by Rose Mary Santiago. Boston: Hoopoe Books, 2000. 32pp. Grades K–3.

In this simply told Sufi tale, a young boy is warned by the frightened people in a village he is visiting to beware of a terrible creature. When he sees it, it is only a melon. He cuts it and eats it, which makes the people afraid of him. He soon shows them not only how good melons are but also how to grow more. Save for the moral about the danger of ignorance, this rather silly story is told visually in appealing cartoon style. The people are clothed in a sort of Middle Eastern costume. The colored illustrations exaggerate gestures and use page layouts for humor.

Shah, Idries. *The Farmer's Wife.* Illustrated by Rose Mary Santiago. Boston: Hoopoe Books, 1998. 32pp. Grades K–3.

This is the Sufi version of the cumulative tale that asks one creature after another to act upon it to start the desired chain of events. Here the farmer's wife begins by asking a bird to fetch the apple she has dropped into a hole. The "rather naughty bird" will not, nor will the "rather naughty cat" jump at the bird, nor the dog chase the cat, and so it goes. She finally gets the chain started for a happy ending. Double-page painted scenes are designed for visual delight, adding sparkle to the repetitious text. The wife is properly dressed in a full-length black robe and red head-covering. All objects are simplified and organized for decorative effect.

Shah, Idries. *The Magic Horse.* Illustrated by Julie Freeman. Boston: Hoopoe Books, 1998. 40pp. Also paper. Grades 1–4.

In this lengthy Sufi folktale, a king has two sons, one a busy producer and the other, Tambal, a dreamer. The king scorns a wooden horse carved for him, which supposedly can take the rider wherever he desires, and gives it to Tambal. The horse takes Tambal on magical adventures that end in his winning a beautiful princess. The text is set in multiple decorative borders illustrated with scenes depicting pieces of the narrative. Costumes and architecture suggest a fanciful Middle East.

Shah, Idries. *Neem the Half-Boy.* Illustrated by Midori Mori and Robert Revels. Boston: Hoopoe Books, 1998. 32pp. Grades K–3.

Because she does not do as she is told by the wise man, the queen of Hich-Hich, "which means 'nothing at all,'" gives birth to a baby who is only half a boy. Prince Neem is told that if he wants to be whole, he must drink a medicine found in the cave of a fire-breathing dragon. In exchange for the medicine, the happy now-whole prince gives the dragon a stove to cook his food on so he doesn't need to blow fire and distress people any more. All ends happily in this Sufi tale. Double-page scenes provide spare contextual details of carpet, arches, distant mountains, with characters in Middle Eastern type dress. The basically naturalistic depictions are relatively emotionless. But the dragon is more of a cartoon, affording some comic relief. The half-boy becomes whole from the front end-papers to the back.

Shah, Idries. *The Old Woman and the Eagle*. Illustrated by Natasha Delmar. Boston: Hoopoe Books, 2003. 32pp. Grades 1–4.

This Sufi teaching tale begins "when cups were plates and when knives and forks grew in the ground. . . ." When an eagle lands at an old woman's door, she assumes he is a pigeon, since she has never seen an eagle. She proceeds to try to make him look like a pigeon, clipping his claws, straightening his beak, brushing his feathers. The unhappy eagle is glad to have another eagle help him make him look like himself again, while warning him of people who think that things are what they are not. "And they never went near that silly old woman again." Naturalistic with eye-pleasing decorations and borders, the illustrations establish a Middle Eastern setting. But the majority of the pictures depict a gloriously feathered eagle in the text's assorted actions. The visual narrative almost needs no text.

Shah, Idries. *The Silly Chicken*. Illustrated by Jeff Jackson. Boston: Hoopoe Books, 2000. 32pp. Grades K–3.

In this Sufi version of the chicken who thinks the sky is falling, a chicken who has been taught to speak tells the town that the earth is going to swallow them up. People run frantically everywhere but of course can't get away from the earth. When they finally ask him how he knows, and he tells them that he doesn't, they are at first furious. But then they realize their own foolishness for believing a chicken—a humorous look at human nature. The comic rendering of the tale includes a cast of appropriately garbed townsfolk, a sandy landscape, a hilarious-looking camel, and a charming white "chicken." Lots of visual actions are designed to make us smile.

Young, Ed. *What About Me?* New York: Philomel/Penguin, 2002. 32pp. Grades K–3.

In this simple but expressive retelling of a traditional Sufi fable, a Grand Master tells a young boy seeking knowledge that he must first bring in exchange a small carpet. In a familiar folktale pattern, this begins the boy's progressive cumulative search; from carpet maker, who asks first for thread; to the spinner requesting goat hair; and on and on in his quest. When he finally finds the last item, a wife for a carpenter, he can go back down the line. But by the time he has the carpet, the Grand Master tells him he has already acquired the necessary knowledge along the way. The Grand Master even offers two morals for our enlightenment. Young designs the bordered pages with elegant simplicity; textured backgrounds hold blocks of text and figures without any context. Collage combines patterned and solid color shapes with watercolor touches. The hints of Asian art are there along with Sufi philosophy.

AFGHANISTAN TODAY

Khan, Rukhsana. *The Roses in My Carpet.* Illustrated by Ronald Himler. New York: Holiday House, 1998. 32pp. Grades 1–4.

A young boy safe in a refugee camp relives in his dreams the horror of bombing in his native Afghanistan. The camp is dirty, school unappealing, food scarce. But after a meager lunch and prayers, he can finally do what he really enjoys, practice carpet weaving. Each color has meaning for him, but he particularly likes red, the color of roses, which the family could never grow. His sister is in an accident; she will be all right. But only in his dreams can he find a really safe place where roses bloom. Watercolor scenes fill most of the double pages with informative pictures that reinforce the emotional content.

TURKESTAN

Hogrogian, Nonny. *The Tiger of Turkestan.* Charlottesville, VA: Hampton Roads, 2002. 32pp. Grades K–3.

Before she dies "in the shadow of Ararat," Little Tiger's grandmother gives him advice: "In this life, never do as others do." He ponders this as he grows up, trying different things; then finally he travels to Asia and Africa and "into the farthest corners of Turkestan," beginning to better understand himself. He dances with great joy; other animals come to learn from him "to find joy in being themselves." This mystical tale is dedicated to G. I. Gurdjieff. The spare visual tale begins on the end-papers, where we find the youngster at rest in the forest. Further watercolors show his development until his adulthood as a spiritual leader. There is little overt action here; we must flesh out the meaning.

Two

THE MIDDLE EAST AND NORTH AFRICA

NO SPECIFIC AREA

ORIGINAL TALES AND FOLKTALES EVOKING THE PAST

Ben-Ezer, Ehud. *Hosni the Dreamer: An Arabian Tale.* Illustrated by Uri Shulevitz. New York: Farrar, Straus, 1997. 32pp. Grades 1–4.

Hosni the shepherd has long wanted to see the city. When he accompanies the sheik on a selling trip, he finds it as exciting as he had hoped. With his pay he buys a verse: "Don't cross the water until you know its depth." Although others laugh at him, the advice saves his life when the others perish. It also enables him to help a young woman. They travel together and finally marry for a happy ending. The mixed media scenes in warm desert colors depict detailed settings of desert hills, city streets, and the roaring flood. No source is given for the tale.

Hughes, Vi. *Aziz the Storyteller.* Illustrated by Stefan Czernecki. New York: Crocodile/Interlink, 2002. 32pp. Grades K–4.

Somewhere in the Middle East, a young boy loves to listen to the old storyteller. When he is offered the carpet filled with "all the stories of the world," Aziz takes it to become the new storyteller, despite his father's scorn. But when his father hears him, he is reassured that Aziz can provide for both of them. Charged by the old storyteller, he travels far, "lighting up the sky" for crowds with his tales, then passing on the carpet to a new storyteller when he is old. Black line drawings are framed in colored borders, depicting the sparest of details: palm trees, camels, archways, and the few characters. The somewhat caricaturing pictures seem drawn for smiles. The type mimics Arabic writing.

LIFE TODAY

Matze, Claire Sidhom. *The Stars in my Geddoh's Sky.* Illustrated by Bill Farnsworth. Morton Grove, IL: Albert Whitman, 1999. Paper, 2002. 32pp. Grades K–3.

Young Alex's grandfather, *Geddoh* in Arabic, comes to visit. He brings many gifts. Alex particularly likes the camel saddle on which he can make believe he is riding in the desert. His grandfather describes his life in the city by the sea and also the countryside, where the farmers till the fields, and five times a day the call for prayer comes from the mosque. Alex and his grandfather play ball, fly kites, picnic on the beach. He does not want his grandfather to go back home. But he is reassured that they will meet again. Meanwhile, he shows him the stars that they will share, like their thoughts, even when far apart. Single- and double-page oil paintings offer details of Alex's home and their interactions. The fully developed scenes along the river or on the busy city streets of *Geddoh's* world help us understand his life, as Alex realizes the pull of the homeland.

CELEBRATING RAMADAN

Ghazi, Suhaib Hamid. *Ramadan.* Illustrated by Omar Rayyan. New York: Holiday House, 1996. 32pp. Also paper. Grades 1–4.

After explaining something about Islam and the Muslim calendar, the author introduces young Hakeem and his family as they climb the hill near their home to see the new moon that signals the start of Ramadan. He explains the routine of fasting and prayer for the month, showing how difficult it is for Hakeem to fast and still go to school. The significance of Ramadan is clearly delineated, as is the joy of Eid ul-Fitr, the celebration of the end of Ramadan throughout the Muslim world. Watercolor scenes in borders drawn from Arabic tiles illustrate the facts, often with a gentle sense of humor but always with a respect for the religious base of the activities.

Hoyt-Goldsmith, Diane. *Celebrating Ramadan.* Illustrated by Lawrence Migdale. New York: Holiday House, 2001. 32pp. Also paper. Grades 3–6.

This very detailed introduction to the Islamic holiday of Ramadan is centered on the actual family of Ibraheem, a fourth grader living in Princeton, New Jersey. After a brief introduction to the religion and the prophet Muhammad along with a map showing the areas where Islam is dominant,

en the
d the
ge, de-
e, and

s. New

wreck,
gigan-
island
sailor
ed and
apyrus
hiero-
lapted
ell the
hs are
scenes.
There
ages of
s, plus

na. San

poetic
ughter
death,

illummnication, and end in a glass case where we see her... etails of life in ancient Egypt are introduced in her story, although no exact date is given. The mostly double-page watercolors emphasize the spirituality of the story, but the depictions of artifacts and the few people are quite naturalistic.

Climo, Shirley. *The Egyptian Cinderells.* Illustrated by Ruth Heller. New York: Crowell, 1989. 32pp. Grades K–4.

The author tells us that the tale of Rhodopis, first recorded in the first century B.C. is partially fable, but a Greek slave girl with that name did marry a pharaoh in the 6th century B.C. This Cinderella is scorned by the other servants because of her fair skin and hair. Her master orders special slippers for her because she dances so beautifully. Rhodopis is left behind when all the others go to the pharaoh's court. She feels even worse when a falcon stea¹ one of her precious slippers. The bird delivers the slipper to the pharaoh, who searches the kingdom until he finds Rhodopis with its mate and makes her his queen. The text is lengthy but entertainingly written. This Western approach to ancient Egypt retains a few stylistic bits, such as a conventionalized lotus blossom, the rigid profile with smooth hairdo, and pharaoh's crown, plus the falcon, hippo, and throne.

Fisher, Leonard Everett. *The Gods and Goddesses of Ancient Egypt.* New York: Holiday House, 1997. 32pp. Also paper. Grades 2–5.

Fisher introduces the major gods and goddesses among the many from this long-lasting culture. Their stories are intriguing and useful to compare to other myths, as well as of interest on their own, told one per page spread. A different color is used for the background for each. They are painted very simply, reflecting the style of the ancient wall paintings, with heavy outlines and flat colors. Also included are their symbols as hieroglyphs. A map, a family tree of the gods, and a pronunciation guide are included.

Hofmeyr, Dianne. *The Star-Bearer: A Creation Myth from Ancient Egypt.* Illustrated by Jude Daly. New York: Farrar, Straus, 2001. 26pp. Grades 1–4.

From darkness and black water rises a lotus flower. The golden godchild Atum inside casts light. Longing for friends, he creates Shu, god of air, and Tefnut, goddess of dew and rain. Their children, Nut of the sky and Geb of the earth stay so close together that Atum has no room to create the world. She lifts Nut up high while keeping Geb on earth. Atum sprinkles stars on Nut so Geb can see her in the darkness. The birth of gods and goddesses to Nut is explained, along with Nut's guidance of Atum's light across the sky. The poetic description of the moods of Nut, the sky, ends the story. Stylized figures resemble ancient Egyptian paintings. Settings are spare and tend to be metaphoric as we see the world come to be, along with the creation of the pantheon of Egyptian gods. The pictures exude a sense of calm mystery. Notes and a pronunciation guide are included.

Kimmel, Eric A. *Rimonah of the Flashing Sword: A North African Tale.* Illustrated by Omar Rayyan. New York: Holiday House, 1995. 32pp. Grades 1–4.

Kimmel has adapted this story, a version of Snow White, from a Jewish folktale from Egypt. Initially an orphan girl, whose wicked stepmother has asked a magic bowl, "Who is the fairest?" is sent off with a huntsman to be killed. Instead of finding refuge with dwarfs, Rimonah joins the Bedouins and becomes a skilled rider and fighter. When the wicked queen tries to kill her again, Rimonah joins forty thieves who also oppose the queen. The queen's final attempt puts Rimonah into the sleep from which the prince's kiss awakens her. This tale continues to a reunion with her father and a triumph over the queen. The action is housed in pages suggesting Persian manuscript paintings. Frames within frames bleed off every page. The watercolor illustrations within them also blend in a bit of Hollywood melodrama.

Kimmel, Eric A. *The Three Princes: A Tale from the Middle East.* Illustrated by Leonard Everett Fisher. New York: Holiday House, 1994. 32pp. Grades 1–4.

The author has heard versions of this story from Saudi Arabia, Egypt, Morocco, and Iran. The heroine is a beautiful and much desired princess. Since the prince she prefers is poor, but of course young and handsome, she sends him and two other suitors on a quest for the "rarest thing." At the end of a year, she is close to death when they return. Each brings something precious to help save her life. Her choice among them is both fair and wise. Fisher's dramatic acrylic paintings flood the double-page scenes. He uses mainly close-ups set against the unmodulated night skies or tan desert sand. His light and shadow accentuate both the solidity of the figures in their traditional robes and headdresses and the emotions evoked by the story.

Lattimore, Deborah Nourse. *The Winged Cat: A Tale of Ancient Egypt.* New York: HarperCollins, 1992. 32pp. Also paper. Grades 2–6.

Lattimore's original story of the temple serving girl Merit's journey through the Netherworld is based on her extensive research and includes some of the spells and ceremonies of which we have records. Pharaoh sends Merit and Waha, the high priest, to be judged in the Netherworld because Merit has seen the priest kill her cat, but he denies it. With the cat's spirit accompanying her, Merit sets bravely forth. The priest tries to rid himself of Merit, but in the final judgment, he is devoured while Merit returns to a good life. Although the text is lengthy, it is action packed and full of information. An afterword adds even more background. The illustrations are closely based on ancient Egyptian scrolls and on the wall paintings from tombs, with fresh colors and settings from conventionalized Egyptian art. Figures are without backgrounds but with some hieroglyphics. The illustrations vary in size, some framed showing an action sequence, some more decorative double pages, all on paper that looks like papyrus. The end-papers contain an "alphabet" chart of hieroglyphics and another of city gods. Not all the included glyphs are translated, however.

PERSIA/IRAN

ORIGINAL TALES AND FOLKTALES EVOKING THE PAST

Balouch, Kristen. *The King and the Three Thieves: A Persian Tale*. New York: Viking/Penguin, 2000. 32pp. Grades K–3.

The King Abbas of this folktale really ruled in Persia in the 17th century. He is a king who loves to eat but eats alone. Told he should share food with his hungry people, the disguised king joins three thieves who plan to rob the king using their special powers. The first thief puts the guard to sleep, the second finds the treasure, the third sneezes the door down, and they take the treasure. The next day, the king has them arrested. Reminded by his vizier that "power can be used for good or evil," he sets them free so their powers can be used for good, so that no one in the kingdom will be hungry again. The stencil-like computer-generated shapes created to tell this tale are composed in scenes jumping with life. Facial features are exaggerated to enhance emotions: they are almost caricatured stereotypes. The effect is consistently comic, with only suggestions of costume and architecture of the time and place, certainly not meant to be taken seriously despite the serious moral.

Hormeyr, Dianne. *The Stone: A Persian Legend of the Magi*. Illustrated by Jude Daly. New York: Farrar, Straus, 1998. 26pp. Grades 1–4.

This version of the Christmas story was recounted by Marco Polo in the 13th century. When passing through the town of Saveh, Persia, he noted three tombs that were said to be those of Jasper, Melchior, and Balthasar. The three are holy men who plot the stars. One night they see a strange new bright object in the sky. They find a legend telling of such a star announcing the birth of a baby "who would bring justice and healing and peace to the world." They follow the star, bearing gifts, to find the child. After receiving the gifts, the child presents them with a box. They later find only a stone inside, but one that produces brilliant light. That light, they realize, is the faith they must carry all over the earth "for all mankind to share." The visualization here is modern: starkly bare settings, smooth desert, tiny shelter. There is a mystic quality to even the market scenes in this allegory of religious faith. The sources are given.

Oppenheim, Shulamith Levey. *Ali and the Magic Stew.* Illustrated by Winslow Pels. Honesdale, PA: Boyds Mills, 2002. 32pp. Grades K–3.

This original tale set in old Persia has the flavor of folklore, including a moral. When his father falls ill and wants a healing stew, young Ali must ask for help from a beggar he has previously scorned. He is told he must purchase the stew ingredients with money he has begged. Dressed as a beggar, the spoiled boy learns compassion and humility in this task. The setting is visualized in multiple patterns combined to create static tableaux in which architectural elements blend with ornately costumed characters and many artifacts to add an exotic flavor. Ali's monkey adds comic bits. A patchwork assemblage of fabrics on the end-papers sets the tone for this very decorative visual narrative.

Zeman, Ludmila. *Gilgamesh the King.* Toronto: Tundra, 1992. 22pp. Also paper. Grades 2–6.

Gilgamesh, cruel ruler of ancient Mesopotamia, was part god and part man. To answer the people's cry for help, the Sun God created Enkidu to challenge Gilgamesh, but first he had to live with the animals and learn compassion. With beautiful Shamhat, who came from the city and became his love, Enkidu approaches the city walls for his challenge. After a terrible battle, Gilgamesh slips and falls, but Enkidu saves him and becomes his friend. Peace and celebration follow. Notes on both the original tale and its historic background are included. Both mythic and humanistic spirituality are inherent in both story and illustrations. Horizontal layouts suggest the friezes on ancient Babylonian walls. Suggestions of the relief carvings on these walls, mostly decorative motifs, frame each illustration. The landscape and architecture are of the period as well. Zeman uses what looks like a scratchboard medium to create illustrations that appear lit from behind. Black lines are used mainly for texture, with smoothly applied pastel colors shining through. The end-papers offer a map of the eastern Mediterranean glowing with the sun. Note that the sequels, *The Revenge of Ishtar* and *The Last Quest of Gilgamesh*, each available in both hardback and paper, complete the saga.

IRAQ

FOLKTALE

Hickox, Rebecca. *The Golden Sandal: A Middle Eastern Cinderella Story*. Illustrated by Will Hillenbrand. New York: Holiday House, 1998. 32pp. Also paper. Grades K–3.

This version of the traditional tale is based on folktales from Iraq. Maha is the girl mistreated by her stepmother. When she spares the life of one of the fish her father catches, the fish promises to reward her kindness. Her angry stepmother sends her back for the fish, who helps her in this and other ways over the years. When there is a wedding celebration, Maha's stepmother takes her daughter but leaves Maha behind. It is the fish who provides the clothing for Maha to attend. And it is a lost sandal and a crowing rooster that lead the right young man to Maha and the happy ending. Hillenbrand supplies scenes that focus on the sequence of narrative events but which are also replete with light-hearted details: strutting chickens, a cat raiding garbage, villagers gossiping. He carefully creates architecture and costumes true to the historical and geographical time and place. Notes by the author cover versions of Cinderella; notes by the illustrator describe his technique, which uses oils, pastels, and watercolors on vellum.

JUDAICA

ORIGINAL TALES AND FOLKTALES EVOKING THE PAST

Forest, Heather, reteller. *A Big Quiet House: A Yiddish Folktale from Eastern Europe*. Illustrated by Susan Greenstein. Little Rock, AR: August House, 1996. 32pp. Also paper, 2000. Grades K–3.

Told in a lively manner spiced with rhymed couplets, this version of the traditional tale has an unhappy man go to a wise old woman for advice. He thinks his house is too small, cluttered, and noisy. But as he follows her suggestions, he finds himself with a house overflowing with a chicken, a goat, horse, cow, and sheep. Of course, when she then tells him to take them all out again, he realizes it "could always be worse" and is content with what he has. Colored woodcuts appropriately tell this rugged tale. The illustrations are direct, with reasonable exaggeration of actions and an appealing innocence to the descriptions of animals, family, and home. A note places the tale in its Old World context with details of the life of the time.

Gerstein, Mordicai. *Queen Esther the Morning Star.* New York: Simon & Schuster, 2000. 32pp. Grades K–3.

This retelling of the story of Esther from the Old Testament begins with the Persian King Ahasueris choosing Esther as his new queen. She is reluctant to leave her cousin Mordecai, but he tells her to go but to be careful because many people at court hate Jews. When Mordecai defies the order of the king's prime minister Haman to bow down, Haman vows to hang him and all Jews. Brave Esther manages to get to the king, save her people, and have the wicked Haman hung instead. The holiday of Purim is the joyous celebration of Esther's success. The visual story is told as a sequence of episodes in sketchy gouache. Each is like a stage set thinly framed with its text. A flat perspective displays details of interior architecture, furniture, gardens, etc. The characters are a bit caricatured, particularly the evil Haman and the fat king.

Jaffe, Nina. *The Way Meat Loves Salt: A Cinderella Tale from the Jewish Tradition.* Illustrated by Louise August. New York: Henry Holt, 1998. 32pp. Grades K–3.

This Yiddish folktale version includes overtones of *King Lear.* When the rabbi asks his three daughters how much they love him, Mireleh, the youngest and his favorite, replies with the title. This angers him so much that he sends her away. On the road, she meets a strange old man who gives her a magic wishing stick and sends her to the house of a rabbi, his wife, and his son. When they leave Mireleh behind to go to a wedding feast, she uses the magic stick for suitable clothes and goes to the wedding. There she enchants the rabbi's son, who carries her lost slipper to find that their poor serving girl is the one he wants to marry. At their wedding, Mireleh arranges to have no salt in the food. It is then that her father realizes the truth of her statement to him. August's heavy black outlined paintings have an earthy folk quality; the characters have simplified features. Descriptions of rituals like the bridal pair under the canopy move this tale into a specific ethnic location. There are notes on Yiddish pronunciation as well as about the tale itself.

Kimmel, Eric A. *Gershon's Monster: A Story for the Jewish New Year.* Illustrated by Jon J. Muth. New York: Scholastic, 2000. 32pp.

Gershon the baker is not "the best person he could be." Every Friday, he sweeps up his nasty, thoughtless deeds, and once a year, on Rosh Hashanah, he drags them down and tosses them into the sea. Gershon and his wife, after wanting children for a long time, are promised by a *tzaddik* that they will have them, but only for five years, until he puts two socks on one foot. One day when he does this, a terrible monster labeled with Gershon's wicked deeds rises from the sea to take away the children. Regretting his past, Gershon offers himself instead. He and the children are saved by his offer of sacrifice. Muth's watercolors transform spiritual abstractions into visual metaphors. Gershon's sins become devilish imps to be swept into a huge black sack, and the retribution is a sea serpent with glaring eyes and foaming mouth. The full-page scenes set in long-ago Eastern Europe are finely wrought, with details of costumes and place and emotional impact. There are added notes on Rosh Hashanah.

Kimmel, Eric A. *The Magic Dreidel: A Hanukkah Story*. Illustrated by Katya Krenina. New York: Holiday House, 1996. 32pp. Also paper. Grades PreS–3.

Kimmel has reset the folktale of "The Tablecloth, the Donkey, and the Stick" at Hanukkah, with an old woman tricking young Jacob out of the magic dreidels given him by a goblin. The first dreidel spins the traditional *latkes* or potato pancakes; the second produces Hanukkah *gelt* or coins. When she spins the third, however, fleas torture her until she returns the others to Jacob so he and his family and neighbors can celebrate the holiday properly. There's an Old World look to these illustrations; the characters wear clothes from another time; a family samovar adds to this background. The pictures create an appealing, semimagical narrative filled with the symbols of the holiday.

Podwall, Mark. *The Menorah Story*. New York: Greenwillow/HarperCollins, 1998. 24pp. Also Harper Trophy paper. Grades K–3.

In this brief, informative account we learn that a menorah is more than what is lit by Jewish people on the holiday of Hanukkah. The traditional story is that the first menorah formed itself when God told Moses to throw a piece of gold into the fire. This menorah had seven lights, with several possible meanings. These were the lights that were extinguished at the time when wicked King Antiochus defiled the Holy Temple. The hero Judah Maccabee, with the help of a miraculous angel, defeated the king's army. It is because of this, and of the miraculous burning of a small amount of oil for eight days, that Hanukkah is celebrated with eight lights, plus one to light the others. Small paintings and vignettes in gouache with colored pencils offer the artist's rather personal, undetailed impressions of some parts of the story, including statues, soldiers, and a variety of menorahs.

Silverman, Erica. *Raisel's Riddle.* Illustrated by Susan Gaber. New York: Farrar, Straus, 1999. 34pp. Also paper. Grades K–4.

The author has combined elements of the Cinderella story with a picture of Jewish life in the "old country" and the celebration of the holiday of Purim. Raisel's grandfather teaches her that learning is precious. When he dies, she must find work. She is taken into the home of a rabbi, where she is cruelly treated. On Purim, when the rabbi's costumed guests go to see the Purim play, Raisel wishes to go in vain. It is an old beggar woman she feeds who provides the magic for her to go to the play, enchant the rabbi's son with her cleverness, and finally win happiness. The large paintings that tell the dramatic visual narrative rely on color to infuse them with emotions, while facial expressions clearly define character. Details are limited to the necessary; the clothing is from past time or the traditional costumes of Purim.

Wisniewski, David. *Golem.* New York: Clarion/Houghton, 1996. 32pp. Grades 2–6.

In 1580, when the Jews in the city of Prague were threatened by angry mobs, legend says that a Golem, a clay giant, was brought to life by magic by Rabbi Loew, to protect them. A mob attacks the ghetto, but the Golem scatters them in terror. The emperor promises the rabbi that he will protect the Jews if the Golem is destroyed. Despite his protest, the Golem is returned to the clay from which it was made. The legend says that "when the desperate need for justice is united with holy purpose, Golem will come to life once more." The historic setting invested with conflict and magic is a challenge to this artist's medium of cut paper. His double-page scenes are replete with local details of architecture, the crowds of people, and the hulking Golem. His powerful narrative is filled with the emotions of danger and awe. There is a note on the historic and the mythological background of the story.

Wolkstein, Diane. *Esther's Story.* Illustrated by Juan Wijngaard. New York: Morrow, 1996. 40pp. Grades 2–5.

The same basic story as Gerstein's *Queen Esther the Morning Star* (above) is told in greater detail in the form of the diary of Esther herself. Her growth from a shy eleven-year-old to a woman strong enough to face the king and then to an old woman watching the happy celebration of Purim is described in a very personal fashion. Elegant full-page gouache paintings tell the story in details of architecture, clothing, furniture, reflecting the time and place. The artist adds drama with his use of lighting for emotional impact. A pronunciation guide is included.

JEWISH AMERICANS AND THE IMMIGRANT EXPERIENCE

Adler, David A. *One Yellow Daffodil: A Hanukkah Story.* Illustrated by Lloyd Bloom. San Diego, CA: Gulliver/Harcourt, 1995. 32pp. Grades 1–4.

The author has a fictional character here who represents several Holocaust survivors he has interviewed. Morris Kaplan runs a flower market, where young Ilana and Jonathan come on Fridays to buy flowers for the Sabbath. In December, they pick up flowers for Hanukkah. He tells them he has not celebrated the holiday since he was young in Poland, so they invite him to join them. He recalls how seeing a daffodil blooming at Auschwitz helped him survive the horror. He still has his family's menorah, which he brings to the children's house to light the candles with them. When he returned home to Poland after the war he had nothing and no one. Now he has friends. The full-page acrylic paintings, in somber tones, maintain the spirituality of the narrative. Naturalistic with just enough detail to create the specificity of time and place, they portray Morris in particular with considerable sympathy.

Bunting, Eve. *One Candle.* Illustrated by K. Wendy Popp. New York: Joanna Cotler/HarperCollins, 2002. 32pp. Grades K–3.

The details of one family's Hanukkah celebration are typical with one exception: Grandma carves a potato as she and Great-Aunt Rose tell of the horror of their time in Buchenwald concentration camp. They smuggled out a potato, not to eat hungry as they were but to light a bit of margarine in for a Hanukkah light. So each year the family remembers and celebrates life with a carved potato. Popp's pastel illustrations are realistic, but washed overall in shades of warm brown and blue, with the concentration camp pages only in the dull browns. The front end-papers show the materials to prepare the holiday food; the back end-papers show the abundance that contrasts with the symbolic potato.

Goldin, Barbara Diamond. *A Mountain of Blintzes.* Illustrated by Anik McGrory. San Diego, CA: Harcourt, 2001. 32pp. Grades K–3.

Blintzes are a kind of filled pancake traditionally served particularly on the Jewish holiday of Shavuot, celebrated in the spring for the day Moses received the Ten Commandments. This lively tale of a farm family in the late 1920s is adapted from a traditional Eastern European folktale of Chelm, the village of fools. Like the couple in that story, Sarah and Max try to work and save a little extra to put into their coin box, so they can afford to make that "mountain of blintzes" they want for the holiday. And like that couple, they fail. But their children save the day and the holiday. The lively, slightly cartoon-y illustrations depict real active American folks who clearly love one another. A recipe is included for the resulting tasty-looking blintzes.

Kimmel, Eric A. *When Mindy Saved Hanukkah*. Illustrated by Barbara McClintock. New York: Scholastic, 1998. 32pp. Grades K–4.

The Klein family, tiny folk similar to *The Borrowers*, live behind the wall of a synagogue on the Lower East Side of New York City at the turn of the last century. Papa has been attacked by a cat, trying to get a candle for their Hanukkah celebration. Brave young Mindy manages the perilous quest with the help of her grandfather. The appealing tale offers details of the celebration, the synagogue, the typical clothing, and a reminder of the story of the holiday, with her grandfather a hero like the Maccabees. A glossary adds information to the charming original story. McClintock's fine lines create a reasonable small world as well as a regular-size cat and synagogue. Transparent watercolors, ink, and gouache supply naturalistic touches.

Rael, Elsa Okon. *Rivka's First Thanksgiving*. Illustrated by Maryann Kovalski. New York: Margaret K. McElderry/Simon & Schuster, 2001. 32pp. Also Aladdin paper. Grades K–4.

Based on the author's own experience as a young immigrant, the story, set in 1919, shows how young Rivka brings the holiday she has learned about in school home to her family. When she wants them all to celebrate Thanksgiving, her grandmother goes to the rabbi to find out whether it is a holiday for Jews to celebrate. It takes Rivka to persuade him and the elders that it is really for everyone. A wonderful Thanksgiving feast is the result. The colored pencil and acrylic illustrations include details of clothing and of the activities in that part of New York at the time. All the characters are believable; Rivka herself is particularly appealing, especially when facing the rabbi and the council of elders. There is a glossary of the included Yiddish words.

Rosen, Michael J. *Chanukah Lights Everywhere*. Illustrated by Melissa Iwai. San Diego, CA: Gulliver/Harcourt, 2001. 25pp. Grades PreS–K.

A young boy counts off each of the eight nights of Chanukah by lighting that number of candles and then spotting the same number of other kinds of lights as well. A different holiday activity is briefly noted for each night. This very simple introduction to the Festival of Lights is followed by details and background information. Double-page acrylic paintings show the proper number of candles for each night as well as a special activity, like family visits or making latkes. There are added details, along with portrayals of the family members, cats, and many different menorahs.

Rosen, Michael J. *Our Eight Nights of Hanukkah*. Illustrated by Dyanne Disalvo-Ryan. New York: Holiday House, 2000. 32pp. Grades 1–4.

A young boy describes the way his family celebrates each night of the holiday. The traditions are all included and explained. But the focus is on the parts of the celebration that are special for this family. They emphasize giving to the less fortunate, making things as well as buying them, enjoying the sharing of their Jewish holiday traditions with their non-Jewish friends, and above all, family togetherness and love. Light-hearted, double-page, mixed media illustrations visualize the family activities and set the actions in the locales mentioned in the text. There is a glossary of Hebrew words used.

Schnur, Steven. *The Tie Man's Miracle: A Chanukah Tale*. Illustrated by Stephen T. Johnson. New York: Morrow, 1995. 32pp. Grades K–3.

On the last night of Chanukah, a young boy impatiently waiting for his father to come home and light the candles is annoyed by the visit of old Mr. Hoffman, who is selling ties. He agrees to stay while they light the menorah. When young Seth wonders why Hoffman has no family and is so sad, he learns for the first time about the terrible war in which all Hoffman's family dies. At dinner, Hoffman tells them how in their village they believed that if all the candles in the menorah went out at once, the smoke would carry their wishes straight to God. Seth watches and makes his wish. The inspirational ending is open to interpretation. The sentiment of the text finds an appropriate partner in the naturalistic watercolors, full-page illustrations effectively displaying strong portraits, particularly of the old man. There is a glossary of words about Chanukah and the Hebrew words in the text.

THREE

AFRICA AND AFRICAN AMERICA

SUB-SAHARAN AFRICA

ORIGINAL TALES AND FOLKTALES EVOKING THE PAST

Aardema, Verna. *Anansi Does the Impossible: An Ashanti Tale*. Illustrated by Lisa Desimini. New York: Anne Schwartz/Atheneum, 1997. 32pp. Also Aladdin paper. Grades PreS–3.

This is an explanation of why the folk stories of West Africa are called Anansi Tales. Anansi the tricky spider is not happy that the Sky God has all the tales of their people. He decides to try to get them back. The Sky God sets him three "impossible tasks." With the help of his clever wife, and to the anger of the Sky God, Anansi captures a live python, a real fairy, and forty-seven stinging hornets and trades them for the stories. The tale is peppered with ideophones, "words that mimic actual sounds," and other words explained in the glossary. The black velvet paper collage pictures that visualize the spider's adventures are inventive in representing the characters and props. They are just naturalistic enough but playful and designed in scenes that project the emotions of Anansi and the anger of the Sky God. The spiders are dressed in the patterns typically seen in the fabric from this area.

Aardema, Verna. *Koi and the Kola Nuts: A Tale from Liberia*. Illustrated by Joe Cepeda. New York: Anne Schwartz/Atheneum, 1999. 32pp. Grades K–3.

After the death of his father, Koi is left with nothing but a kola nut tree. As he travels with some of the nuts, he uses them to help a snake, some ants, and a crocodile. They, in turn, help him with the difficult tasks set for him by a chief in order to win his daughter. At the wedding celebration, Koi gives the message of the story: "Do good and good will come back to you—in full measure and overflowing." The characters are almost cartoons. The settings of the double-page oil-painted scenes are equally spare of details. But Koi is spirited in his colorful loincloth; the creatures he befriends, particularly the crocodile, are engagingly defined. The glossary includes both meaning and pronunciation, plus notes on the many ideophones, "words that mimic actual sounds," that are liberally sprinkled through the text.

Aardema, Verna. *Why Mosquitoes Buzz in People's Ears: A West African Tale*. Illustrated by Leo and Diane Dillon. New York: Dial, 1975. 32pp. Also Penguin paper. Grades K–3.

The classic *pourquoi* tale is told with Aardema's usual rhythmic and repetitious text. The Dillons use airbrushed smooth shapes with white line separations that give a cloisonné effect to the double-page scenes with stylized animals and careful designs.

Bryan, Ashley. *Beautiful Blackbird*. New York: Atheneum, 2003. 34pp. Grades PreS–3.

In this adaptation of a traditional story from the Ila-speakers of Zambia, all the other birds agree that Blackbird is the most beautiful. They beg him to paint them with a touch of black. The dots or rings he gives them are those they have today. The text is rich with rhythm, rhymes, and interspersed accents like "coo-coo-coo" and "uh-huh!" Not only is the "black is beautiful" message clear, but Blackbird himself also emphasizes the fact that it is what's inside, not outside, that counts. Bryan's cut paper birds fill the pages with a constantly changing pattern of colors as the multihued birds flit and fly and strut around. Silhouettes provide suggestions of bird types that lend themselves to design manipulation. With Blackbird's help, they attain more decorative appearances.

Cummings, Pat, reteller and illustrator. *Ananse and the Lizard: A West African Tale*. New York: Henry Holt, 2002. 40pp. Grades K–3.

This tale of how the trickster Ananse the Spider is outwitted comes from Ghana. When he hears that whoever guesses the name of the Chief's daughter can marry her, Ananse decides that should be easy. How he discovers the name but is tricked in turn by Lizard makes for a funny tale, along with an explanation of why lizards are always scurrying nervously and looking about. Angry Ananse has vowed revenge. Blocks of text are set into the complex double-page, richly patterned scenes with thin frames. The many traditional patterns of local fabrics vie for our attention with sculpture-like representations of both creatures and humans. Mixed media, watercolors, gouache, and colored pencil create the sequence of actions that compel us to turn the page.

Day, Nancy Raines. *The Lion's Whiskers: An Ethiopian Tale*. Illustrated by Ann Grifalconi. New York: Scholastic, 1995. 32pp. Grades 1–4.

This lively story with a universal lesson is from the predominantly Christian Amhara people of Ethiopia. Fanaye feels fortunate when she marries the widower Tesfa, so she works hard to take care of their home and her stepson Adebe. When he continues to reject her, she asks the medicine man for help. He demands three whiskers from the chin of a fierce lion. How she obtains these and what she learns make for a satisfying story. Double-page collages project a mythic quality. Integrating photographic details, prepared papers, and other textured materials, the artist creates the vastness of the searing desert as well as the mysteries of the wise man's cave. The striking illustrations, however, have been criticized for not being accurate for the area.

Diakité, Baba Wagué. *The Hatseller and the Monkeys: A West African Folktale*. New York: Scholastic, 1999. 32pp. Grades K–3.

BaMusa, the happy hat seller, travels from town to town, singing his song, selling the hats made by his family. One day, on his way to a festival where he expects to sell many hats, but not having eaten, he stops to rest and falls asleep under a mango tree very attractive to monkeys. When he wakes up, they have taken all his hats, and they will not give them back. But after eating and seeing how they copy him, he gets them finally to throw the hats down so he can sell them at the celebration. For "it's with a full stomach that one thinks best." There is an innocence to the highly decorative paintings on ceramic tile which tell the antic tale. The hats all have distinctive designs; the mango tree is also designed so that the leaves and fruit make attractive patterns. The monkeys are obviously happy making mischief both in the tree and in the drawings that create bands around each page. There is a note on the source of the tale and the lessons taught. Esphyr Slobodkina did the most famous version of this story in her *Caps for Sale*.

Diakité, Baba Wagué. *The Hunterman and the Crocodile: A West African Folktale*. New York: Scholastic, 1997. 32pp. Grades K–3.

When Donso the Hunterman agrees to help Bamba the Crocodile and his family back to the river, they promise not to bite him. But when they get to the river, hungry Bamba seizes Donso's hand and won't let go. One by one a cow, a horse, and a chicken come to the river and refuse Donso's pleas for help because men have treated them so badly. Even the mango tree has no sympathy. After rabbit tricks Bamba and his family back into Donso's control, they find that crocodile tears are required to cure Donso's sick wife. The crocodiles shed the needed tears when they are freed. After this, Donso always remembers that man must live in harmony with nature. The language of the telling is lively, with animal sounds. The full-page illustrations, similar to those mentioned above, are full of implied action. The author's note gives his sources.

Diakité, Baba Wagué. *The Magic Gourd.* New York: Scholastic, 2003. 32pp. Grades K–3.

At a time of drought, Rabbit is searching for food for his family when he is asked by Chameleon to help him out of some thorny bushes. Being kind-hearted, he not only rescues Chameleon but also his beautiful magic gourd, which Chameleon then gives to him as thanks. The gourd fills itself with food and water on request. Rabbit and his family share their bounty with their friends. The greedy king Mansa Jugo steals the gourd and has it fill with gold, while poor Rabbit's family goes hungry. Luckily, Chameleon gives him the means to get back the gourd and teach the king "the importance of generosity and friendship." Pictures depicting the characters are painted on plates and bowls in a stylized fashion that is both vigorous and informative. Borders and end-papers derived from the "mud cloth" patterns of the Bamana people of Mali add to the visual impact. Many notes add information on praise songs, story backgrounds, the patterns, similar folktales, and there is also a glossary.

Gershator, Phillis. *Only One Cowry: A Dahomean Tale.* Illustrated by David Soman. New York: Orchard, 2000. 32pp. Grades K–4.

When King Dade Segbe is ready to marry, he offers only one cowry shell as a gift to the bride's family. Clever young Yo says that he will find the king a wife for that price. He begins to build from there, trading the shell for a flint, which he uses for a fire to make grasshoppers jump into his sack. He moves on to acquire beans in exchange for the grasshoppers, trades the beans for fish, fish for tools, tools for oil and flour, and those for bread. These he gives to a chief as gifts to make his daughter the king's bride. But he sends word back to the king that he has given only one cowry. The daughter, as clever as Yo, has the king send wine, food, clothes, and jewelry, so he can feel that he has a wonderful wife for "only one cowry." Collage is used effectively to create proper clothing, shelter, utensils, etc., while paint produces the many characters in this lively, multitextured visual narrative. There are notes on the importance of cowry shells, on the source of the tale, and on Yo as a trickster.

Gershator, Phillis. *Zzzng! Zzzng! Zzzng!: A Yoruba Tale.* Illustrated by Theresa Smith. New York: Orchard/Scholastic, 1998. 32pp. Grades PreS–3.

"In the days when all things came together to make the world as it is," Mosquito flies around looking for someone to marry. First she admires Ear, and hums and sings her rhyming song, punctuated by *zzzum-zzzum's* and *zzzng-zzzng's*. Ear declines, declaring she is too small and weak to last. So Mosquito thinks about Head but then decides that Arm is as handsome. But the joyful song doesn't impress Arm either; he also feels she is too small and weak. Mosquito moves past Chest to admire Leg and try the song again. Turned down by Leg, Mosquito becomes angry. Her song becomes one of biting and stinging. Leg, Arm, and Ear feel her bite and realize that she is stronger than they thought. And since then, we all feel her sting, and we scratch. Long double-page scenes, smoothly rendered in pastels and crayon, show Mosquito flitting from body part to part with an arabesque of her song twisting around her. As she grows angrier, we note that she grows larger and more aggressive. The author adds background on the tale.

Gregorowski, Christopher. *Fly, Eagle, Fly!: An African Tale.* Illustrated by Niki Daly. New York: Margaret K. McElderry/Simon & Schuster, 2000. 32pp. Also paper. Grades K–4.

A farmer finds an eagle chick and raises it among the chickens. When a friend claims it is an eagle, he tries to make it fly, but it continues to scratch among the chickens. The determined friend insists on taking the bird up into the mountains at sunrise to a high ledge. He tells the bird about the sun and how it must rise with the sun to the sky. Finally the eagle soars off, "never again to live among the chickens." The parable is attributed to a teacher, Aggrey, who wanted to encourage people to soar rather than be limited, and was adapted by the author for his dying child. Daly fills the large double-page scenes with details of the clothing, village life, and surrounding landscape, sometimes framed in typical patterns of the area. There is a deftness to his watercolor painting and animation in his visual narrative. The final scenes take on a reverential tone as the eagle prepares to take off into the sunlight.

Grifalconi, Ann. *The Village That Vanished.* Illustrated by Kadir Nelson. New York: Dial/Penguin, 2002. 40pp. Grades K–4.

In a tale the Yao told in the style of an African storyteller or *griot,* the fearful ordeal of those threatened by slave traders in African history is made vividly real. A young girl, her mother, and her grandmother, inspired by ancestor spirits, move the people out and dismantle their village so that the slavers cannot find them and the people are saved. Nelson's black line drawings in pencil are subtly colored with transparent oils to create the jungle village and its many inhabitants. One can feel the humidity and sense the anxiety. The lines build sculptural forms, model bodies, trees, and huts, while the strong personalities of the three generations are clearly delineated.

Hunter, Bobbi Dooley. *The Legend of the African Bao-bab Tree.* Trenton, NJ: Africa World Press, 1995. 32pp. Also paper. Grades K–3.

Annoyed by his arrogance and constant complaints, the Great Spirit of the Wild Plains seized a shade tree, yanked it from the earth, put it back upside-down, and named it the bao-bab. This is the legend the author retells after a visit to Botswana. The spare text is supplemented by several pages of "keys to the legend" giving further information about the tree, the many animals of Southeast Africa, and the people. Double-page naturalistic watercolor scenes show the animals mentioned, always with the tree in a fixed landscape, sometimes at a distance and sometimes up closer. The changing skies reinforce the evolution.

Kimmel, Eric A. *Anansi and the Magic Stick.* Illustrated by Janet Stevens. New York: Holiday House, 2001. 34pp. Also paper. Grades PreS–3.

Lazy Anansi wants to know how Hyena gets all his work done and can rest. He discovers the Hyena has a magic stick that works on command. Anansi steals the stick and puts it to work for him, with fine results but unpleasant consequences for his friends. When he lies down for his nap, he commands the stick to keep watering the seeds in his yard. Of course the stick doesn't stop until there is a flood that carries away all the characters, including the author and illustrator in the illustrations. Anansi has forgotten the words to make the stick stop. Luckily Hyena floats by in time to call a halt, leaving a lovely lake behind. And although his friends think he has been swept away, Anansi is still "planning new tricks, which is just what Anansi does best." Digitally manipulated naturalistic watercolor crayon and acrylic illustrations create a robust cast of convincing actors. Most of the visual fun is found in the scenes involving the flood. How they all adopt to the newly formed lake adds more comedy. Little is particularly African, however, except for the animals. The source of the tale is given.

Knutson, Barbara, reteller. *How the Guinea Fowl Got Her Spots: A Swahili Tale of Friendship*. Minneapolis: Carolrhoda/Lerner, 1990. 32pp. Grades K–4.

The author, who was born and has lived in Africa, retells this *pourquoi* tale of a natural phenomenon. After Nganga the Guinea Fowl has saved her friend Cow twice from the hungry lion, Cow cleverly speckles the previously black fowl to help her escape the lion. Realistic creatures in believable but minimal grass, rocks, or water are placed on wide expanses of white paper. Knutson uses black ink and watercolors on scratchboard, so that although the illustrations do not look typically "African," the technique mimics some traditional Swahili designs seen incised on utensils from that culture. This is clearly seen on the vertical designs placed under the bold black initial letters on the left side of most pages.

Kurtz, Jane. *Fire on the Mountain*. Illustrated by E. B. Lewis. New York: Simon & Schuster, 1994. 34pp. Grades 1–4.

Kurtz, who grew up in Ethiopia, retells a story she heard there many times but notes that she has added a sister, since there is a "tradition of strong women in Ethiopian stories." Alemayu, a young shepherd, plays his flute in the mountains and dreams. When his parents die, he goes to find his sister, who gets him a job with her rich employer. The boastful master is challenged when Alemayu claims he can stay a night on the cold mountain with only his thin cloak. He survives, but the master says he cheated by looking at a distant fire, so he must leave without his reward. The employer orders a rich feast to celebrate his victory. Alemayu's clever sister, however, has the servants prepare the feast but not serve it, making the master's enjoyment come the same as Alemayu's warmth from the faraway fire. The rich man agrees and pays what he promised. The naturalistic watercolors focus on the major characters in action. We have portraits of the place and some of its people, with landscapes, interiors, village streets, all with minimum details. Most are full or double page without margins, drawing us into the action.

McDermott, Gerald. *Anansi the Spider: A Tale from the Ashanti*. New York: Henry Holt, 1972. 40pp. Also Owlet paper, 1986. Grades PreS–2.

In this tale of the trickster, Anansi is swallowed by a large fish. One of his six sons, "See Trouble," tells his brothers that their father is in danger. "Road Builder" makes the road for them to take to find him. "River

Drinker" drains the river, "Game Skinner" opens the fish to let Anansi out. Falcon then snatches Anansi away. "Stone Thrower" hits Falcon. "Cushion" catches Anansi as he falls. Happily back at home, Anansi finds a great globe of light but cannot decide which helpful son deserves it. So he gives it to Nyame, the God of All Things, to hold until they can agree. While they argue, Nyame takes the globe up to the sky, where it still shines. This mythic tale is imaginatively portrayed in geometric shapes, mostly derived from African sources. There are no landscapes or other representational objects; rather, symbols are used in striking color contrasts with the brief, caption-like text. A map locates Ghana in Africa. Traditional patterns decorate the end-papers.

McDermott, Gerald. *Zomo the Rabbit: A Trickster Tale from West Africa.* San Diego, CA: Harcourt, 1992. 32pp. Grades K–3.

Zomo the trickster rabbit of West African oral tradition jauntily hops through this humorous tale. Although he is clever, Zomo also wants wisdom, a distinction that may be difficult for children to discern. Asking Sky God to give him wisdom, Zomo is given three seemingly impossible tasks. He uses his cleverness in amusing and successful encounters with Big Fish, Wild Cow, and Leopard, only to receive some sly wisdom in return. Figures and objects influenced by African designs tend to exploit geometric, sharp-edged, stencil-like shapes for characters, even landscapes. Saturated gouache pigments produce intensely colored double-page scenes. The boldness of the paintings match that of the rabbit hero.

Mollel, Tololwa M. *Ananse's Feast: An Ashanti Tale.* Illustrated by Andrew Glass. New York: Clarion/Houghton, 1997. 32pp. Also paper. Grades K–3.

During a time of drought, Ananse the traditional spider trickster decides to feast secretly on the food he has stored. His friend Akye the turtle smells the cooking, and Ananse cannot turn him away. But each time the hungry turtle starts to eat, Ananse sends him away to wash his hands, until the food is all gone. When the drought ends in floods, Ananse has little food, so looks forward to eating at Akye's. In order to arrive there underwater, however, he has loaded his pockets with pebbles. Akye insists that he be polite and remove his robe. Up he goes to the surface. This time the trickster is the tricked. These characters express human emotions and even use objects and furniture like ours, all depicted naturalistically. Glass creates animated characters with great personality, along with attractive landscape, with oils and colored pencil. Little is really "African" beyond Ananse's hut and the patterns on the clothing. A note adds information on Ananse stories and on the included exclamations.

Mollel, Tololwa M. *The King and the Tortoise.* Illustrated by Kathy Blankley. New York: Clarion/Houghton, 1993. 32pp. Grades 1–4.

In this sprightly retelling of a story from Cameroon, a king challenges all creatures to prove that they are smarter than he is by making him a robe out of smoke. Many animals brag, try, and fail. Then the tortoise asks for seven days' time, plus the king must give him whatever he needs for the job. When the week has passed, tortoise says he just needs more thread to finish. To fulfill his promise, the king must give him "thread of fire" to finish the robe of smoke. The king has to admit that the tortoise is as clever as he is. The double-page scenes are enlivened by a variety of decorative borders, using geometric devices like those on the end-papers. Textured pastels in black outlines create naturalistic animals and humans in appropriate clothes. The text is unobtrusively integrated into scenes composed to focus on the sequenced trials. Turtle and king are particularly individualistic; the king's ornately colorful throne is simply splendid.

Mollel, Tololwa M. *Kitoto the Mighty.* Illustrated by Kristi Frost. Toronto: Stoddart Kids, 1998. 34pp. Grades K–3.

The author has set his variation of the traditional tale of the Mouse Bride on the African Savannah. There Kitito, a small mouse, seeks a strong friend to protect him from predators. First he asks the rapid river. But the river says the sun is more powerful because he can dry up the river. The sun says the wind blows the clouds over him. But the wind says the mountain is stronger because it cannot be moved. The mountain, in turn, says that whatever is chomping at its roots must be the most powerful of all. Kitoto searches deep within the mountain only to find to his surprise Kigego, the mountain mouse, proud of what she has built with just her teeth and hard work. He finds a good friend at last. The mice are appealing, full of personality. The African settings are pleasant landscapes with a few friendly animals. The forces of nature are imaginatively portrayed. The soft-edged paintings fill the pages with attractive imagery and action. The author notes how he has changed the traditional tale.

Mollel, Tololwa M. *Shadow Dance.* Illustrated by Donna Perrone. New York: Clarion/Houghton, 1998. 32pp. Grades K–3.

Salome is happily dancing when she hears a cry for help. Crocodile is trapped in the gully. When she pulls him out, he asks her to walk him back to the river and into the water. Then the treacherous beast grabs her to eat her, saying he will spare her if he can find a good reason. First a tree, then an old cow tell long stories about their mistreatment by little girls, saying he should not spare her. Only a pigeon offers reasons, but Crocodile says he will eat her anyway. How the pigeon tricks him and saves Salome makes an amusing happy ending. Oil crayons produce a translucency to landscapes and river, nasty crocodile, and to the pigeon's gloriously patterned wings. Color pencils add fine details like teeth, Salome's dress decorations, and pigeon feathers. Information on the background and changes to the tale are included, along with a Kiswahili song.

Mollel, Tololwa M. *Song Bird*. Illustrated by Rosanne Litzinger. New York: Clarion/Houghton, 1999. 32pp. Grades K–3.

This adaptation of a traditional tale from Southern Africa has been modified by the author, who explains in a note the origins among the Zulu and the Xhosa. Swahili is used for the bird's song, which is set to a Tanzanian tune on the last page. One night, all the cattle of the Kung'ombe disappear. Without milk to sell, young Mariamu and her parents must clear a field to plant food. A bird arrives, sings a song, and the field is clear no longer. The bird needs the field for her eggs and promises to provide them with milk if they leave it alone. Mariamu helps the bird and in return is magically taken to the land of Makucha, the monster who has taken the cattle. They manage to defeat him and bring the cattle back. Life goes on well from then on with Song Bird's help. Watercolors and colored pencil are applied delicately to depict the stylized bird and people and the nonspecific landscape, with suggestions of clothing. Mariamu is charming, while Makucha is so big and ugly that he can't fit on even double pages. A glossary is included.

Mollel, Tololwa M. *To Dinner, for Dinner*. Illustrated by Synthia Saint James. New York: Holiday House, 2000. 32pp. Grades PreS–3.

Juhudi is the rabbit trickster in this tale in which the author has combined universal folktale themes and added his own emphasis on friendship and celebration of life. When Leopard wants to dine on Juhudi, she persuades him to wait until she grows fatter. When the confrontation can no longer be avoided, her friends help her frighten Leopard away. The story is filled with fun with African-based nonsense words and a song from Tanzania to sing them in. The illustrations are also light hearted, with only a bit of the melodrama of the animal confrontation. The flat, stencil-like pictures of animals and vegetation seem symbols designed more for decorative eye-appeal than natural history. The author clearly states both the sources and the themes he wishes to emphasize in his original plot. The artist describes in detail how she painted the illustrations with acrylic paint on nonstretched primed canvas. There are four or five coats of paint for each color, applied over an outline drawn with nonphoto blue pencil. There is a pronunciation guide included.

Musgrove, Margaret. *The Spider Weaver: A Legend of Kente Cloth*. Illustrated by Julia Cairns. New York: Blue Sky/Scholastic, 2001. 34pp. Grades K–4.

Told among the weavers in the Ashanti region of Ghana, this story goes back to the mid-1600s. Two skilled weavers have made only simple cloth for everyone. One evening, they come upon a wonderfully designed web. But when they try to bring it home, it collapses. So they search for the maker, a large, yellow and black spider. They do not want to destroy her beautiful web, but they watch her weave all day. She has shown them wonderful new designs that they try to imitate on their looms. This is the Kente cloth of today. Watercolors depict the dense leafy patterns against which the weavers discover and admire the web. Several village scenes show them at work among the round-roofed houses. A final procession of rows of folks almost in silhouette offers six striking Kente patterns. Notes are added on pronunciation and on Kente cloth then and now.

Paye, Won-Ldy, and Margaret H. Lippert, retellers. *Head, Body, Legs: A Story from Liberia*. Illustrated by Julie Paschkis. New York: Henry Holt, 2002. 32pp. Grades PreS–2.

There is humor in this creation legend from the Dan people. As Head rolls around wishing he could reach some tasty cherries, he encounters Arms. Together they can do some things. Body and Legs appear, and at first can't get it all together to make sense. Finally, to show how each part is necessary, as is cooperation, they find that together they can pick and enjoy a mango. In Paschkis's imaginative, almost geometric illustrations, body parts are solid black set against roughly brushed gouache backgrounds that vary from browns and yellows to the blue of the river. The text is set in small swatches of contrasting hues, all filled with lively fun.

Rumford, James. *Calabash Cat and His Amazing Journey*. Boston: Houghton Mifflin, 2003. 32pp. Grades K–3.

The cat sets out one day from the middle of Africa "to see where the world ended." Each time a creature tells him he has reached the end, another takes him on to show him another "end," from desert through grasslands, jungle, over ocean, until an eagle flies him home again. The cultural interest in this story lies in the art inspired by the burned designs on a gourd the author bought in Chad and in the calligraphy of the writing in the Arab dialect of Chad on the pages opposing the English text. Heavy black ink outlines, with interior patterns produced with thinner lines, and figures set against blank backgrounds, all create an exotic visual narrative.

Shepard, Aaron. *Master Man: A Tall Tale of Nigeria.* Illustrated by David Wisniewski. New York: HarperCollins, 2001. 32pp. Grades K–3.

This traditional tale describes the cause of thunder. A boastful man named Shadusa is told by his wife that although he thinks he is the strongest, some day he will meet someone stronger. When he hears of a man who calls himself Master Man, he wants to see him. When the huge man returns home, Shadusa hides in fear, then escapes with Master Man after him. As he flees, he meets another gigantic man who challenges Master Man. Together they fight on up to the sky, where they make thunder whenever they start to fight again. Shadusa "never called himself Master Man again." Cut paper creates the characters and everything else in the illustrations, which are so crowded that they overflow the boxes used to house them. Everything is exaggerated for comic effect, including speech balloons. The sources of the tale are given.

Sierra, Judy. *The Mean Hyena: A Folktale from Malawi.* Illustrated by Michael Bryant. New York: Dutton Lodestar/Penguin, 1999. 32pp. Grades K–3.

Fisi the hyena, the trouble-making trickster, sticks poor Kamba the tortoise in a tree. There Kamba makes a brush and offers to paint a new coat for a zebra. Then the leopard wants a change, but not stripes like the zebra. Soon other animals are lining up for the new coats Kamba is offering. Fisi the hyena decides he wants a change too. First Kamba asks to be taken out of the tree. Then Kamba "paints" Fisi, but with sticky gum, so that he ends up looking like "a garbage heap." By the time he chews it off, he has the patchy coat he deserves for tricking Kamba. Watercolor scenes provide a "feel" for the African landscape with its grasses, small trees, and misty skies. More specific are the naturalistic representations of the animals. The sources of the tale are noted.

Souhami, Jessica. *The Leopard's Drum: An Asante Tale from West Africa.* Boston: Little, Brown, 1995. 30pp. Grades K–3.

Osebo, the proud, boastful leopard, refuses to share his wonderful drum with the Sky-God Nyame, so the god offers a reward to the animal who can bring the drum to him. Other animals are scared away. Then little tortoise, with no shell, tricks Osebo into the drum and brings it to Nyame. As a reward, tortoise gets the protective shell she wears today. The tale is told simply, with rhythmic repetition. No sources are given. The end-papers start a visual rhythm with multicolored geometric patterns, like those in Nyame's clothing, made of the cut papers also used to create the abstract figures in the double-page scenes.

Steptoe, John. *Mufaro's Beautiful Daughters: An African Tale*. New York: Lothrop, 1987. 32pp. Grades 1–5.

Inspired by a folktale collected from near the ruins of a once important city in Zimbabwe, this story includes elements familiar from European fairy tales. One beautiful daughter, Nyasha, is as good as she is lovely, but her sister Manyara is vain and selfish. When the king invites the daughters of the land to come to his city so that he can choose a wife, Manyara pushes herself ahead and reveals her true character. Nyasha takes the time to be kind and considerate and so is chosen to be queen. Steptoe creates a lush and vibrant community—the jungle verdant, the blossoms exotic, the birds technicolor. The city is splendidly built on stone terraces with sculptures and patterned inlays. On the double-page spreads are real people, each perceived in portraits that express individual personality. The lengthy text is integrated into spaces carefully left for it. Forms are developed using fine cross-hatching and limited paint in this grandly romantic presentation of another time and place.

Tchana, Katrin, reteller. *Sense Pass King: A Story from Cameroon*. Illustrated by Trina Schart Hyman. New York: Holiday House, 2002. 32pp. Grades K–4.

Young Ma'antah is such an exceptional child that the villagers call her "Sense Pass King," meaning that she has more sense than the king. Hearing this, the angry king tries in vain to have her killed. When this fails, he decides to listen to her advice. She helps him to gain the bride he desires, then slays a threatening monster. When the king claims the credit, the people decide to make her their queen instead. Her reign is a long and happy one. The author has changed the traditional "hero" from boy to girl. A delightful cast of characters is painted in acrylics in a properly luscious tropical setting. The clothing stimulates our eyes with its patterns; the textured round houses up on stilts contrast decoratively with the dark green forests. Ma'antah is bursting with self-assurance. Assorted animals contribute their own visual subtext, with the seven-headed sea dragon an added treat. A note on the Pidgin English spoken in northwest Cameroon is added, as is one on the adaptation of the original story.

Wisniewski, David. *Sundiata: Lion King of Mali*. New York: Clarion/Houghton, 1992. 32pp. Also paper. Grades 2–6.

This tale from the oral tradition of the *griots*, or storytellers, has a basis in the facts we know about the king of Mali and 13th-century Africa. Prince Sundiata does not speak or walk as a child, so when his father dies, the crown goes to a stepbrother, the child of a rival wife of the king. The prince and his mother go into exile, while the adviser given to Sundiata by his father is sent to the court of the wicked sorcerer Sumanguru. When Sumanguru begins to conquer all the land, Sundiata defeats him in an exciting battle, saves his people, and rules them "for many golden years." Although lengthy, the story is rich in adventure and detail. Extensive notes explain historic facts and accuracy of illustration along with the art technique. Multiple razor-cut layers of paper photographed for the effect of light and shadow make pictures that are fine foils for the mythic qualities of a hero's story. Using designs and artifacts adapted from several west African groups, in brilliant colors, the artist creates double-page scenes as stage sets on which the characters play out their roles with dramatic effectiveness.

Wolkstein, Diane. *The Day Ocean Came to Visit*. Illustrated by Steve Johnson and Lou Fancher. San Diego, CA: Gulliver/Harcourt, 2001. 40pp. Grades PreS–3.

In this adaptation of a creation myth from Nigeria, Sun leaves his home with Moon to travel. When he meets Ocean, he enjoys talking to her so much that Moon suggests inviting Ocean to visit. She is so big, bringing everything including her whales with her, that Sun expands their house greatly. But still, when Ocean arrives, she fills everything. The only thing Sun and Moon can do is leap up to the sky, where they remain now, with their children the stars. The artists barely hint at anything African except for the bamboo house. The scenes use decorative patterns in their work in oils for water and forest. The figures are dominated by moon- and sun-shaped heads.

SUB-SAHARAN AFRICA TODAY AND IN RECENT HISTORY

Alexander, Lloyd. *The Fortune-Tellers*. Illustrated by Trina Schart Hyman. New York: Penguin Putnam, 1992. 32pp. Grades 1–5.

This original, richly told adventure has the qualities of legend, although not set in ancient or mythical times. A young man, not content with his life, seeks to learn his future from an old fortune-teller. The predictions will be obviously silly and self-evident to the readers, but the young man believes and acts upon them. A series of wild, humorous, and romantic adventures follows, ending in success for the hero. Though timeless in concept, Hyman has set the tale in a town in contemporary Cameroon, complete with bars, oxcarts on the unpaved main road, and stalls selling items of mundane living. Her mixed media paintings create an environment one can almost hear and smell. The double-page scenes are rich with the wonderfully varied colors and patterns of local dress, the details of shops, pottery, carvings, even the animals that coexist with the individually portrayed characters. The pictures are designed to accept the many lines of text. Her visit to Cameroon is evident in the joy and humor Hyman brings to these wonderfully alive illustrations.

Angelou, Maya. *Kofi and His Magic*. Illustrated by Margaret Courtney-Clark. New York: Crown paper, 2003. 42pp. Grades 1–4.

Seven-year-old Kofi tells us he is a magician living "near the Ashanti golden stool," a weaver of Kente cloth. Sometimes he closes his eyes and finds himself in different places north of his town of Bonwire, places where the cloth is woven differently and where the boys wear strange hats. Back home, he describes his school for us and the harvest festival called Durbar. After taking another mind-trip with a friend, this time to the sea, he urges the reader to close eyes and make the magic trip to visit him. Bold typography in many sizes tells the story, while clearly printed color photographs of many sizes supply the local details of dress and settings. The end-papers display close-ups of pieces of woven cloth important in Ashanti life.

Angelou, Maya. *My Painted House, My Friendly Chicken and Me*. Illustrated by Margaret Courtney-Clarke. New York: Crown paper, 2003. 40pp. Grades 1–4.

Thandi, an eight-year-old Ndebele girl, tells us about her chicken, along with showing us how her mother teaches her the art of painting designs on her house and other places and of stringing beads to make traditional dance costumes. The design of the book is an imaginative combination of several sizes of type set as visual elements along with several sizes of clear color photographs. We also see the many house decorations that characterize the cultural traditions of the area.

Asare, Meshack. *Sosu's Call.* La Jolla, CA: Kane/Miller, 2001. 40pp. Grades K–3.

In a village in Ghana between the sea and a lagoon lives young Sosu, who cannot walk. When he is said to bring bad luck, he is unhappily confined to his house, comforted during the day only by his dog. One day when everyone is away working or at school, a storm brings the sea close enough to menace the village. Bravely Sosu drags himself to the drums in the chief's shed and beats a warning that brings help. He is acclaimed a hero for saving the village and, with a wheelchair, is finally able to go to school with the other children. Misty watercolor paintings in gray-green tones with accents of orange and yellow depict Sosu and the other villagers with simplified naturalism. The huts and trees provide sufficient background across double pages for this intense drama.

Bognomo, Joël Eboueme. *Madoulina: A Girl Who Wanted to Go to School: A Story from West Africa.* Honesdale, PA: Boyds Mills, 1999. 24pp. Grades K–3.

Madoulina, who tells her story, lives with her mother and younger brother in Yaoundé, Cameroon. She has to help her mother selling fritters at the market. One day Mr. Garba, the new teacher at the school, asks why she doesn't attend. She explains that they are too poor. Her mother sends her brother to school because as a girl, she doesn't think she needs an education. Mr. Garba disagrees. He makes arrangements so that Madoulina can go to school as well, which makes her very happy. By working hard, she can catch up with her class. The very simply told story is based on real experiences of children in Cameroon today. The full-page pictures are colored drawings, almost child-like depictions of people, street scenes, Madoulina's home. There is a stiffness of pose, a naive application of color. The author/illustrator is a member of an organization devoted to creating picture-books for African children.

Daly, Niki. *Jamela's Dress.* New York: Farrar, Straus, 1999. 32pp. Grades K–3.

Jamela's mother has found beautiful fabric for a dress to wear to Thelma's wedding. Instead of looking after it as she was asked, Jamela struts off down the street with it draped around her. The children sing "Kwela Jamela African Queen" as she shows it off through the town. She even gets her photo taken in it by photographer Archie. By the time she reaches Thelma, however, it is dirty and torn. Everyone is cross with her. But when her photo appears in the newspaper, Archie assures the unhappy girl that her sad story will have a happy ending. With the money he has earned from the photo, he buys her mother more material, and the ending is happy indeed. Jamela couldn't be more beguiling. The picture of life in a South African town to-day is clearly detailed. Paintings vibrate with the young girl's exuberant spirit. Equally energetic are the responses of the local citizens to her antics; some all smiles while a few others display horror.

Daly, Niki. *Not So Fast, Songololo.* New York: Margaret K. McElderry/Atheneum, 1987. 32pp. Also Aladdin paper. Grades K–3.

Young Malusi helps his granny Gogo go shopping in a city in South Africa. They ride the bus and look in the shop windows. After Gogo finishes shopping, they stop in a store where Malusi had admired new red-and-white tackies, or sneakers. His old ones have holes. Fortunately Gogo has enough money to buy him new ones. With these he walks so happily and proudly that his granny has to call out the title of the story, "Not so fast, Songololo," to him, using her pet name for him, so she can keep up with him. Watercolors that suggest rather than define do a convincing job of creating real people and a sense of a particular place. The double-page illustrations use the whiteness of the pages for the simple text while focusing our attention on the adventures of the characters. The loving relationship between grandmother and grandson is evident.

Daly, Niki. *Once upon a Time.* New York: Farrar, Straus, 2003. 40pp. Grades K–3.

This description of life on a South African sheep farm today centers around Sarie. She dreads being called on to read aloud at school because it is so hard for her. But with her friend, Auntie Anna, she shares the love of story as they read together. She finally succeeds in reading as she also gains a new friend. The universal story goes beyond the African setting. A lively cast of characters is depicted with a gentle watercolor palette. The arid landscape contrasts with the spiritually rich actions of Sarie and company. The visual narrative makes the reading success a subtext to the intergenerational love.

Daly, Niki. *What's Cooking, Jamela?* New York: Farrar, Straus, 2001. 32pp. Grades K–3.

Jamela and her mother buy a chicken for part of the Christmas celebration. Jamela cares for the chicken, which she names Christmas. As the holiday approaches, her mother wonders whether Jamela will be able to part with her friend the chicken when cooking time arrives. On the day before Christmas, when Mrs. Zibi arrives with her tools, suspicious Jamela takes off with her chicken. In traffic, Jamela loses her. Soon the hunt, and a wild chase, is on. But all turns out happily for Jamela and her new friend in the end. The delightful story with its charming heroine is also a picture of South Africa today. The lively watercolors are similar to those in *Jamela's Dress* above. This is a worthy sequel.

Hoffman, Mary. *Boundless Grace.* Illustrated by Caroline Binch. New York: Dial/Penguin, 1995. 28pp. Grades 1–4.

The ebullient heroine of the more lengthy *Amazing Grace* (Dial, 1991) returns in a story that links Grace's life as an ordinary African American girl with Africa. Grace's father, who has moved to Africa and remarried there, sends tickets for Grace and her grandmother to visit him and his new family in Gambia. Along with Grace, we can feel the adjustment to both different people and places as we observe many aspects of life in this part of Africa today. Binch conveys a real sense of place with her combination of watercolors and colored pencils. Her emphasis on fabrics worn and displayed in the market is especially effective.

Hoffman, Mary. *The Color of Home.* Illustrated by Karin Littlewood. New York: Phyllis Fogelman/Penguin, 2002. 26pp. Grades K–3.

Hassan cannot feel comfortable in the classroom so different from his former one in Somalia. The language and the food are strange; his attempt at painting is ruined by his memories. But when a Somali lady comes to school to help him, he is able to tell his teacher about the horrors he left behind. At first all the colors seem gone from his life as well. But soon he is on his way to feeling more at home, and his art shows the change. The watercolor illustrations clearly show the transition from apprehension and sorrow to comfort and some joy as well. There's a vitality to the paint's application with loose brushstrokes leaving bits of paper unpainted. Hassan's mother, incidentally, has her head appropriately covered.

Ichikawa, Satomi. *The First Bear in Africa.* New York: Philomel/Penguin, 2001. 32pp. Grades PreS–1.

One morning a car of tourists arrives to visit Meto's little village in the African savanna. Among them is a small girl holding an animal Meto tells us he has never seen. After taking photographs, they leave, but Meto notices that the animal has been left behind. Meto runs to catch up with them, passing his friends and neighbors, the hippos, the lions, elephants, giraffes, all of whom wonder at the strange creature in his arms. With the help of a giraffe, Meto reaches the girl before her plane leaves: perhaps a bit too much fantasy?

Happy to have her teddy bear returned, she gives Meto the ribbon from around its neck for his goat. Meto realizes that it was a bear, truly the first one in Africa. Watercolor scenes paint sympathetic pictures of the African family and the various animals and landscape. The end-papers display a map of sorts, showing where the various animal groups live, including those domesticated ones in pens. There is a glossary of the Swahili words used.

Kurtz, Jane, and Christopher Kurtz. *Water Hole Waiting.* Illustrated by Lee Christiansen. New York: Greenwillow/HarperCollins, 2002. 32pp. Grades PreS–2.

In a poetic voice of hushed anticipation, the authors recreate a scene at a water hole on the African savanna. As the sun rises, a small monkey is stopped by his mother while going for a drink. He must wait for a safe time, while hippos, then zebras, lions, elephants, and giraffes arrive in turn to drink. The monkey gets ever more thirsty as the day goes by. Finally, avoiding a lurking crocodile, all the monkeys can drink their fill. Attractively composed pastel illustrations describe the various drinkers naturalistically, getting under the bellies of kicking zebras or alongside a snapping croc. Emotional content pervades the sense of being there. The authors note that although the story is fiction, the factual information is accurate. The facts include an emphasis on the vervet monkey.

Mbuthia, Waithira. *My Sister's Wedding: A Story of Kenya.* Illustrated by Geoffrey Gacheru Karanja. Norwalk, CT: Soundprints, 2002. 32pp. Grades PreS–3.

We share the excitement as the wedding day of Wambui's sister approaches and also her anticipation of future loneliness. The traditional wedding day of the Gikuyu is always a surprise to the bride. She is carried to her new home amid singing, dancing, good food, and gifts from her many friends. Further facts about Gikuyu ceremonies are included, along with a glossary, a map, and information about Kenya. Double-page paintings are filled with scenes of village activities. Although the pictures are impressionistic, the information about local houses, clothing, animals, and landscape is directly accessible while conveying the anxieties and joys of the wedding.

Mollel, Tololwa M. *Kele's Secret.* Illustrated by Catherine Stock. New York: Lodestar/Dutton, 1997. 32pp. Grades PreS–2.

It is his job, Yoanes tells us, to find the eggs that Grandmother Koko's hens lay. When he fills the big bowl with them, it will be time to go to market. One hen, Kele, seems to have found a secret hiding place, and Yoanes is determined to find it. After following her for a long time, he has to brave entering a frightening shed. But there he finds enough eggs for the trip to the market and his reward. This story of life on a Tanzanian farm is based on the author's experiences. Naturalistic watercolors recreate a rural life style with buildings, typical farm animals, assorted trees, and fringes of jungle, along with Kele's nesting place. The market is a wonderland of local details. A glossary is included.

Mollel, Tololwa M. *My Rows and Piles of Coins.* Illustrated by E. B. Lewis. New York: Clarion/Houghton, 1999. 32pp. Grades K–4.

Saruni is saving his hard-earned money to buy a bicycle, so he and his mother can take their produce more easily to the market. Meanwhile, he is counting his coins and learning to ride a laden bicycle. He is shattered to learn that a bicycle costs much more than he has saved. It is a wonderful surprise when his father comes home with a new motorbike and "sells" his old bicycle to Saruni. Then it's time to save for a cart to pull behind the bike. The author adds a note on the time of the story, when he was a child in Tanzania in the 1960s, plus a list of Maasai and Swahili words in the story. Lewis's naturalistic watercolors present clear, even vivid pictures of the local life with busy markets, rural roads, and of course the people engaged in routine activities. The extra double-page scenes of Saruni's adventures with the bicycle add emotional involvement.

Njeng, Pierre Yves. *Vacation in the Village: A Story from West Africa.* Honesdale, PA: Boyds Mills, 1999. 24pp. Also paper. Grades K–3.

On their last day of school, Nwemb tells us, his father informs him and his sister that they are going to spend their vacation with his grandparents in a village outside the city. His sister is delighted, but Nwemb is concerned because he doesn't know anyone there and he can't take all his toys. But he soon has a friend and is enjoying many new experiences. He even acquires a pet turtle. By the end of vacation, he is sad to leave but looks forward to returning soon. The illustrations add local details to the sparse text. The village, in a dense green forest, is very different from the city where Nwemb lives. The paintings have the look of an unschooled artist but of someone familiar with the settings and able to present them directly.

Onyefulu, Ifeoma. *Ogbo: Sharing Life in an African Village.* San Diego, CA: Gulliver/Harcourt, 1996. 26pp. Grades 1–4.

We learn about family and village life in Igboland, Nigeria, from six-year-old Obioma. An *ogbo* is an age group to which all children born in a five-year period belong. Obioma tells us about the activities of each of the *ogbo* of her family using many native words. The masquerade celebrating the new planting season and the making of a chief are two happy ceremonies described. Sharp, clear color photographs provide considerable visual information.

Onyefulu, Ifeoma. *A Triangle for Adaora: An African Book of Shapes.* New York: Dutton, 2000. 26pp. Grades PreS–1.

The story has a young girl introducing her younger cousin to the shapes around her: a square *apkasa,* or colander, in which her sister is sifting grated cassava roots; a rectangle on Uncle Eze's *agbada,* or robe, etc. Each item mentioned has added information about it in a small colored rectangle on the page. The children encounter many aspects of African life, probably from the author's birthplace in eastern Nigeria. Clear, brightly colored photographs illustrate the objects mentioned in the text. They also offer specific images of the village and its inhabitants.

Sisulu, Elinor Batezat. *The Day Gogo Went to Vote: South Africa April 1994.* Illustrated by Sharon Wilson. Boston: Little, Brown, 1996. 32pp. Grades 1–5.

Six-year-old Thembi's great-grandmother, the *Gogo* of the title, tells about her ancestors as she takes care of Thembi. When election days are announced by the new South African government, Gogo shocks everyone by her determination to vote, despite the difficulties of getting to the polls. Gogo tries to explain to Thembi the importance of the right to vote, one that blacks have been denied but finally achieved. On election day and afterward, there is excitement and celebration. The pastel double-page scenes describe the settings effectively to convey the several emotions as well as the scenes associated with Gogo's adventure. There is a glossary and pronunciation guide.

Stanley, Sanna. *Monkey for Sale.* New York: Frances Foster/Farrar, Straus, 2002. 32pp. Grades K–3.

When Luzolo takes her five francs to the village market, her father reminds her to shop around, to bargain, and her mother adds "no one gets something for nothing on market day." Luzolo shops carefully, but when she and her friend Kiese find that a monkey is for sale, they despair at not being able to buy it. Their wheeling and dealing finally allows them to purchase the monkey and set it free. Meanwhile, we have had a tour of the people and products of a village market in the Democratic Republic of the Congo as recalled from the author's childhood. Colored illustrations made using etching and hand-painted *Chine collé* on mulberry paper create almost double-page scenes that detail the specifics of Luzolo's village life and something of the unhurried rhythm of that life.

Stock, Catherine. *Gugu's House.* New York: Clarion/Houghton, 2001. 32pp. Grades K–3.

Kukamba loves to leave the city to visit her grandmother's house out in the veldt. It has paintings and sculptures everywhere. Every day Kukamba helps Gugu with the chores. Then they work together with mud and dung to make new walls and shape animals. After that, they grind colors to paint. The rain is late in coming this year; everyone is worried about the crops. At night, at the fire where the villagers gather, Gugu tells the story of the Tortoise and the Hare to cheer them up. When the rains finally arrive, everyone celebrates. But Kukamba is upset, because the paint is washed away and the walls are becoming mud. Gugu takes her out to see that the colors are outside now in the flowers. Gugu is based, the author tells us, on a real person, Mrs. Khosa, and her colorful house. Watercolor paint is used to illuminate the changing weather in the pictures of this Zimbabwe village. Stock wraps up the information about both house decoration and agriculture in a pleasantly accessible story. We see people at work and at rest amid the decorated walls, happily demonstrating the concept of community. A glossary is included.

Stuve-Bodeen, Stephanie. *Babu's Song.* Illustrated by Aaron Boyd. New York: Lee & Low, 2003. 32pp. Grades K–3.

In Tanzania today, Bernardi would like to go to school and to have a real soccer ball to play the game he loves. But he and his grandfather, Babu, have barely enough money for food from selling the toys Babu crafts from scraps of wood and metal. One day in the market, Bernardi is offered a lot of money for a special music box Babu has made for him. Although he loves the box and would also like to have the soccer ball the money could buy, he sells the box and brings the money to Babu, who figures out a way to get Bernardi all he wishes anyhow. Boyd's watercolor scenes give emotional charge to this story of family love and sacrifice. Naturalistic, but more concerned with suggesting the village settings than with details, the pictures focus on Bernardi's actions and feelings.

Stuve-Bodeen, Stephanie. *Elizabeti's Doll.* Illustrated by Christy Hale. New York: Lee & Low, 1998. 32pp. Grades PreS–3.

When a new baby brother arrives, Elizabeti wants her own baby to care for. Not having a doll, she finds a rock that feels just right. She names her rock

Eva, and finds her much better behaved than her brother Obedi, as she bathes her, feeds her, and changes her. But when Elizabeti leaves Eva for a while, she can't locate her. She is very happy when she finally finds Eva supporting the cooking pot. Her mother helps her find another rock to replace Eva under the pot. When cleaned up, Eva is ready for her lullaby at bedtime. Elizabeti is a heart-warming charmer. Mixed-media paintings create affectionate impressions of Elizabeti and her village life. Special attention is given to the patterned clothing, even those hanging on the line.

Stuve-Bodeen, Stephanie. *Elizabeti's School.* Illustrated by Christy Hale. New York: Lee & Low, 2002. 32pp. Grades K–3.

Elizabeti, the charming heroine of *Elizabeti's Doll* above and *Mama Elizabeti* below, is off for her first day of school in Tanzania. All through the day she is learning but also worrying how everything is at home. Back there after school, comfortable in her old clothes doing her usual activities, she wonders whether she wants to go back to school. But after she shows everyone what she has learned, she decides to give school another try. Illustrations, with collage using decorated papers added for the textiles, hint at the home and school settings, while creating real youngsters involved with school, lessons, games, and home chores. A Swahili pronunciation guide is included.

Stuve-Bodeen, Stephanie. *Mama Elizabeti.* Illustrated by Christy Hale. New York: Lee & Low, 2000. 32pp. Grades K–3.

Despite the fine practice Elizabeti had in *Elizabeti's Doll,* she finds that taking care of her brother Obedi when her mother has a new baby is a lot harder than caring for a rock doll. He squirms and pulls her hair as she tries to do her chores with him tied on her back with her *kanga.* When she has to fetch water, she puts him down on the *kanga,* but when she returns, he is gone, and she feels as if she has failed. Luckily he comes toddling back. Somehow a kiss from him is better than Eva. This is another look at village life later than *Elizabeti's Doll* above, with views of different pieces of her life presented with the same mixed media and appeal.

Winter, Jeanette. *Elsina's Clouds.* New York: Frances Foster/Farrar, Straus, 2004. 34pp. Grades K–3.

A young girl dreams of rain in a time of drought. As is traditional for Basotho women of southern Africa, her mother has painted their house as a plea to the ancestors for rain. Elsina wants to paint the house herself, while dreaming of clouds. She is allowed to paint a new part, then waits, until finally the clouds come, bringing the rain to make everything grow. The cycle continues, as happily "the ancestors listen" every year and the rains come. The sequence of framed scenes effectively demonstrates the cycle of the seasons. Each border is a different combination of stripes and dots and other geometric shapes that reflect those on Basotho houses. The pictures of the action all share the same shapes, colors, and simplified, almost symbolic naturalism. The end-papers tell their own simplified sequential version of the story.

AFRICAN AMERICANS

ORIGINAL TALES AND FOLKTALES

Allen, Debbie. *Brothers of the Knight*. Illustrated by Kadir Nelson. New York: Dial/Penguin, 1999. 34pp. Grades K–3.

The traditional tale of the Twelve Dancing Princesses moves to a "once upon a time" Harlem, with amusing consequences and an unusual family dog as narrator. The Reverend Knight cannot understand why every morning the shoes of his twelve sons are all worn out, although his housekeepers have always locked them in at night. Sweet Sunday at first seems the answer to his problems. She cleans and cooks up a storm. But the boys are determined that she won't find out their secret. Of course she does, after some wild dance moves, followed by a happy ending. This modern fairy tale visualized in pencil drawings and oil paint on photocopy depicts a modern Harlem and a musical comedy-like cast of lively dancers. The comedy is moderated by a genuine respect for the people and their actions.

Battle-Lavert, Gwendolyn. *The Shaking Bag*. Illustrated by Aminah Brenda Lynn Robinson. Morton Grove, IL: Albert Whitman, 2000. 32pp. Grades K–3.

Miss Annie Mae never lets the birds go hungry. But one night as she is wondering how she will be able to feed them plus her dog and herself, a young man asks to stay the night. When she apologizes for the cold, he simply shakes her old seed bag and produces a warm fire in her stove. To a repeated refrain he also shakes out a chair, great food, and a large table. After enjoying the meal and conversation, they go to sleep. When he leaves the next morning, she offers him all she has, the bag. But he says that it is hers, and because of her generosity, it will never be empty. The folk quality of the story is enhanced by the appearance of the young man named Raven after she has fed the ravens and the magic he then produces for her. There's also a lively folk art quality to the directness of the colored line drawings that provide both a richly detailed context and the two characters who play out the drama. Miss Annie Mae's house is right out of a European fairy tale.

Medearis, Angela Shelf. *Tailypo: A Newfangled Tall Tale*. Illustrated by Sterling Brown. New York: Holiday House, 1996. 32pp. Grades 1–4.

This a version of the old scary story in which a boy and his dog confront a beast who loses his "tailypo" and wants it back. In this case it is Kennie Ray, home alone with his ferocious chihuahua Fang while his parents are working in the fields, who confronts the nasty beast. He and Fang chase it around to protect their meager meal and are left with the tailypo after the critter goes out the window. They trade it for needed groceries and are crossing the swamp when the beast demands his tailypo back. It chases them home, asking louder and louder. The terrified boy finally gains the courage to save the day. Washy watercolors fill the double pages with pictures of the characters and cabin, and of course, the beast, a long-snouted, multitoothed, hairless invention with that shaggy "tailypo."

Nolen, Jerdine. *Big Jabe*. Illustrated by Kadir Nelson. New York: Lothrop/Morrow, 2000. 32pp. Grades 1–4.

This original tall tale offers some amusement while it details the difficult life of the slaves. Addy finds a small boy floating in a basket who brings both magic and freedom. When grown, Jabe makes the plantation work easier for all. He infuriates the overseer, who takes his anger out on others. But they seem to disappear to freedom when Jabe takes them to the magic pear tree he has planted. When the overseer chains Addy up, she disappears as well. Jabe then moves on to lift burdens elsewhere. These naturalistic watercolor and gouache scenes of life on the plantation contrast with the magic in the text, except for the illustration of all those fish jumping out of the river as Jabe calls them. Slave shacks, fields, hound dogs, all are seen as part of the slave history.

Nolen, Jerdine. *Thunder Rose*. Illustrated by Kadir Nelson. San Diego, CA: Silver Whistle/Harcourt, 2003. 32pp. Grades K–3.

The author wrote this humorous, twang-y original African American tall tale as a folk tale from the Old West "out of love and joy." The strong African American heroine is in the Paul Bunyan tradition, amazingly strong, making her own thunderbolt, defeating outlaws, conquering a storm with her mighty song from the music in her heart. Nelson gives us a sassy, confident youngster. These are naturalistic oil, watercolor, and pencil illustrations of heroine and cows with lots of prairie and an exciting tornado.

Rosales, Melodye Benson. *Leola and the Honeybears: An African-American Retelling of Goldilocks and the Three Bears.* New York: Cartwheel/Scholastic, 1999. 34pp. Grades PreS–3.

This retelling of the old fairy tale has only a few phrases associated with African Americans. Otherwise it's a step-by-step adaptation. Visually, the large book's naturalistic paintings offer a very attractive, detailed, and energetic visual narrative sequence. Leola is as charming a youngster as one could imagine, fully involved in her mischief. The bear family gets more attention. There's even an early scene where they entertain several animal friends at a brunch. The food described is an adventure in itself. Background notes are included.

San Souci, Robert D. *The Secret of the Stones: A Folktale.* Illustrated by James Ransome. New York: Phyllis Fogelman/Penguin, 2000. 40pp. Grades K–3.

A hard-working, childless couple come back from the fields every day to find all their work at home done and supper ready. They do not understand who is doing this until "Aunt Easter," a local healer, tells them that two white rocks they had brought home were previously transformed by a conjure-man. The rocks turn into an orphan boy and girl while the couple are away and do their work. The healer tells them how they can see the children. When they do, they want to change them permanently back into children. "Aunt Easter" tells them how. They challenge the conjure-man, do what is necessary, and joyously welcome their new family. The story is told with dialect, but clearly and with excitement and wonder. Large oil paintings create naturalistic scenes with details of landscape and cabin. The characters are well defined, reflecting the range of emotions in the tale. The healer is a particularly strong character. There are notes on the sources.

San Souci, Robert D. *Sukey and the Mermaid.* Illustrated by Brian Pinkney. New York: Four Winds, 1992. 32pp. Also Aladdin paper. Grades 2–6.

The lengthy text is based on a fragmentary South Carolina tale, as noted by the author. A young girl who is made to work hard by her lazy stepfather takes a break on the beach and sings a song to "Mama Jo." A mermaid appears, bringing her treasures but warns that she must keep it secret. When her mother and stepfather discover it, however, and try to catch the mermaid, she will no longer come. Life at home becomes so bad that young Sukey decides to join the mermaid under the sea. When she pines for home, the mermaid sends her back with gold and with the name of the man she is to marry. Her stepfather steals the gold and kills the man, but the mermaid returns to set everything right one last time. Some of the mythic quality of the story is expressed in the scratchboard illustrations on creamy-toned pages. Full-page and double-page scenes depict realistic characters and settings with details of dress, interiors, and the sea, to produce a mood of exotic anticipation.

AFRICAN AMERICAN HISTORY THROUGH SLAVERY AND THE CIVIL WAR

Altman, Linda Jacobs. *The Legend of Freedom Hill.* Illustrated by Cornelius Van Wright and Ying-Hua Hu. New York: Lee & Low, 2000. 32pp. Also paper. Grades 1–4.

In California during the Gold Rush, two young girls become friends. Both are isolated, Rosabel because she is black and Sophie because she is Jewish. Although Rosabel is free, her mother Miz Violet is a runaway slave who could be shipped back to her owner. When the slave catchers take her away, Rosabel comes to stay with Sophie. Together the girls search frantically until they find enough gold to buy Miz Violet's freedom and that of others as well. The up-beat story is told in colloquial language and naturalistic watercolors. The double-page scenes are replete with historical details of the town, the gold mining digs, the several characters, and even Sophie's family Sabbath dinner. The girls' friendship is convincingly depicted as the central core of the story.

Bearden, Romare. *Li'l Dan the Drummer Boy: A Civil War Story.* New York: Simon & Schuster, 2003. 34pp. Grades K–3.

Young Dan learns that he is free when Union soldiers arrive at the plantation where he has been a slave. He joins up with them and follows them to a battle. He is told to go away but notices Confederate troops approaching. From a tree, he makes the drum sound like cannons to warn his friends. General Sherman appreciates his help and makes him part of the Army's Drum Corps. Bearden's mixed media impressions of both plantation and army life suggest rather than specify particular events or details. There is a child-like innocence to the bloodless rendering of war, a focus on the adventure and companionship rather than the real horrors. Henry Louis Gates Jr. describes his meeting with Bearden in the Foreword. A CD of the reading of the story by Maya Angelou is attached.

Hopkinson, Deborah. *Sweet Clara and the Freedom Quilt.* Illustrated by James Ransome. New York: Alfred A. Knopf, 1993. 36pp. Also paper, 2003. Grades 2–5.

Set on a plantation in slavery days, the lengthy story of the quilt is told by Clara, the young slave seamstress who made it. Learning to sew helped her move from field work to the Big House, where she first heard of the Underground Railroad and the need for a map of it. She begins using scraps of cloth and the pieces of information she can collect to make a quilt showing the route to freedom. She leaves the quilt behind for others when she and Jack flee, first to find her mother, then on to Canada. The focus is on the people, with mere suggestions of interiors or landscape. Opaque paints are used like clay to model forms rather than define them in detail. Episodes build visually as Clara works on her quilt, which is displayed on the end-papers.

McGill, Alice. *Molly Bannaky.* Illustrated by Chris K. Soentpiet. Boston: Houghton Mifflin, 1999. 32pp. Grades 1–4.

The title character escaped a death sentence in England because she could read but was shipped off to the Colonies in the late 17th century for seven years of bondage. Surviving that, the brave, strong woman stakes a claim and builds a farm. Finding she cannot manage it alone, she buys a slave whose name is Bannaky. They get along so well together that they decide to marry, even though interracial marriage is illegal. The grandson of this couple is Benjamin Banneker. A Historical Note adds information on Molly's life, the laws of the time, and the outstanding career of the boy who was also Molly's pupil. Fully detailed, very naturalistic but dramatically interpreted watercolor paintings fill the large double pages with information about the living conditions only suggested in the text. The visual narrative is both informative and moving.

Morrow, Barbara Olenyik. *A Good Night for Freedom.* Illustrated by Leonard Jenkins. New York: Holiday House, 2004. 32pp. Grades K–3.

Through the eyes of young Hallie, who is white, we see two young runaway slaves take refuge in the house of Levi Coffin, a real person who was called "President of the Underground Railroad." Her father wants no trouble from the slave hunters, but Hallie sends them away in the wrong direction despite her father's warning not to "meddle," for she has come to sympathize with the brave young girls. She hopes that they will finally be free. The illustrations are naturalistic, made in acrylic, pastel, spray paint, and colored pencil. The drama is played in expressionistic scenes where color provides emotional effectiveness. Information on the Coffin family and their role in the Underground Railroad, along with other sources, is included. The illustrator explains his use of dark and bright colors to mirror the brutality and Hallie's victory.

Nelson, Vaunda Micheaux. *Almost to Freedom*. Illustrated by Colin Bootman. Minneapolis: Carolrhoda, 2003. 40pp. Grades 1–4.

Inspired by a doll seen by the author in a museum, the story is told in dialect by the doll. A "bunch of rags," Sally the doll is young Lindy's only precious possession on the plantation. They escape one night on the rough road, the Underground Railroad to freedom. In her hurry out of a hiding place, Lindy accidentally drops Sally, who sadly misses her. But soon another frightened girl takes comfort from her. The full- and double-page naturalistic paintings are set primarily at night, with faces lit by the moon. Tense drama comes to a satisfying conclusion. The author notes both the inspiration for and the historic background of the story. There is a glossary of historic words and phrases.

Ransom, Candice. *Liberty Street*. Illustrated by Eric Velasquez. New York: Walker & Co, 2003. 32pp. Grades 1–4.

A young girl and her mother work long and hard all week as slaves in the town of Fredericksburg; her father has been sold away. Before Kezia can be sent away as well, her mother has tried to buy her freedom, in vain. So she decides to send her alone to Canada. She sends and receives signals about the Underground Railroad when hanging her laundry, using the "clothesline telegraph." Kezia is afraid to make the journey without her mother but bravely sets off toward freedom, vowing to learn and to send for her mother. Oil paintings tell the visual story of the slaves' lives with details of dress and locale. The author's note adds information on the time and place and of the use of the "clothesline telegraph" by slaves to signal. The bright red shirt blowing across the end-papers fairly shouts "Run!"

Rappaport, Doreen. *Freedom River*. Illustrated by Bryan Collier. New York: Jump at the Sun/Hyperion, 2000. 28pp. Grades K–4.

One thrilling incident in an ex-slave's adventures taking slaves across the Ohio River to freedom is dramatized. John Parker was a real person. Here he manages to get a man, his wife, and their baby away from a cruel master and safely the thousand feet from Kentucky to Ohio. Although the characters are portrayed in naturalistic detail with watercolors, collage is used for clothing, architecture, and landscape. This combination gives a mythical quality to the visual narrative in the emotion-packed sequence of action. The artist notes that he has incorporated people who are not part of the narrative. These are "ancestors or protectors" modeled on people in his life, portrayed with wavy lines across their faces to represent the river, "the key to freedom." Notes also add historic details to the story of John Parker.

Raven, Margot Theis. *Circle Unbroken: The Story of a Basket and Its People*. Illustrated by E. B. Lewis. New York: Melanie Kroupa/Farrar, Straus, 2004. 42pp. Grades K–4.

A grandmother begins her poetic story, told with affectionate asides to her granddaughter, of how she came to weave baskets. The tale begins with her grandfather back in Africa. He was taught to weave baskets tight enough to hold water, along with many other skills. When he was brought to America in chains as a slave, he continued to make baskets at night and to remember. He married a woman who also made baskets. After they were freed, they moved to islands that were at first isolated. But a bridge now brings tourists who buy the sweet-grass baskets now in museums and still made in the old way. The circle that connects the generations continues to grow as the girl learns about "the knot that ties us all together." Lewis's large watercolors parallel the text's poetry and cadences, helping us feel the spirituality of the historic events while depicting them with affectionate naturalism. The basket remains the central theme as the book ends, with the grandmother starting the youngster on a new one. Notes offer "More About Sweetgrass Baskets" and a bibliography. A close-up of the basket weave stretches across the end-papers.

Riggio, Anita. *Secret Signs Along the Underground Railroad*. Honesdale, PA: Boyds Mills, 1997. 32pp. Also paper. Grades 1–4.

Luke fears that his mother is in danger. She is a link in the information chain for the Underground Railroad. Slave catchers have set fire to the barn of neighbors who had been hiding runaway slaves. Luke, who is deaf, communicates with his mother in sign language. Together they paint scenes in sugar eggs to sell at the general store. When the slave catchers come to their home, one of them accompanies Luke to the store to sell the eggs. There he must also safely contact the black girl his mother was to meet. Quickly painting in an empty egg, Luke bravely pictures the new safe house for her, showing her where to take the fugitives to safety. Full page, detailed watercolors highlight the dramatic action of this quasi-historical tale. The tension of the sequential events is made clear. Notes are added on both education for deaf children at that time and on the Underground Railroad.

Ringgold, Faith. *Aunt Harriet's Railroad in the Sky*. New York: Crown, 1992. 32pp. Also paper. Grades 2–6.

Cassie and her brother Be Be fly again, as they do in the author's *Tar Beach*, below. This time it is to the days of slavery in the South. Cassie learns from Harriet Tubman something of the hardships of her ancestors and of the Underground Railroad that helps them to freedom. There's a child-like simplicity in the illustrations, which have decorative patterning. History is worked into the details.

Vaughn, Marcie. *The Secret to Freedom*. Illustrated by Larry Johnson. New York: Lee & Low, 2001. 32pp. Grades K–4.

A young girl's Great Aunt Lucy tells her the story behind a scrap of cloth on her wall. She and her family were hard-working slaves. After her mother and father are sold away, her brother Albert begins searching for a way to get them to the Underground Railroad. He brings her what looks like ragged quilts but tells her that each pattern has a message about escape. She agrees to hang certain ones on the fence to deliver the message needed whenever he tells her to. One night he is caught coming in late and is whipped. Lucy tells him that he must leave without her. She gives him a quilted star and hopes that he can make it. Years later, after slavery, they can finally meet and rejoice together. The cloth on Lucy's wall is the star she made for Albert. There's a roughness to the way the acrylic paint is applied in creating the rather literal double-page scenes. The effect is strongly emotional, including not only the broad context but also a more sensitive exploration of character. The particular patterns of the quilt squares on the jacket/cover are named and described inside in a note that lists their meanings, along with information on the Underground Railroad.

Vaughn, Marcia. *Up the Learning Tree*. Illustrated by Derek Blanks. New York: Lee & Low, 2003. 32pp. Grades 1–4.

A young slave named Henry Bell tells his story in the direct present tense. He is given the job of walking the son of his owner back and forth to school every day. It stings him that they think he is stupid; his master reminds him that slaves are not allowed to learn to read. But when he happens to hear the teacher read, the magic of it makes him determined to listen and learn. Miss Hattie, the teacher, soon begins to teach him in secret. She is forced to leave when this is discovered. But Henry is on his way. Naturalistic oil paintings depict the plantation and provide sensitive portraits of Henry's attempts at education. A note fills in the history of some of the slaves who wanted to learn to read, with quotations.

Weatherford, Carole Boston. *The Sound That Jazz Makes*. Illustrated by Eric Velasquez. New York: Walker & Co, 2000. 32pp. Grades K–3.

In brief verses, the author traces the evolution of jazz from its roots in African chants, dance, and instruments; through the capture and sale of slaves and their lives on plantations; the songs of church worship; the music played on steamboats; to Harlem and to the rappers of today. Each double page illustrates a verse in painted scenes that create melodramatic settings from early history on.

Winter, Jeanette. *Follow the Drinking Gourd*. New York: Dragonfly paper, 1992. 48pp. Grades 2–4.

Winter tells how the actual song taught by the sailor Peg Leg Joe helps fictional characters to follow the route of the Underground Railroad to freedom. When her husband James is about to be sold away from her, Molly remembers the song and sees the "gourd" or Dipper in the sky. She, James, and three others follow the trail as described in the verses of the song until they reach the Ohio River, where Peg Leg Joe takes them across and sends them on through other secret houses to Canada. The song is reproduced in the book. Added notes further describe the Railroad, the white sailor, and how the song worked to guide the runaways. Opaque paint is used in a flat manner to create a series of rectangular scenes, each framed with a thin black line and set on the white page. There is a mythic quality, as shapes are abstracted to create patterns in the clouds, rows of corn, ripples on a river.

AFRICAN AMERICANS TODAY AND IN POST–CIVIL WAR HISTORY

Coleman, Evelyn. *To Be a Drum*. Illustrated by Aminah Brenda Lynn Robinson. Morton Grove, IL: Albert Whitman, 1998. 32pp. Also paper. Grades K–3.

Out in the misty field, Mat and Martha's daddy tells them of the rhythm of the earth that first beat in Africa. He talks of the slavers taking away the people and their drums from Africa and how they made their own songs and drums in America: courage drums, mind drums, communities drums, art drums, finally all the drums of freedom. Together Mat, Martha, and their dad "drum the earth's heartbeat together." The double pages seem bursting with the combined energies of organic images created by Robinson with materials like old cloth scraps, buttons, sawed bits of wood, thick paints, etc. People emerge from the vibrating surfaces to act out the poetic and symbolic history in ways that almost make the reader feel the drum beats.

Collier, Bryan. *Uptown*. New York: Henry Holt, 2000. 32pp. Also paper. Grades K–3.

In just a few words per double page, a young African American boy introduces us to his neighborhood, Harlem in New York City—its brownstones, its food, its entertainment, its shopping, its underlying jazz. The combination may be odd, but he celebrates it all. Watercolors, collage, and cut-up colored photographs create complex scenes that pulse with the life inherent in the events of the text. Interiors and street scenes provide the details that help define the visual culture of Harlem.

Crews, Donald. *Bigmama's*. Greenwillow/HarperCollins, 1991. 32pp. Grades K–3.

Simply written memories of Crews's childhood summers at his grandmother's house in the Florida countryside include the three-day ride South, the outhouse, the pump for water, the farm animals, and most of all, the fun and the warm family togetherness. Double-page watercolors display the sort of joy only possible in the memories of age. Crews fills the pages with myriad details, bold-faced text, and all sorts of happy activities of youngsters.

Herron, Carolivia. *Nappy Hair*. Illustrated by Joe Cepeda. New York: Alfred A. Knopf, 1997. 32pp. Grades K–3.

The author has based the story on her own childhood experience. The text reads like a tape recording of the family's comments on Brenda's hair, with a sort of call and response using different typefaces. For that hair "intended to be nappy. *Indeed it did.*" The remarks about her hair go on and on, all in good fun, with comparisons, praises, even speculation on the angels complaining to God, who replies that He wants some nappy hair on earth, and Brenda has the nappiest. A serious note on slavery creeps in, but then the celebration continues. "And she's got the nappiest hair in the world. *Ain't it the truth.*" The cast of characters beginning with old Uncle Mordecai in his rocking chair is a happy, frequently exuberant bunch of friends and relatives. Cepeda keeps changing his background colors as his paints supply enough details to fill in the community and its spirit. The pictures keep jumping as they follow Brenda's frenetic actions, never losing sight of that wonderful hair.

hooks, bell. *Happy to Be Nappy.* Illustrated by Chris Raschka. New York: Jump at the Sun/Hyperion, 1999. 32pp. Also board. Grades PreS–3.

This celebration of African American hair is light hearted and jolly, to "let girls go running free." The brief, poetic lines printed in script run across and all over the pages along with the active dancing girls and their wonderful, versatile hair. Watercolors create small areas of background colors, while a series of free brush strokes produces a cast of happy youngsters and, on some pages, adults who mess with their hair. Some of the black hairstyles are a bit wild, but they obviously satisfy the gang as they join hands and circle around.

Howard, Elizabeth Fitzgerald. *Virgie Goes to School with Us Boys.* Illustrated by E. B. Lewis. New York: Simon & Schuster, 2000. 26pp. Grades 1–3.

After the Civil War, some schools are open for black children in the South. Our narrator is one of five brothers who have been going to a Quaker school. Their little sister Virgie wants to go too, even though it is seven miles away. She keeps begging all summer, until her father agrees that "All free people need learning." Finally school is about to begin. They prepare and start the long trek. Virgie keeps up and doesn't falter. They finally arrive, and Virgie can't wait to start learning. There is humor running throughout this simple story along with the more serious message. Double-page watercolors recreate the farm environment and the family with sensitive reality. The paintings exude a vitality that propels the story ahead; Virgie and the boys have individual personalities. Facts about the historic situation and the real school in the story, which was attended by the author's grandfather, are included. There is even a photograph of Virgie's brothers.

Johnson, Angela. *Just Like Josh Gibson.* Illustrated by Beth Peck. New York: Simon & Schuster, 2004. 32pp. Grades K–3.

A young girl listens to her grandmother's reminiscences of growing up loving baseball, gaining great skill but not being allowed to play because she was a girl. When the team is short a player, however, she helps win the game. Her idol at the time was Josh Gibson, "the Babe Ruth of the Negro Leagues." Here is an example of not only the former rules against girls playing baseball but also the much bigger issue of the prejudice that kept black players out of the major leagues for years. Pastels effectively create the vivacity of youngsters at play. Double-page scenes vigorously depict the events of the brief text, extending them with simple settings as backdrops for the drama of the story and its satisfying end. Facts on Josh Gibson and the Negro League are included.

Joosse, Barbara. *Stars in the Darkness*. Illustrated by R. Gregory Christie. San Francisco: Chronicle, 2002. 30pp. Grades 1–4.

When his brother doesn't come home one night, a young boy fears he is becoming involved with the "gang bangers" who seem to run their inner city neighborhood. Together with their mother, he helps organize the neighbors. Every night families walk the streets, their flashlights and their children being the "stars" that they hope will shine in the darkness. The author has based the character of the brother on a real person, writing it in dialect to reach "little brothers and sisters" and has added a list of "Resources on Gang Prevention." Double-page acrylic paintings make much of the mythic quality in this all-too-real story while depicting characters in settings that we recognize as real. Large areas of solid color are backdrops for the few objects needed for the action.

Kroll, Virginia. *Faraway Drums*. Illustrated by Floyd Cooper. Boston: Little, Brown, 1998. 32pp. Grades K–3.

Young Jamila is left in charge of her little sister Zakiya in their new neighborhood while their mother goes to work. Strange noises from outside frighten them both, but Jamila thinks back to the stories of Africa her great-gramma told. "Listen to the faraway drums," she reassures her. They imagine that their spaghetti is West African *fou-fou*. Howling in the street is just bickering hyenas. Tooting horns are the elephants at the water hole. After the next-door neighbor checks to see that they are OK, the bath becomes the waterfall of the Zambezi. And so the dreams of Africa take away the fear of the unknown. Cooper's misty scenes created with washes of oil paints on board convincingly portray the characters and setting. He designs the double pages so that the appealing sisters and the evoked African visions blend into a single reality.

Littlesugar, Amy. *Freedom School, Yes!* Illustrated by Floyd Cooper. New York: Philomel/Penguin, 2001. 40pp. Grades 1–4.

The original story is based on the 1964 Mississippi Summer Project, when young volunteers, black and white, faced terrible hostility when they went there to teach. The author interviewed three of those teachers for background. In the story, a white teacher, nineteen-year-old Annie, is staying with Jolie's family when a brick is thrown through their window. The next day, the church where Annie urges the children to come to school is set on fire. But the school begins anyhow, under a tree. Jolie learns about Black History as the church is rebuilt. And she learns to appreciate Annie and what she has taught her: to be brave like her ancestors. Cooper's double-page scenes combine sufficient background to set the narrative, while his focus is on each character's response to events. His naturalistic images are grainy but reflect a nobility of spirit, a sense of determination, an inspiration.

Littlesugar, Amy. *Jonkonnu: A Story from the Sketchbook of Winslow Homer.* Illustrated by Ian Schoenherr. New York: Philomel/Penguin, 1977. 32pp. Grades 1–4.

Around the Winslow Homer painting *Dressing for the Carnival,* the author has built a story of a young girl who observes the painter at work in a small town in Virginia as the country prepares to celebrate the centennial of Independence Day in 1876. Homer is sketching and painting in the African American part of town. One day, he is invited to see the preparation for their freedom holiday from slavery time called "Jonkonnu." This is when he does the painting of the young man dressing for the carnival with children holding American flags. Homer faces the anger of the white townspeople at his interest in the freed slaves. After he leaves, the girl thinks, "That's what an artist does. He lights up the darkness." The illustrations create genuine people whose gestures clearly display how they feel. We note the contrast in life styles between the two areas of town. By the placing of the town toughs starkly against the blank white page, the artist has us sense the tension and anger and the painter's stoic silence in the confrontation.

Littlesugar, Amy. *Tree of Hope.* Illustrated by Floyd Cooper. New York: Philomel/Penguin, 1999. 40pp. Also Puffin paper. Grades 1–4.

There really was a Tree of Hope in Harlem. It stood beside the Lafayette Theatre, once the busy center of performances but in the Depression decayed and empty. Florrie's father had been an actor there, which is where he met her mother. Now in hard times, he fries donuts and her mother cleans houses. Florrie's heartfelt wish on the tree is for her father to be able to act again. In 1935, Orson Welles did stage a version of *Macbeth* at the Lafayette. Although it was by a white author, it was made relevant by its African setting and sparked the revival of black theater. Here the author thrills Florrie with her father's performance in the successful play. Cooper's illustrations are moody, textured, naturalistic pictures, saturated with the browns of the streets. But Florrie's face shines brightly with hope. The large double pages create a detailed sequence of a deeply troubled African American community and its eventual recovery. The play production is brought vividly to life.

McKissack, Patricia C. *Goin' Someplace Special.* Illustrated by Jerry Pinkney. New York: Anne Schwartz/Atheneum, 2001. 34pp. Grades K–3.

This story about the indignities suffered by a young girl in the segregated South of the 1950s, based on the author's experience, is uplifting for both the portrait of the eager, appealing young girl and because of the sign on the library that says "All are welcome." 'Tricia Ann is excited about going by bus to her favorite Special Place all by herself. But she has to stay behind the Jim Crow sign on the bus. She can't rest on the park bench that says "Whites Only." She is angry about other restrictions; she can't eat inside a restaurant, and she is not allowed in the hotel lobby. She needs reassurance but feels better when she finally reaches her Special Place, the library that welcomes all. The detailed watercolor and pencil scenes paint a real picture of 'Tricia Ann's world. They also create distinct personalities in that world, along with insights into her emotions. Pinkney helps us feel a bit of what segregation meant.

McKissack, Patricia C. *Ma Dear's Aprons.* Illustrated by Floyd Cooper. New York: Anne Schwartz/Atheneum/Simon & Schuster, 1997. 32pp. Also Aladdin paper. Grades K–3.

The author has based the title on what she was told of her great-grandmother who raised her three children in rural Alabama by doing housework for a living. A young boy describes the days of his week by the aprons his Ma Dear wears each day as she takes him to her jobs—washing, ironing, cleaning, baking, visiting the sick—but always taking special time together. Only Sunday is a no-apron day. A sentimental, happy story is illustrated naturalistically in scenes dominated by mother and son in the context of each day's work. There's a mistiness to the oil wash on board paintings that makes fine details superfluous while enhancing the emotions.

Miller, William. *The Bus Ride.* Illustrated by John Ward. New York: Lee & Low, 1998. 32pp. Grades K–3.

This fictional account of a young African American girl who refuses to sit in the back of the bus in the segregated bus is "loosely based" on the case of Rosa Parks, who has written the introduction. Sara and her hard-working mother always sit in the back of the bus, but one day Sara moves to the front to see what it's like and then refuses to move back. A policeman then carries her to jail. Sara can't understand the law. Meanwhile, a reporter has written her story in the newspaper. She thus inspires a boycott by African Americans that finally changes the law. Naturalistic, double-page acrylic paintings leave out all but the details needed to further the narrative. Sara makes a very appealing heroine.

Miller, William. *Night Golf.* Illustrated by Cedric Lucas. New York: Lee & Low, 1999. 32pp. Also paper. Grades K–4.

The Author's Note sets the stage for the original story. Back in the 1950s, African Americans were not allowed to play at private, even at many public, golf courses, much less to play professional golf. So when young James discovers how he loves to play golf, he has to settle for being a caddy to get on a course. An older caddy who once wanted to play himself, takes James into his confidence. He plays at night and invites James to join him, teaching him all summer. One day James gets the chance to show what he can do, and his future looks brighter. Pastel and colored pencil illustrations are rather literal visualizations of the text. The night scenes are particularly effective.

Miller, William. *Rent Party Jazz.* Illustrated by Charlotte Riley-Webb. New York: Lee & Low, 2001. 32pp. Grades 1–4.

A rent party is a traditional way for family and friends to party along with helping someone who is having financial trouble. In this story, young Sonny is already working hard during the Depression in New Orleans. When his mother loses her job, there is a question of how they will pay the rent. Sonny enjoys listening to the jazz played by Smilin' Jack in Jackson Square. When he looks so sad, Jack asks him what his trouble is. Jack then describes how the folks back in Mississippi, when in financial trouble, invited friends and neighbors to bring food and hear music, leaving a bucket out for contributions. With Jack's trumpet, the party Sonny plans is a big success. An Afterword fills in the history and details of rent parties. The acrylic paintings have the look of metaphors for the music. Colors of all kinds are applied expressionistically to produce barely recognizable objects along with emotionally charged people. When Jack plays, the pages seem to move.

Miller, William. *Richard Wright and the Library Card.* Illustrated by Gregory Christie. New York: Lee & Low, 1997. 28pp. Also paper. Grades 2–5.

This is a fictionalized account of events from the life of the African American author. An avid listener to the stories his mother and grandfather told, Richard couldn't get to school regularly because his poor family moved so often. He couldn't use the local libraries because he was black but read avidly whatever he could. He finally moves to Memphis when he is seventeen. There he finds a white man to whom he feels he can express his need for books. The man gives him his library card, and with a note, Richard is allowed to enter the stacks. Although challenged, he manages to get the books he wants. He reads constantly. He knows "[h]e would never be the same again." When he finally has enough money to move to Chicago, he feels that every page he has read was "a ticket to freedom." The expressionistic, opaque acrylic and colored pencil illustrations cover double pages but offer minimal contextual details. They focus on the characters, emphasizing their psychological sensibilities. A note adds additional information on Wright.

Mitchell, Margaret King. *Uncle Jed's Barbershop*. Illustrated by James Ransome. New York: Simon & Schuster, 1993. 32pp. Also paper, 1998. Grades 1–5.

The story of life in the South in the 1920s and 1930s is told in the voice of Sarah Jean, whose favorite Uncle Jed was the only black barber in the county. He traveled around to cut hair, since he had no shop, but knew just what he wanted when he finally saved enough money to open one. When Sarah Jean needs an operation, Uncle Jed gives $30 from his dream fund. A few years later, a Depression bank failure takes his savings and defers his dream again. At seventy-nine, he finally sees it come true and dies happy. In her story, the author discusses unpleasant historic facts such as segregated rest rooms, water fountains, schools, and hospital services as part of her otherwise warm picture of African American life in that time and place. Double-page oil paintings bring us into the rural world and the life of the period. The wallpaper pattern that appears on the end-papers is used as a unifying theme from rooms in Sarah Jean's house to the eventual barbershop; the patchwork quilt on Sarah Jean's bed is a glorious creation.

Pinkney, Andrea Davis. *Fishing Day*. Illustrated by Shane W. Evans. New York: Jump at the Sun/Hyperion, 2003. 32pp. Grades 1–4.

"[W]e sure love fishing," says Reenie about her mother and herself, as they take off for the Jim Crow River. They are disturbed by the arrival of Mr. Troop and his fidgety son Peter who frequently fish there. But they do it to eat, not for fun. Tossing corn in for bait, Reenie and her mother catch some carp. Resenting his lack of success, Peter throws some stones at them. But Reenie brings some corn to Peter and lends him a helping hand. Peter happily catches fish then and waves at Reenie when he sees her again. Reenie has done her best to ignore the Jim Crow line, explained in the author's note, where she also discusses the events in her life as she experienced prejudice and racism. There's a meandering blue ribbon that flows across all the pages, suggesting the river. The visual action is superimposed with some small scenes framed as if to focus our attention on the personal interactions, with a few large enough to give room for actions. There's a crudeness to the general naturalism of the illustrations.

Pinkney, Andrea Davis. *Mim's Christmas Jam*. Illustrated by Brian Pinkney. San Diego, CA: Gulliver/Harcourt, 2001. 32pp. Grades K–3.

In the early 1900s, many African Americans were working on the construction of the New York City subway. Royce and Saraleen's Pap is far away working there instead of celebrating Christmas with them. Mim decides to make her traditional belly-hum jam to send him. Magically, a taste of the jam seems to soften the hearts of Pap's bosses. They give the crew time for Pap and his friends to get home for Christmas. Double-page illustrations done with colored Luma dyes and acrylic on scratchboard display the family loneliness as well as the dark, hard work of the men underground. Colors reinforce the mood of each place, with scenes seemingly frozen in time. The recipe for Mim's belly-hum jam is an added feature.

Ringgold, Faith. *Tar Beach*. New York: Crown, 1992. 32pp. Also paper, 1995. Grades 1–5.

Ringgold takes us back, in a deceptively brief, simple story, to her memories of the rooftops of Harlem in the 1930s, when the tar on the roof became her beach on hot summer nights. There, in the story, Cassie's imagination flies her above the city, the George Washington Bridge, the union building her father helps construct, even the ice cream factory. She'd like to change the discrimination her father faces because he's black, the tears her mother cries when he looks for work and "doesn't come home." Meanwhile, Cassie finds the freedom she seeks by flying away "among the stars." A long addendum details the history on which her story is based. It also describes the quilt Ringgold created about *Tar Beach*, now in the Guggenheim Museum in New York. The quilt is pictured in its entirety at the end of the story; parts of its border run along the bottoms of the pages, tying the narrative together. Qualities of the same decorative patterning appear in various scenes; a few details of city life are pictured as well. There's a child-like simplicity to the paintings, in keeping with the directness of the text, while the compositions reveal the artist's sensibilities.

Smalls-Hector, Irene. *Irene and the Big, Fine Nickel*. Illustrated by Tyrone Geter. Boston: Little, Brown, 1991. 32pp. Also paper, 2004. Grades K–3.

Drawing on her own experiences growing up in Harlem in the 1950s, the author details the events of a sunny Saturday in the life of seven-year-old

Irene. While her mother sleeps and her younger brothers and sisters are away, Irene gets herself up, goes out to play, argues with Charlene, plays in the park with her friends, plants some seeds, finds a glorious nickel to buy a raisin bun to share, makes up with Charlene, and still has a wonderful day to look forward to. The lengthy test is filled with details of time and place, showing us the Harlem where "nobody locked the door and you never questioned being black because there were a million people who looked just like you." Full-page opaque paintings show interiors and street scenes not mentioned in the text, creating atmosphere and depicting children engaged in spirited activities.

Shange, Ntozake. *Ellington Was Not a Street*. Illustrated by Kadir Nelson. New York: Simon & Schuster, 1983 and 2004. 35pp. Grades 3 and up.

The text of Shange's emotion-packed free verse is spread, a line or two, across the tall double pages. It is rich with the memories of a Harlem childhood, warm with family love, and filled with encounters with men of vision at the time "who changed the world," such as Paul Robeson, W. E. B. Dubois, "Dizzy" Gillespie, and Duke Ellington. All those mentioned appear again at the end with small portraits and descriptions of exactly who they were. Naturalistic oil paintings, like a family album of color photographs, record the details of place and the people in them. A posed group shot of thirty friendly folks adds specific vitality to the text's more general remembrances. The final full-length portrait of Ellington is stunning in its elegant directness, illuminating the man's gentle spirituality.

Smothers, Ethel Footman. *The Hard-Times Jar*. Illustrated by John Holyfield. New York: Frances Foster/Farrar, Straus, 2003. 32pp. Grades 1–3.

Emma's family can't afford even paper and pencils, much less books. For migrant workers, every penny counts and is saved in a jar, just in case. Emma loves writing stories and reading books. She wants to work and earn money but is told she must go to school. At first unhappy and apprehensive, she is overwhelmed by the school library. She takes a book home without permission. She must confess, but her teacher is sympathetic, while her mother gives her some of the precious money to buy a book of her own. The story, based on the author's childhood, not only reveals something of migrant worker life but also discusses Emma's discomfort in a classroom of white students, having had only black classmates in the South. Full-page paintings illustrate Emma's house, school, and the apple orchard with sufficient details to make the action flow. Girl and mother are portrayed with mutual love in visuals totally positive in feeling.

Strickland, Michael R. *Haircuts at Sleepy Sam's*. Illustrated by Keaf Holliday. Honesdale, PA: Boyds Mills, 1998. 32pp. Also paper. Grades K–3.

Three brothers set off for haircuts with the money and their mother's instructions to the barber. "Not too short on the top," she writes, but they get a lot more advice on the way. The barbershop is a center of African American life, and the boys enjoy the exchanges between barbers and customers. When the narrator is finished, "no longer nappy," as the barber says, he and his clipped brothers go home to show their mom their new "do's" as she smiles and shakes her head. Three engaging, smiling faces take us through the neighborhood, background for their more detailed reactions depicted in airbrush and pastel chalk. A bit slickly done, the overall effect of the illustrations is positive and reasonable.

Tarpley, Natasha Anastasia. *I Love My Hair!* Illustrated by E. B. Lewis. Boston: Little, Brown, 1998. 26pp. Also paper. Grades PreS–2.

The author introduces the story with her own memories of her mother combing her hair and her subsequent experiments with it. African American girls can identify with the heroine as her mother gently combs out the tangles in her hair while telling her all the ways she is lucky enough to be able to wear it. Other girls can get an insight into their own feelings. Double-page naturalistic watercolors focus on a young girl's adventures with a variety of hair arrangements in a loving atmosphere.

Thomas, Joyce Carol. *I Have Heard of a Land*. Illustrated by Floyd Cooper. New York: Joanna Cotler/HarperCollins, 1998. 32pp. Grades 2–4.

Drawing on the experiences of her family in their journey to the Oklahoma Territory in the late 1800s, Thomas writes poetically of the open land available for the pioneers, "where the land runs on forever." The winters may be bitter but life, even for African Americans, is rich and sweet, with neighbor helping neighbor. A woman's possibilities "reach as far / As her eyes can see." An Author's Note adds information on both the family and national history of that time, in particular of the African American flight from the South. Cooper's misty oil paintings illustrate the particulars of each "I have heard" phrase on double pages golden with good feeling. Strong, happy people are hard at work at the tasks demanded of the pioneer in a vast landscape.

Wiles, Deborah. *Freedom Summer.* Illustrated by Jerome Lagarrigue. New York: Anne Schwartz/Atheneum, 2001. 32pp. Grades K–3.

A young white boy describes what happens in his town when the formerly segregated swimming pool is ordered to be open by law to all. He and his best friend John Henry, son of the family's black housekeeper, have always had wonderful fun together, but John Henry hasn't even been able to go into the General Store to buy his own pop. Unfortunately, when the excited boys arrive at the pool, they find that trucks are filling it with asphalt rather than allow blacks in. Swallowing their disappointment, the boys decide to walk to the General Store together. The cruelty of segregation and the power of friendship are brought to life in this original story based on the author's own experience. There's a fuzziness to the full-page and vignette paintings that give them an aura of history. They successfully depict the small town and particularly the sense of friendship the boys share. We sense the joy, then the pain, and finally a hope for positive change as the boys go into the store together.

Williams, Sherley Anne. *Working Cotton.* Illustrated by Carole Byard. San Diego, CA: Harcourt Brace, 1992. 32pp. Also Voyager paper, 1997. Grades K–4.

In a spare text written in black English and based on her poetry and her childhood experience, Williams tells of a day in the life of a migrant family who pick cotton. Shelan, too small to have her own sack but big enough to help, tells of the smells, the sights, the long hard day, and the fatigue at the end. Acrylic paintings totally fill the wide double pages with expressionistic pictures that provide the soul for Shelan's bare-bones descriptions. We can feel the speed of her Daddy's picking in the diagonal of his sack as he leans forward across both pages. The beauty of the cotton fields stands ironically in opposition to the sweat-dripping faces of the family. Close-ups focus attention on the human scale of the endless labor.

Woodson, Jacqueline. *The Other Side.* Illustrated by E. B. Lewis. New York: G. P. Putnam's Sons, 2001. 32pp. Grades K–3.

Clover's mother has told her that it isn't safe to climb over the fence because white people live there. But one summer, a white girl climbs on the fence, all alone. She asks if she can play with Clover and her friends, but another girl says "no." Because "that's the way things have always been." As the summer passes, Clover and Annie begin to talk to each other, sitting on the fence. One day Annie joins the friends, jumping rope and sitting on the fence together. "Some day somebody's going to come along and knock this old fence down," Annie says, with hope for a better future. The double-page watercolor scenes clearly depict the two worlds separated by the shoulder-high slat fence, demonstrating the tentative moves made over time that, for these genuine youngsters, end in friendship.

Wyeth, Sharon Dennis. *Something Beautiful.* Illustrated by Chris K. Soentpiet. New York: Dragonfly/Random paper, 1998. 32pp. Grades 1–4.

A young African American girl has learned the word *beautiful* in school but wonders where in her grim inner city neighborhood of trash, graffiti, and the homeless she can find anything beautiful. But she discovers as she encounters her neighbors and friends that there are beautiful things that can make her heart happy. She finally decides to do what she can to clean up. When her mother comes home, she tells her what she knows she has that is truly beautiful: her. The double-page watercolors bring our narrator's quest for something beautiful up close, creating an ongoing reality. These naturalistic pictures include details of mundane living like the children's paintings on the classroom wall, the litter of overflowing garbage cans, the barred windows. The final illustration of mother and daughter makes the more abstract concept of spiritual beauty tangible.

FOUR

THE CARIBBEAN, SOUTH AMERICA, AND CENTRAL AMERICA

THE CARIBBEAN AND CARIBBEAN AMERICANS

ORIGINAL TALES AND FOLKTALES EVOKING THE PAST

Alvarez, Julia. *The Secret Footprints*. Illustrated by Fabian Negrin. New York: Alfred A. Knopf, 2003. 34pp. Also Dragonfly paper, 2002. Grades K–3.

Guapa is a beautiful young *ciguapa,* one of the Dominican Republic's legendary creatures. The *ciguapas* live in underwater caves, fearful of humans, coming to the land for food only at night, and difficult to detect because their feet face backwards, making misleading footprints. Despite warnings, Guapa is curious and doesn't fear humans. One day she is caught by them. Having been told she must protect her people from disclosure, she manages to escape undetected with the help of a young boy. He keeps her secret and leaves her sweets in his pockets. There is a seductive lushness to the painted scenes of sea and leafy jungle. The daylight illustrations seem to ooze yellow while enhancing the details of the foliage. There is a note on the background and the many versions of this story in Dominican and Taino tradition.

Gershator, Phillis. *Tukama Tootles the Flute: A Tale from the Antilles*. Illustrated by Synthia Saint James. New York: Orchard/Scholastic, 1994. 32pp. Also paper. Grades 1–4.

A wild but brave boy plays on the beach of his Caribbean island, tootling on his flute, while his Grandma warns him about the dangerous two-headed giant. Late one night, the giant catches Tukama and takes him home for his wife to fatten up. The clever boy plays his flute, charming the wife into letting him go. After that, he minds Grandma. The rhyming refrain of his song is repeated throughout the tale. The illustrator uses large shapes of solid color to emphasize the emotions of the story. Some of her oil paintings look almost nonobjective, as when Tukama deals with the giant as a small green shape against a page overflowing with red and purple shapes.

Hallsworth, Grace. *Sing Me a Story: Song-and-Dance Tales from the Caribbean.* Illustrated by John Clementson. Little Rock, AR: August House, 2002. 44pp. Grades PreS–3.

Five traditional folktales from Caribbean areas like Jamaica and Haiti, Trinidad and Tobago are told in a succinct but entertaining fashion. They are followed by a song from the text with music and, in three cases, with instructions for a dance children can do to that song. Both people and animals are characters in these sometimes funny, sometimes a bit ghostly stories. Cut paper pictures depict the characters, also providing strong decorations, surrounding the text and contributing to the overall light-hearted feeling. There is a glossary of Caribbean words and notes on the background of the selections.

Hamilton, Virginia. *The Girl Who Spun Gold.* Illustrated by Leo and Diane Dillon. New York: Blue Sky/Scholastic, 2000. 32pp. Grades K–4.

This lengthy West Indian version of the "Rumpelstiltskin" folktale is told with a lilt in its language. Here a mother boasts to the Big King that her daughter can spin gold thread. The greedy king decides to marry her. After a splendid wedding, he demands that she spin three rooms full of golden items. Lit'mahn, the magic mischief maker, comes to her aid. But she must guess his name or he will carry her away with him. Luckily she discovers his name, but she is so annoyed at the king's greed that she waits three years to forgive him before they can live "happily ever after." The Dillons have combined acrylic paintings of an exotic place with elaborately patterned costumes and palace architecture; there are golden touches everywhere in the complex, detailed scenes. Sources are given. There are also notes on the difficulty of reproducing the sumptuous original art.

Keens-Douglas, Richardo. *Mama God, Papa God: A Caribbean Tale.* Illustrated by Stefan Czernecki. Brooklyn, NY: Crocodile/Interlink, 1999. 32pp. Also Tradewinds paper, 2000. Grades PreS–2.

This creation tale begins "before there was time," when Mama God and Papa God are living in empty darkness. After he says, "Let there be light" and sees how beautiful Mama God is, Papa God wants to make something beautiful for her. So he creates the world, and together they fill it with beautiful growing things and other creatures. Then they make people but enough different from each other to be "beautiful" and a "masterpiece." The people speak different languages, to keep it from being boring. Mama God and Papa God are pleased with the wonderful world. Using folk art symbols from Haiti as a springboard, Czernecki has brought his personal vision into play to create the very brightly colored characters in flat color areas, bringing definition to the sparse words. This is visualized as a happy, open-ended story.

Montes, Marisa, reteller. *Juan Bobo Goes to Work: A Puerto Rican Folktale.* Illustrated by Joe Cepeda. New York: HarperCollins, 2000. 32pp. Grades K–3.

Juan Bobo is the simple folk hero of Puerto Rican folktales. He tries to do the right thing but frequently does it completely wrong. When he finds work, he either does the opposite of what he is told or he does what he was supposed to do with one thing with something completely different. For example, he is supposed to put his wages in a sack to bring home. But he is paid in milk, which of course leaks out. This sort of mix-up continues until he does his last foolish thing. This is seen by a very sick girl who is about to die if she doesn't laugh. When she laughs at Juan, her rich father gratefully provides for Juan and his mother. The visual context produced primarily in stylized double-page paintings shows the simplicity of Juan's life as well as the interactions of the characters in the country setting. Here, honest humor rather than ridicule should generate frequent smiles. There is a note on the Juan Bobo tradition and the changes made, as well as a glossary of the included Spanish.

San Souci, Robert D. *Cendrillon: A Caribbean Cinderella.* Illustrated by Brian Pinkney. New York: Simon & Schuster, 1998. 40pp. Also Aladdin paper, 2002. Grades K–4.

The island of Martinique is the setting for this version of the familiar fairy tale. The narrator, who has a magic wand of sorts, is the nurse of the motherless Cendrillon. The young girl's father has married again, and her stepmother treats her cruelly. The ball she wishes to attend is a birthday celebration for Monsieur Thibault's handsome son Paul. After the transformation of Cendrillon, the young man spends all his time with her until she races away at midnight, losing one pink slipper. Paul finds her, of course, for the happy wedding celebration. Scratchboard, luma dyes, and opaque gouache and oil paints create the local color, the characters, and the landscape. They also form fanciful borders to house the blocks of text. Pinkney's nervous white lines produce tensions and an energy that helps propel the visual narrative to its anticipated ending. There are notes on the sources and additions to the tale, plus a glossary of the included Creole words.

San Souci, Robert. *The Faithful Friend.* Illustrated by Brian Pinkney. New York: Simon & Schuster, 1995. 40pp. Also paper. Grades 2–4.

This version of a familiar theme from European folklore is retold as it is in Martinique. Two boys grow up together: Clement, motherless son of a plantation owner, and Hippolyte, son of the widow hired to care for Clement. Clement wishes to marry the lovely Pauline, so the friends go together to see her and her uncle, Zabocat, who is said to be a wizard. When the wicked uncle opposes the marriage, the young people leave together, and Zabocat sets many traps for them. Hippolyte tries to foil them but is finally turned to stone when he reveals the truth. All ends well, however, because of the good character of the friends. Pinkney's scratchboard medium effectively creates double-page scenes that emphasize the lush mysteries of the island, the magic, and the character and feelings of the protagonists. The varying shades of color of the characters, while not mentioned, reflects those on the island. A glossary with pronunciation explains the included Creole words.

San Souci, Robert D. *The Twins and the Bird of Darkness: A Hero Tale from the Caribbean.* Illustrated by Terry Widener. New York: Simon & Schuster, 2002. 40pp. Grades K–3.

The terrible Bird of Darkness has demanded and taken away Princess Marie in exchange for lifting the darkness he had spread over the land. Poor twin brothers live in the kingdom; they look alike but are very different. Soliday is brave, good, and hardworking while Salacotta is the opposite. When Soliday, with help and advice from a sorcerer, sets out to rescue the princess; Salacotta, hoping for richness, joins him. After Soliday has braved dangers to kill the Bird, treacherous Salacotta tries to take Marie back for the reward, leaving his brother behind. But justice prevails, for the happy ending. Acrylic paintings depict the characters and landscape in a sculptured style that adds a melodramatic tone. Strong color contrasts add to the sense of high adventure. The Bird of Darkness is created to seem the epitome of evil. There are notes on the sources of the story and a glossary.

THE CARIBBEAN TODAY AND IN THE RECENT PAST

Belafonte, Harry, and Lord Burgess. *Island in the Sun*. Illustrated by Alex Ayliffe. New York: Dial, 1999. 24pp. Also Puffin paper, 2001. Grades PreS–2.

The lyrics of the song written about Belafonte's memories from his child-hood in Trinidad form the brief text. The praise of "your forests, waters, your shining sand" also includes the hot sun, the hard work of men and women, and the drums and music of Carnival. Double-page collages express the vibrancy of the island landscape and the activities of the people. Most scenes are overloaded with colors of flowers, markets, harvests, and dances, all including small details cleverly used to produce patterns for the blooms, foliage, and clothing.

Binch, Caroline. *Gregory Cool*. New York: Dial, 1994. 26pp. Grades 1–4.

On a visit to his grandparents in Tobago, the apprehensive Gregory finds fault with everything, from the climate and the bug bites to the food and lack of TV. With the help of his cousin, however, he begins to discover what he can enjoy that is special to the island. Realistic watercolors, sometimes vignettes and sometimes fully developed double pages, offer appealing portraits of the characters and a good sense of the lushness and attractiveness of the island.

Figueredo, D. H. *The Road to Santiago*. Illustrated by Pablo Torrecilla. New York: Lee & Low, 2003. 32pp. Grades K–3.

The author has based the story on events in his childhood in Cuba in the late 1950s, while Fidel Castro and his rebels were fighting the Cuban dicta-tor, Fulgencio Batista. Figueredo's family is hoping to join the rest of their relatives as usual at their grandmother's house on the other end of the island for Christmas. Because of the fighting, the trains are not running. They man-age to reach a bus after taking a car and having a flat tire. When they finally arrive, all the family is waiting. At last they can celebrate despite the troubled times. Double-page acrylic paintings accurately depict the details of place, autos, and clothing at the time. The events of the improvised journey are conveyed with an appealing sense of reality. The assembled family appears to be enjoying themselves.

Garne, S. T. *By a Blazing Blue Sea*. Illustrated by Lori Lohstoeter. San Diego, CA: Gulliver/Harcourt, 1999. 25pp. Grades K–3.

Brief verses take us to "a crescent of land, / Between craggy black rocks" to "a white strip of sand." On this Caribbean island lives a "wrinkled old man," a simple fisherman. Although some think he is a fool, he lives a contented life with his cat and his parrot amid the beauty of the sea, the shore, and the sky above. Opaque acrylic paints naturalistically depict this peaceful seascape and its inhabitants, offering many details of the place and activities mentioned in the brief verses.

Hanson, Regina. *The Tangerine Tree*. Illustrated by Harvey Stevenson. New York: Clarion/Houghton, 1995. 32pp. Grades 1–4.

Ida is distressed when her father must leave her to go to New York, where he can earn what he cannot in Jamaica, the money to support his family. As they tour the home he must leave, Papa gives Ida a book to learn to read by the time he comes home and also the tangerine tree to care for while he is gone. Ida squeezes juice, the essence of sunshine, for him to take along. Both words and pictures are full of the sunny flavor and language of Jamaica, along with the sadness of the poverty-driven separation. Acrylic paintings create scenes that emphasize the emotions, blurring details of the tropics.

Lauture, Denize. *Running the Road to ABC*. Illustrated by Reynold Ruffins. New York: Simon & Schuster, 1996. 32pp. Grades 1–3.

Three boys and three girls rise before the sun and run a long way every day to school. The author describes the Haitian countryside where they run. The long, overstuffed gouache paintings have the look of murals; the sinuous stylization, rich color, and emphasis on decorative composition produce attractive pages.

Leiner, Katherine. *Mama Does the Mambo*. Illustrated by Edel Rodriguez. New York: Hyperion, 2001. 34pp. Grades K–4.

Havana, Cuba, is the setting for this story of a young girl and her mother. Sofia's mother hasn't danced since her father died, although many men would like to dance with her. Sofia feels sad about it. Finally, at Carnival time, Sofia becomes her mother's partner, to the delight of all. Although the tale could happen anywhere, here it completely reflects the music, the excitement, and the taste of Havana, along with Sofia's joy. Rodriguez uses pastel, gouache, and spray paint on colored papers with monoprinted woodblock ink line work to exploit the warm colors of this tropical country. The double- and single-page scenes display the spirit of a community involved with the positive qualities of life. There are local street scenes with architectural facades on the end-papers, backyards hung with laundry, baskets loaded with fruit, while the scenes of dancing almost get our feet moving. The Spanish included is explained in a glossary.

Mitchell, Rita. *Hue Boy*. Illustrated by Caroline Binch. New York: Dial/Penguin, 1993. 28pp. Also Penguin paper, 1999. Grades K–3.

The author, who grew up in Belize, has based this story about a boy on a Caribbean island on the experience of a nephew in Belize. The text has a repetitive refrain: Hue Boy doesn't seem to grow "at all, at all." His schoolmates tease; he feels bad. His mama tries feeding him extra food, his gran gives him larger clothes to grow into, he tries to stretch himself, even visits the wise man and healing woman of the village. But nothing helps until his father, who has been away working on a ship, comes home. Then he's so happy he doesn't "feel small at all, at all." The end-papers present the lush, tropical environment. Watercolor paints exploit the white of the paper to produce a sun-drenched world that includes humans with genuine character. The illustrations form a page of sequenced vignettes showing Hue Boy's exercises, then a double-page view of him in school with his uniformed classmates.

Orr, Katherine. *My Grandpa and the Sea*. Minneapolis: Carolrhoda, 1990. 32pp. Grades K–3.

Lila remembers her grandfather, a fisherman on the island of St. Lucia, and his dugout canoe. When fish become scarce, he tries to do other things. But he misses his life on the sea, where he feels God lives. He finally begins to cultivate scarce sea moss in special frames and can thus return to the life he loves. Lila has gone away to school but has never forgotten him and the lessons he taught, in this simply told, sentimental story. Smoothly applied opaque paints create full-page pictures and attractive vignettes on facing text pages. Details of everyday life and backgrounds of the local seascape and landscape depict time and place and appealing characters.

Rahaman, Vashanti. *A Little Salmon for Witness: A Story from Trinidad*. Illustrated by Sandra Speidel. New York: Lodestar/Dutton, 1997. 32pp. Grades 1–4.

Rajiv needs a birthday present for his grandmother, Aaji. Since it is Good Friday, a holiday in Trinidad, Aaji would like to have something extra, but the traditional salmon is too expensive. Rajiv decides to try to earn enough money to buy her some. He tries several places without success, until he remembers his teacher's problem with the weed called Ti Marie. He offers to dig it out for just a bit of salmon. After much hard work, he is delighted with his payment. The author has based the lengthy story on her Caribbean memories. The pastel illustrations are frequently more atmospheric than representational, but they provide a sense of place and a character we care about.

CARIBBEAN AMERICANS AND THE IMMIGRANT EXPERIENCE

Dorros, Arthur. *Isla*. Illustrated by Elisa Kleven, New York: Dutton/Penguin, 1995. 42pp. Also Puffin paper, 1999. Also Spanish edition, *La Isla*. Grades K–3.

Rosalba's *abuela*, or grandmother, takes her on an imaginary flight from New York to the tropical island she came from. Poverty is absent in this jolly view of the original family home, the rain forest, harbor, market, and beach. The text is laced with Spanish, all understandable in context, with a glossary and pronunciation. The illustrator has over laden the pages with tiny details of flowers, buildings, fish, and people, mainly from a bird's-eye view.

Figueredo, D. H. *When This World Was New*. Illustrated by Enrique O. Sanchez. New York: Lee & Low, 1999. 32pp. Grades K–3.

Young Danielito describes his feelings as he leaves his home on a Caribbean island to travel with his parents to live in the U.S. The city and the language are strange, and he is very apprehensive about going to school. But his first morning, his father wakes him to take him outside, to the wonder of falling snow. They climb a hill to see their footprints behind them. When his uncle arrives to drive him to school, Danielito is no longer so frightened. The illustrations tell a rather literal story, adding some visual specifics to the text's generalities. As the family is driven from the airport we are shown a suburb emerging from the distant cityscape. The characters are depicted honestly in simplified naturalism. The final textless page's picture of Danielito ice skating is symbolic of a positive future. Some Spanish words are included.

Velasquez, Eric. *Grandma's Records*. New York: Walker, 2001. 32pp. Grades 1–4.

The narrator recalls spending his summer holidays with his grandmother in El Barrio, Spanish Harlem. Music is a vital part of their lives together. His grandmother also tells stories of her childhood in Puerto Rico, but above all, she loves to play her records and dance. Sometimes he gets to choose the records as well. Grandma's nephew plays percussion in Rafael Cortijo's band, "the best band in Puerto Rico." Her nephew brings the band over for dinner when they are in town along with additional treats: their latest record and two tickets to their first New York concert. The experience is a thrill for them both, especially when the band plays grandmother's special song about having to leave their hearts behind in Puerto Rico. The emotional song, in English and Spanish, is included, along with information about the real members of the Cortijo band. Naturalistic paintings illuminate the characters with honest emotions. The visual narrative creates a genuine family memoir of happy memories.

SOUTH AMERICA

ORIGINAL TALES AND FOLKTALES EVOKING THE PAST

DeSpain, Pleasant. *The Dancing Turtle: A Folktale from Brazil.* Illustrated by David Boston. Little Rock, AR: August House, 1998. 32pp.

Turtle is caught by a hunter, brought home by him, and put in a cage to be cooked for soup. While the hunter is out in the fields, Turtle entertains his children by playing her flute, then persuades them to let her out so she can show them how she dances. Of course she promises not to run away, and of course she does. The children, in turn, try to trick their father. Turtle is the clever trickster here. Lush tropical jungle plants and animals on the endpapers set the stage for the fanciful tale. The humans, turtle, and other animals seem stuck into the foliage-laden scenes. Notes trace the background of the story along with the author's journey to trace it.

Ehlert, Lois. *Moon Rope / Un Lazo a la Luna.* San Diego, CA: Harcourt Brace, 1992. 32pp. Also paper. Grades K–4.

In this legend told in two languages, Fox and Mole try to reach the moon. They can't make their woven grass rope reach, until the birds help. But Mole slips, falls back to earth, and is so upset that he prefers to stay in his hole underground thereafter. Whether Fox makes it back remains a question. Notes detail the source of the story and the inspiration for the illustrations. Motifs influenced by Peruvian crafts have been modified into sharply defined symbols made of cut-out shapes with lots of silver and red. These are set against solid, intensely colored backgrounds to illustrate the brief text. These large-size pages with stunning pictures reflect some of the mysticism of ancient Peruvian art objects.

Gerson, Mary-Joan. *How Night Came from the Sea.* Illustrated by Carla Golembe. Boston: Little, Brown, 1994. 32pp. Grades 1–3.

The influence of African slaves who came to Brazil is evident in this retelling. At the beginning of time it was always daytime. When the daughter of the African sea-goddess Lemanja marries a man from earth, she enjoys earth's brightness but misses the cool, restful dark. Her husband sends servants to her mother in the sea to bring some darkness back. When they drop the bag and night spirits escape, the daughter is there to calm and welcome them. She then sets the morning star, the rooster, and the birds to herald the beauty of the day she has come to appreciate, but some night remains for all to rest. Notes cover both African sources and the Candomble religion. Double-page monoprints present flat black figures on intense blue backgrounds with just enough flora and fauna to add decorative details to the appealingly mysterious settings.

Jendresen, Erik, and Alberto Villoldo. *The First Story Ever Told*. Illustrated by Yoshi. New York: Simon & Schuster, 1996. 34pp. Grades 2–5.

"Inspired by the creation tales of the Incas of Peru," the authors begin their story with an explorer finding a map at a museum, which shows the way to the legendary Vilcabamba, the lost City of Gold. He travels through the Mountains of the Moon and the Valley of the Shadow to the River of Rainbow. There, while he sleeps, Grandfather Fire comes to him in a dream to tell him "the first story ever told." This is a creation tale, relating the importance of gold to the Incas. When the Spanish took the gold, what is left is not in a real place but in the mind and heart. The explorer wakes to feel it all around him. The mostly double-page watercolor illustrations depict the mountainous setting, local and historic costume, and some of the jungle creatures along with the other-world feeling of parts of the tale.

McDermott, Gerald. *Jabutí the Tortoise: A Trickster Tale from the Amazon*. San Diego, CA: Harcourt, 2001. 32pp. Grades preS–3.

Although the songs Jabutí plays on his flute are sweet, many of the animals resent the tricks he has played on them. The birds, however, enjoy singing when he plays, except for Vulture, who is jealous of the tortoise. When all the birds are invited to a festival by the King of Heaven, Jabutí wants to go too. Vulture offers to take him but then drops him through the sky. His shell shatters. When the King of Heaven discovers from Vulture where the tortoise is, he then sends the birds to find him. They piece him together, receiving a new color as thanks. But not Vulture. He stays the same dull color, and he still can't sing. These flamboyant double-page scenes in gouache, colored pencil and ink are set on a hot pink background. Geometric stylizations employing saturated colors of every description create birds, foliage, turtle's shell, with grays and black to personify Vulture's evil. Designed cinematically, the sequence of images tells the tale with enthusiasm and visual splendor. There are background notes on the tale.

Pitcher, Caroline. *Mariana and the Merchild: A Folk Tale from Chile.* Illustrated by Jackie Morris. Grand Rapids, MI: Eerdmans, 2000. 26pp. Also paper. Grades K–4.

After a storm, a lonely old woman who loves the sea finds amid the seaweed she has collected, in a crab shell, a beautiful baby girl with a fish tail. A wise woman tells Mariana that the child is a Merbaby whose mother is a sea spirit. The Sea Spirit comes from the ocean to thank Mariana for saving her child. She asks Mariana to care for her, while she comes daily to nurse her and teach her to swim. Much as Mariana loves her, she realizes that she must let the Merchild return to the sea. Meanwhile, however, the child has helped Mariana get to know the village children, who comfort her when the child leaves. The Merchild and the Sea Spirit still come to see her and send her bounty from the sea. Mariana is depicted with brown skin and indigenous features compared with the pale child. Naturalistic watercolors in full page scenes and vignettes offer details of local dress, the seashore with its birds and marine life, and of course the characters on land and sea.

Tompert, Ann. *The Pied Piper of Peru.* Illustrated by Kestutis Karaparavicius. Honesdale, PA: Boyds Mills, 2002. 32pp. Grades 1–4.

The story is based on an incident in the life of Saint Martin de Porres, a Dominican lay brother in colonial Lima, Peru. Ordered by his prior to remove the hungry mice who are eating the cheese and sheets, kind-hearted Martin figures out a way to save them, because he cannot hurt any of God's creatures. The story is told here from the mouse's point of view by the mouse who works with Martin to solve the problem. Finely detailed naturalistic colored drawings use warm tints of brown and brick red with subtle touches of blue to tell the visual story. The illustrations add contextual information on architecture and clothing as the action moves from room to room. All the characters, even the cat, are drawn with considerable sensitivity in this message of universal peace. Notes on the real St. Martin are included.

Van Laan, Nancy. *The Magic Bean Tree: A Legend from Argentina.* Illustrated by Beatriz Vidal. Boston: Houghton Mifflin, 1998. 32pp. Grades K–3.

One summer, when no rain falls, young Topec sets out to find the rain and save the people. The North Wind blows him under the only tree growing on the pampas. Topec asks the tree if it has seen the rain. The tree explains that the wings of the Great Bird of the Underworld are keeping the rain from falling. The bird cannot be killed but must be driven away. Topec leads the people and animals to where the bird is sleeping in the tree. They make so much noise that the bird is frightened away, the rains arrive, and the bonus for Topec's bravery is the gift of the beans of the carob tree. All over Argentina, the tree is supposed to bring good luck. Double-page scenes painted in gouache depict the regional animals and people with simplicity, treating them more symbolically than realistically. The carob tree and Great Bird are designed to enhance their decorative appeal, with feather and branch patterns creating striking images. Some appropriate costume is shown. There is a glossary and list of sources.

SOUTH AMERICA TODAY

Ancona, George. *Carnival.* San Diego, CA: Harcourt, 1999. 48pp. Also paper. Grades K–5.

The color, the excitement, the build-up to the climactic parades of Carnaval in Olinda, Brazil, all are here to experience and enjoy. The celebration lasts five days just before Lent, but the preparation begins in January. The three cultures of Brazil—indigenous, European, and African—are all seen blended in the songs and dances. Costumes, masks, and gigantic puppets are created, and traditional songs and dances practiced. Finally the festivities begin on Friday; by Ash Wednesday, it's all over. But "It's hard to stop when you're having so much fun!" The large, full-page clear color photographs offer aspects of the performers and milling crowds; the smaller pictures and vignettes focus on individuals. The impression is of wild diversity, happy competitiveness, serious preparation. The included Portuguese words are explained; notes on other Carnavals are added.

Cherry, Lynne, and Mark J. Plotkin. *The Shaman's Apprentice: A Tale of the Amazon Rain Forest.* Illustrated by Lynne Cherry. San Diego, CA: Gulliver Green/Harcourt, 1998. 34pp. Also Voyager paper, 2001. Grades 2–5.

Since Kamanya's life was saved by the shaman, the medicine man Nahtahla, he hopes to learn enough from him to become the next shaman. One day, a strange new sickness arrives in Kwamla village, one Nahtahla cannot cure. Several months later, white missionaries come with white pills to cure the sickness they call "malaria." The villagers begin to doubt their gods as well as their shamans. But four years later, a young woman comes to study the healing plants of the forest, for the quinine that cured malaria came from the forest people of Peru. She returns five years later with a book she has made of their medicinal plants, to place alongside those of the whites. Meanwhile, Kamanya learns from Nahtahla and becomes the next shaman. The double-page illustrations bring the reader into the Amazon rain forest with its dense foliage, brilliant flowers, assorted lizards and monkeys, etc. Watercolors and detailed linear representations show the village and people with a focus on the activities of the shaman. The end-papers display botanical paintings of some of the plants and the illnesses they cure. There are notes on the value of preserving such plants.

Díaz, Katacha. *Carolina's Gift: A Story of Peru.* Illustrated by Gredna Landolt. Norwalk, CT: Soundprints, 2002. 32pp. Grades PreS–3.

Carolina and her mother go to the village market to find a birthday present for her grandmother. They go from one stall to another, enjoying the activities, but nothing seems suitable until they see the walking sticks a wood carver has made. The gift is perfect for grandmother; with its help she can manage to go with them to enjoy the market. The double pages are loaded with information on local life, from flowers and produce to ceramics, jewelry, and of course, the bright and varied patterns of the women's clothing. The paintings reveal Carolina's world, perhaps a bit cleaner than reality but otherwise accurate, even to the guinea pigs living on the floor of their house. There are additional notes on the country, the market, and the language.

Fraggalosch, Audrey. *Land of the Wild Llama: A Story of the Patagonian Andes.* Illustrated by Michael Denman and William Huett. Norwalk, CT: Soundprints, 2002. 32pp. Grades 1–4.

In the grasslands at the base of the Chilean Andes, we follow the life of a chulengo, a baby guanaco. He and his family group go through the seasons, encountering other creatures of the area, going from the scarcity of food in the winter to the lushness of spring, until he is old enough to be off on his own before starting his family. The story is followed by a wealth of information on the area, including a map and a double fold-out scenic panorama with all the included creatures, which are then individually pictured and named. The brief text is inserted in rectangular blocks onto double-page scenes of the chulengo's family adventures. These naturalistic pictures provide considerable natural history information about the plant life, indigenous animals, birds, etc. All the details are attractively composed to hold our interest.

Torres, Leyla. *Liliana's Grandmothers*. New York: Farrar, Straus, 1998. 32pp. Also in Spanish. Grades PreS–3.

Liliana loves both of her grandmothers. Mimi lives down the street from her in her small New England town, where Liliana can visit her often. Mama Gabina lives a plane ride away, so Liliana visits for a week or two at a time but not so often. The visits are very different. At Mama Gabina's, Liliana speaks Spanish and helps with the work in the garden. The food is also very different from that at Mimi's, as are the activities. But both grandmothers tell wonderful stories and fill Liliana's thoughts with joy. Large, naturalistic watercolors make visual comparisons in life styles that go beyond the text. The architecture, inside and out; furniture; objects on the walls and shelves; clothing; even the pets all contribute in subtle ways to the differences in the cultures.

CENTRAL AMERICA AND MEXICO

ORIGINAL TALES AND FOLKTALES EVOKING THE PAST

Ada, Alma Flor. *The Lizard and the Sun / La Largartija y el Sol*. Illustrated by Felipe Dávalos. Translated by Rosalma Zubizarreta. New York: Doubleday, 1997. 40pp. Also Scott Foresman paper, 1999. Grades 1–4.

The story, told in two languages, begins long ago when the sun disappears, and the world is desolate. All the creatures search for the sun in vain, but only the lizard perseveres. She finds a glowing rock and goes back to the city to tell the emperor. He sends her back to move the rock, but she cannot. So the emperor calls the woodpecker to come with him and the lizard to the rock. The woodpecker pecks open the rock, but the sun sleeping there won't come out until the emperor arranges music and dancing. This then happens every year to keep the sun happily shining. And since then, "all lizards like to lie in the sun." Grainy double-page illustrations combine symbolic representations of the sun with naturalistic images of people, costumes, ornaments, plants, animals, and architecture. Without sunshine, the pictures are muted; the final celebration when the sun wakes up is a splendid display of decorative arts as dancers and musicians perform in bursting colors. An author note fills in background and source information.

Argueta, Jorge. *Zipitio*. Illustrated by Gloria Calderón. Translated by Elisa Amado. Toronto: Groundwood/Douglas & McIntyre, 2003. 32pp. Grades 1–3.

The title legendary character from the Pipil/Nahua of El Salvador is very old, small as a child, with feet that point backward. Rufina's mother tells her about the Zipitio, who wants to be "the first boyfriend of every girl" as she becomes a woman. He will appear to her, but she should not be frightened. When Rufina sees him and runs away, he cries. Rufina's mother tells her what to do if he keeps bothering her. It is a clever idea and it works. The full-page paintings and vignettes describe the landscape and the two main characters in native dress. There is a folk quality to the illustrations, contributing an earthiness to an otherwise rather mystical story open to many interpretations. There is also a glossary.

Argueta, Manlio. *Magic Dogs of the Volcanoes / Los Perros Mágicos de los Volcanes*. Illustrated by Elly Simmons, translated by Stacey Ross. San Francisco: Children's Book Press, 1990. 32pp. Also paper, 1995. Grades K–4.

This bilingual story based on the traditional "magic dogs" of El Salvador was written for the children of El Salvador by a noted native author. After describing how the people love the *cadejos,* or magic dogs, that always protect them, the tale relates how a wicked man and his brothers try to destroy the *cadejos* who stop them from exploiting their workers. The soldiers they send almost succeed, until the volcanoes come to the rescue of the *cadejos.* Full-page paintings are crammed with heavy black-outlined figures and abstract representations of trees, landscape, and the two key mountains. They and the sun have human faces. The pages intermix people, objects, and text in ways that emphasize the emotional content of the symbols more than the literal. This surrealism is appropriate as it may relate to the political situation in El Salvador.

Climo, Shirley. *The Little Red Ant and the Great Big Crumb: A Mexican Fable*. Illustrated by Francisco X. Mora. New York: Clarion/Houghton, 1995. 40pp. Also paper, 1999. Grades 1–3.

This tale has elements with parallels in those from many cultures. In Mexico in the fall, a red ant smaller than the rest finds a large cake crumb, too large for her to haul back herself for winter storage. Looking for help, she is turned down by lizard, spider, rooster, coyote, and man, each stronger than the last. When she manages to frighten the man, strongest of all, she finds that she is really strong enough to carry the crumb herself. The story has repetitive themes and Spanish words that can be understood in context. Translations and pronunciations are also included. Watercolors offer an ant's-eye view of the action in unemotional but carefully designed scenes.

Coburn, Jewell Reinhart. *Domitila: A Cinderella Tale from the Mexican Tradition.* Illustrated by Connie McLennan. Auburn, CA: Shen's Books, 2000. 32pp. Also in Spanish. Grades K–3.

When a storm destroys her family's adobe home in Mexico, Domitila goes to work in the kitchen of the governor's house. One day, she makes her family's favorite dish, *nopales.* At first it is scorned by the governor's son Timothy, but when he tastes it, he finds it delicious. Unfortunately Domitila is called home to find that her beloved mother has died. She is reminded in her grief of her mother's advice: Do your tasks carefully and all will be well. Meanwhile, Timothy goes in search of the girl who made the delicious *nopales* and left a piece of her sandal behind. Another woman, Malvina, persuades Domitila's father to marry her, brings her daughter into the house, and treats Domitila cruelly. Timothy finally finds Domitila by her sandal, and her *nopales,* for the happy ending. Full-page oil paintings supply the details of the settings: interiors with appropriate household objects, a busy market, the landscape, architecture, etc., and the characters. Although the action is visualized in a somewhat frozen series of pictures, the sequence clearly tells the romantic story. There are notes on the many versions of the story. A proverb goes across the frame of each illustration in both English and Spanish. The recipe for *nopales,* a dish made from cactus, is also included.

DePaola, Tomie. *Adelita: A Mexican Cinderella Story.* New York: G. P. Putnam's Sons, 2002. 34pp. Grades K–3.

This original variation on the old tale is set in Mexico and told with verve and generous seasonings of Spanish. All the words are listed with pronunciation guide and meanings in the back. There are no magical transformations here, however. The hero is the son of a local ranch owner. He falls in love with the stranger at his party who calls herself *Cencienta* like the Cinderella of the fairy tale but who leaves no slipper behind. Our orphan heroine is helped by a faithful family servant. The hero recognizes Adelita from her mother's *rebozo* or shawl, which she hangs out her window, for the happy ever after. The acrylic painted scenes are created in typical dePaola style but are framed in different colored tiles with frequent use of rounded archways to suggest a Mexican locale. Costumes and artifacts are Mexican as well; the glorious end-papers are imprinted with birds and flowers to add a celebratory tone.

DePaola, Tomie. *The Legend of the Poinsettia.* New York: Putnam, 1994. 32pp. Grades 1–4.

This tale from a Mexican legend concerns a girl whose mother becomes too ill to finish a blanket for the baby Jesus in the Christmas procession. Lucinda cannot do the weaving; she despairs at having nothing to take to the church as a gift for Jesus. When she brings weeds that grow in the hills, a miracle turns them and the rest outside into "red stars," the flower of the Holy Night in Mexico ever since. A note also tells of Joel Poinsett, who first brought cuttings of the plant named for him to the United States from Mexico in 1830. The illustrations are typically dePaola in style, all appearing like stage sets.

Fisher, Leonard Everett. *Gods and Goddesses of the Ancient Maya.* New York: Holiday House, 1999. 34pp. Grades 1–4.

After an introduction to the Maya, their culture, and history, Fisher presents twelve of the Mayan gods, each on a double page with large illustration on one side and a summary of the role and character of that god on the other. These are from the glyphs we see on buildings in the excavated Mayan cities in Central America. Some are benevolent, while others are frightening, like the gods of war, death, and human sacrifice. The importance of agriculture is clear from the gods of sun, rain, wind, and corn. Different colors are used for each spread. The glyphs are reproduced with thick black outlines and flat areas of many different colors. The visual effect is stunning, designed so that we can appreciate the complexity of the composition of each glyph. There is a bibliography and pronunciation guide. The end-papers show a map and the Mayan numbers.

Harper, Jo. *The Legend of Mexicatl.* Illustrated by Robert Casilla, translated by Tatiana Lans. New York: Turtle Books, 1998. 40pp. Also paper. Also in Spanish as *La Leyenda de Mexicatl.* Grades K–4.

The Spirit of the Light of Dawn, or Morning Star, calls on young Mexicatl to lead his people to their promised land in this retelling of the traditional tale of early Mexico. He is brave, but he must also learn to be humble, to have all the people work together to build the city of Tenochtitlán, which is today the location of Mexico City. The symbolism of the eagle and the serpent on the Mexican flag is explained here, as well as the source of the name of Mexico, in this inspirational story. Full-page watercolor paintings focus on an appealing hero and on an occasional other person or crowd, all in a rather barren landscape. With little action, the thrust of the story comes from the text.

Hayes, Joe. *El Cucuy!: A Bogeyman Cuento in English and Spanish.* Illustrated by Honorio Robledo. El Paso, TX: Cinco Puntos, 2001. 32pp. Also paper. Grades 1–4.

The traditional threat to Mexican children is that the ugly old man called *el Cucuy* will carry them away if they don't behave. This cautionary tale is of three sisters. One of them works hard to cook and clean for their widowed father. Her sisters mock her and make her life very difficult. Finally, their exasperated father calls on *el Cucuy,* who takes them to a deep cave. When they are finally rescued, they have learned their lesson. The paintings that accompany this folktale clearly depict the actions in a setting that shows the tiled houses and surrounding mountains. Above all is the scary, very ugly monster looming hugely over the town. The text is in both English and Spanish, with added background information.

Kimmel, Eric A. *Montezuma and the Fall of the Aztecs.* Illustrated by Daniel San Souci. New York: Holiday House, 2000. 32pp. Grades 1–4.

Kimmel makes history come alive as he recounts the story of the end of the Aztec empire. After briefly describing the cruel aspects of the Aztec civilization and the threatening portents before the arrival of the Spaniards, he tells the tale of Cortés's march to the capital city of Tenochtitlán, his capture of Montezuma, and the conflicting reports of what happened next. Many died in the battles. But eventually, helped by the native enemies of the Aztecs, the Spaniards won. The double-page watercolors supply details of place and people, also describing the variety of Spanish armor and Aztec ceremonial dress and artifacts. Dramatic tableaus of the action can only suggest the extent of the tragedy. A glossary is included.

Mathews, Sally Schofer. *The Sad Night: The Story of an Aztec Victory and a Spanish Loss.* New York: Clarion/Houghton, 1994. 40pp. Also paper. Grades 1–4.

The book includes background on the legends of the people about their origin, but the focus is on the arrival of the Spanish and the actual events leading to their final triumph. The story is brought up to the present, with much additional factual material appended, making this a rich resource as a transition from myth to reality. The author/illustrator borrowed the style of picturing people and architecture from the Aztec codices but depicted them in a modern sequence.

McDermott, Gerald. *Musicians of the Sun*. New York: Simon & Schuster, 1997. 40pp. Also Aladdin paper. Grades K–4.

Because the earth is sad, dark, and silent, the Lord of the Night sends Wind to the house of the Sun to bring to Earth the four musicians imprisoned there: Red, Yellow, Blue, and Green. Armed with a turquoise shield, a black thundercloud, and silver lightening and aided by Turtle Woman, Fish Woman, and Alligator Woman, Wind challenges Sun and brings the musicians back to fill the world with color and joy. The brief, lyric tale dealing with powerful protagonists is visualized in acrylic, fabric paint, opaque ink, oil, and pastel on handmade paper with potent images drawn from Aztec stone carvings. Very sculptured and complex, they help fill the double pages with mystery and emotions, ultimately symbolized by a radiant rainbow. The background of the tale is explained.

Mora, Pat. *The Night the Moon Fell: A Maya Myth*. Illustrated by Domi. Toronto: Groundwood/Douglas & McIntyre, 2000. 32pp. Grades PreS–1.

One night, the grandfather of Luna the moon shoots his blowgun. Surprised, Luna rolls from the sky to the earth and down to the bottom of the sea, broken in pieces, leaving the sky dark. Sad and lost at first, Luna sighs in rhymes. The little fish cheer her as she tries to collect herself together with their help. When they have glued her pieces back, Luna can float back up, with the fish accompanying her, to twinkle in the sky. The author explains how her mystical, lyrical retelling differs from the original tale. Impressionistic watercolors fill the double pages with suggestions of birds and fish, cloudy amorphous forms, and a cubistic moon. There's an exotic suggestion of a magical dance as the sea creatures work to rebuild the moon. Only some patterns suggest the source.

Mora, Pat. *The Race of Toad and Deer*. Illustrated by Maya Itzna Brooks. Toronto: Groundwood, 2001. 32pp. Grades K–2.

This Guatemalan folktale, similar to the traditional Tortoise and Hare, is another tale of trickery. When Sapo the toad challenges Venado the deer's claim to be the fastest, he needs the help of his toad friends and a little foolery to win the race. Gouache paintings fill double pages with flatly painted vegetation and animals, somewhat similar to patterned Guatemalan folk art. The source of the tale is cited.

Mora, Pat, and Charles Ramirez Berg. *The Gift of the Poinsettia/El Regalo de la Flor de Nochebuena*. Illustrated by Daniel Lechon. Houston, TX: Piñata Press/Arte Público, 1995. 32pp. Grades 1–4.

This legend of the flower, different from some others, is told in both English and Spanish. Here, a Mexican boy, living with his grandmother, celebrates the nights from December 16 to Christmas of the traditional *posadas*, the words and some music for which are at the end of the book. When he and his grandmother go to church on Christmas Eve, he has no gift to take, so he brings a common plant from outdoors. In this version, his tear turns the leaves red, because "love makes small gifts special." The ink and watercolor full pages are framed in multiple borders. The characters have a stiff, almost cartoon-y look; many details of daily life are shown.

Morales, Yuyi. *Just a Minute: A Trickster and Counting Book*. San Francisco: Chronicle, 2003. 32pp. Grades PreS–3.

Clever Grandma Beetle isn't at all upset when the skeleton Señor Calavera arrives, demanding that she go with him immediately. She just tells him he'll have to wait because she still has much to do for her coming party. Counting in English and Spanish, she and then he enumerate her chores, from one house to sweep, through the party preparations, to the eight platters of food on the table and the nine beautiful grandchildren sitting there. The table is set for ten, and Señor Calavera makes the tenth guest at her wonderful birthday party. It's so good that he decides not to take her until after her party next year. Doll-like characters and simple stage props are organized in inventive ways to describe the growing impatience of the skeleton and the many comic ways Grandma devises to keep him waiting. The lively illustrations filling the double pages inform us of the local food preparation, utensils, and piñatas. The humor surrounding the symbol of death is in keeping with the spirit of the Day of the Dead celebrations in Mexico.

Petersen, Patricia. *Voladores*. Illustrated by Sheli Petersen. Columbus, OH: Peter Bedrick/McGraw-Hill, 2002. 32pp. Grades 1–4.

Voladores were chosen men who flew across the sky at feast time to honor the sun, seeking a good harvest. Young Tigre lives in the village where his uncle is one of the legendary flyers and his Uncle Quiche plays the flute. All is well until the volcano and the rain god, jealous of the sun, make it impossible for the men to fly. Tigre bravely volunteers to ask the wind to sweep away the clouds. In exchange for Tigre's flute, the wind agrees and Tigre has saved the people. There's a hint of Mayan glyphs in the heavy black-outlined figures in their ornate costumes. The double pages are designed to emphasize the energy of the flyers and the potency of the gods. The exotic imagery enhances the magical qualities. Part of the "Legends of the Americas" series.

Rockwell, Anne. *The Boy Who Wouldn't Obey: A Mayan Legend*. New York: Greenwillow/HarperCollins, 2000. 24pp. Grades K–3.

When Chac, the rain and wind god, decides that he needs a servant, he does not know that the boy he snatches away to the sky is very disobedient. The boy tries in vain to escape. He finally promises not to disobey and works hard, still missing his home and family. One day he cleans and cooks for a feast, but when he returns with flowers for the table, he finds frogs dirtying it. He chases them away, only to find that they were the guests. After punishment, he determines to get away. He steals Chac's rain-making tools and, after a terrible storm arises, is lucky enough to have the disgusted Chac send him home. Using imagery derived from Mayan ceramics, the pen and ink and watercolor illustrations tell the tale more with humor than horror. The plants of the forest are fanciful, the monkey impish, even Chac is a bit comic. A Foreword gives the Mayan art sources and background.

Wisniewski, David. *Rain Player*. New York: Clarion/Houghton, 1991. 32pp. Also Houghton paper, 1995. Grades 2–6.

This original story is based on the art, language, traditions, and culture of the ancient Maya. In a time of drought, rash young Pik challenges the rain god Chac to a game of ball. If Pik wins, the rains will come; if he loses, he will become a frog. With the help of the jaguar, the quetzal bird, and ritual *cenote,* or well, Pik succeeds. Many details of Mayan history and life are included in the author's note. Intricately cut paper illustrations create double-pages of dramatic intensity. Costumes with elaborate headdresses; jungles with animals, birds, and foliage; temples, all are incorporated into settings of great complexity.

CENTRAL AMERICA AND MEXICO TODAY
AND IN THE RECENT PAST

Amado, Elisa. *Barrilete: A Kite for the Day of the Dead*. Illustrated by Joya Hairs. Toronto: Douglas & McIntyre, 1999. 32pp. Also paper. Also Spanish edition. Grades 1–4.

In the 1970s, Hairs took the photographs for these illustrations in Santiago Sacatapéquez, Guatemala, where the people fly some of the largest kites in the world on the Day of the Dead. For that year's celebration, Juan, with the help of his brother José and some friends, wants to build a kite. His grandfather used to make kites with them, but he has died so they must work alone. They purchase the necessary materials, as do the others in town. The final assembly is not easy. But on the Day of the Dead, everyone goes to the cemetery to be with those who have passed on. Juan will fly his kite there for his grandfather, when all the kites are in the air. The photographs in both black and white and color describe the village, the fields, and the folks engaged in village life. A score or more of the color photos show the making and the flying of a very large kite. Notes fill in the background.

Amado, Elisa. *Cousins*. Illustrated by Luis Garay. Toronto: Groundwood/ Douglas & McIntyre, 2004. 32pp. Grades 1–4.

The narrator of this tale is a girl caught between two sides of her family in an unnamed Spanish-speaking country. She lives with her father and one grandmother but visits her Catholic grandmother regularly for snack time. There she becomes jealous of her cousin Mariana who will be making her First Communion. So she takes the rosary near the statue of the baby Jesus. She knows she has sinned and feels guilty but can't go to confession because she is not Catholic. A talk with a priest finally straightens everything out. The lengthy story offers food for thought about jealousy as well as different cultural values. The full-page acrylic paintings supply details of place in a static, studied fashion. The emotion comes through in the portraits of the characters. There is a glossary.

Ancona, George. *Pablo Remembers: The Fiesta of the Day of the Dead*. New York: HarperCollins, 1993. 48pp. Grades 2–5.

Pablo and his family first go through the Oaxaca market, gathering what they need for the fiesta, all pictured and labeled in English. The next day, the cooking and the preparations for visiting relatives are followed by the trip to the cemetery. Because Pablo is remembering his beloved dead grandmother, the holiday takes on added meaning for him. The layout, number, and size of the clear color photographs make this an informative as well as attractive book, readily projecting the emotions of the celebration.

Ancona, George. *The Piñata Maker / El Piñatero*. San Diego, CA: Harcourt Brace, 1994. 40pp. Grades 3–6.

Details on the making and the breaking of this important part of any Mexican or Mexican American party are given here in two languages. Don Ricardo shows us all the steps of making both a beautiful swan and a more traditionally designed *piñata*. Finally we see the excitement of breaking one at a birthday party. Clear color photographs invite us to get involved as we gather information.

Andrews-Goebel, Nancy. *The Pot That Juan Built*. Illustrated by David Diaz. New York: Lee & Low, 2002. 32pp. Also paper. Grades K–5.

Using a cumulative rhyme like "The House That Jack Built" that is rich with description, the author takes us through the steps that Juan follows, from fueling "the flames so sizzling hot / that flickered and flared and fired the pot" all the way back to the finding and the digging of the clay. As the rhyme grows on one of the double pages, a factual story in prose goes along on the other. This tells the story of Juan Quesada, "the premier potter in Mexico." His career from his beginning as a farm laborer to his start as a potter is traced; his method of working is detailed. The Adobe Photoshop computer-generated illustrations rely on tones of yellow and blue for atmospheric effect and on a nondetailed, isolated Juan with animals and decorative plants for eye appeal. Bordered with typical indigenous motifs, a five-page detailed account of the history of the area and of Juan's creation and production of his pots is illustrated with small color photographs.

Castaneda, Omar S. *Abuela's Weave*. Illustrated by Enrique O. Sanchez. New York: Lee & Low, 1993. 32pp. Grades 1–4.

Writing about Guatemala, the country of his birth, the author tells how young Esperanza is learning from her *abuela,* or grandmother, how to weave on the backstrap loom. They work hard together in the family compound to prepare for selling at the fiesta in Guate. Because she fears that her birth-marked face may deter customers, Grandmother stays away from Esperanza. So the girl must negotiate alone the bus ride, the busy city streets, the placing of the weavings on display, and the anxious wait for customers. Her work sells well, however, and they return home happy. Opaque acrylic paintings depict the countryside and city scenes. But the focus is on the weaving under a magical tree and on the fabric patterns of blouse and headband. Text pages include fabric designs in the borders along with a splendid large tapestry, with the theme of love of grandmother and child strong throughout.

Cohn, Diana. *Dream Carver.* Illustrated by Amy Córdova. San Francisco: Chronicle, 2002. 34pp. Grades K–3.

After their work in the fields near Monte Alban, Mexico, Mateo and his father carve the traditional small animals that his mother and sister paint to sell at fiestas. But in Mateo's dreams he sees large, wildly colored creatures that he would like to make despite his father's discouragement. One day, he begins to practice making these on his own. Finally, despite his fear of ridicule, he feels ready to take them to the fiesta. Their success there has his father asking him to teach him the "new way to carve." There is a rugged quality to the double-page illustrations, created in acrylic on gessoed board with colored pencil, showing the landscape, the family, and the dreams. Plants and flowers are stylized. The carved animals, both in dreams and reality, are fancifully based on those created by successful carver Manuel Jimenez, on whose life the story is based.

Corpi, Lucha. *Where Fireflies Dance / Ahí Donde Bailan las Luciérnagas.* Illustrated by Mira Reisberg. San Francisco: Children's Book Press, 1997. 32pp. Grades 1–4.

The author reminiscences about her childhood in Mexico. She and her brother visit an old house supposedly haunted by ghosts. Their grandmother tells them the story of Juan Sebastián, the supposed ghost of the haunted house, who died fighting for Mexico's freedom. Their father sings their favorite songs. When she leaves home to travel north and follow her "destiny," these are the memories she carries with her. Each full-page painting is framed in a different color border. The figures are simplified and painted flat. Much of the setting, like the trees, is produced for decorative rather than naturalistic or informative effect.

Crandall, Rachel. *Hands of the Maya: Villagers at Work and Play.* New York: Henry Holt, 2002. 32pp. Grades K–3.

The author, an elementary teacher whose students are pen pals with Maya children in Belize, has visited Mayan villages and lived with the people. After a brief introduction to their history, she discusses the activities of the village, including the wood gathering, the house building, the farming, the crafts of weaving, basket making, and carving, and the music. Each double page includes a brief, simple text and a large close-up and smaller composite clear color photograph of the people and their work. This appealing, informative volume includes a map and glossary.

Estes, Kristyn Rehling. *Manuela's Gift.* Illustrated by Claire B. Cotts. San Francisco: Chronicle, 1999. 26pp. Grades K–3.

When Manuela's Mama and Abuela asked her what she wanted for her birthday, she said, "a new party dress." She tries not to show her disappointment when she is given a dress made over from one of Mama's. She dreams of what good things she would like to have in her birthday *piñata:* eggs and chicks for Mama, for whom the chickens have not been laying; rain for Papa's thirsty corn plants; a horse for tired Abuela to ride. She realizes how much her Mama and Abuela worked to make her dress in these hard times and finally looks forward to her party with her loving family and friends. Opaque, full-page acrylic paintings illustrate the facing page of texts. We are given glimpses of interiors, but primarily the visual story is told through Manuela's dreams as we see her relationships with her family. Solid figures and rather static poses are appropriately costumed; the decorations resemble Mexican folk art, while the end-papers are filled with typical paper cut-outs.

Fine, Edith Hope. *Under the Lemon Moon.* Illustrated by René King Moreno. New York: Lee & Low, 1999. 32pp. Also paper. Grades 1–4.

Rosalinda is very distressed. First a man steals all the lemons from her tree; then the tree seems to be sick. She asks advice from her parents, friends, and finally from her grandmother. Grandmother tells her that perhaps *La Anciana,* the Old One who helps things grow, will come when needed. Rosalinda seeks her in vain. At the market, Rosalinda sees the man who stole her lemons, selling them. Then, the Old One magically appears. She tells Rosalinda that perhaps the man really needed the lemons. Then she tells her how to heal her tree. The magic works. Rosalinda has many large lemons, which she gives away, except for one. That she gives to the man, telling him to plant the seeds. Watercolor and pastel illustrations convey information about clothing, architecture, and the market. Details are simply presented, market browsing encouraged. Spanish words are listed with meaning and pronunciation.

Franklin, Kristine L. *When the Monkeys Came Back.* Illustrated by Robert Roth. New York: Atheneum, 1994. 32pp. Also paper. Also in Spanish. Grades 1–4.

When Doña Marta was young in a Costa Rica valley, there were trees and the chattering of monkeys. Then men from the city came and cut down most of the trees. The monkeys were soon gone. When she marries, she asks her husband for some land and she plants small trees. As an old woman, she can see a rich forest there and can hear again the sound of the monkeys. Watercolor illustrations on full or half pages make a strong case for the conservation example Marta sets.

Freschet, Gina. *Beto and the Bone Dance*. New York: Farrar, Straus, 2001. 32pp. Grades K–3.

This view of the traditional Mexican celebration of the Day of the Dead sees it through the eyes of young Beto. As the family gathers the materials they need, Beto tries to think of something of his own to place on the altar on his grand-mother's grave. She died in the spring, and he misses her, but someone else has already brought everything he can think of. As the celebration goes on around him and the family tells stories about her all night, Beto dreams of his grand-mother and finally knows what to put on the altar. This holiday about death may be a bit frightening, even to Beto, but the emphasis is on joy and love. Al-though the many objects relating to the occasion, like skeletons, skulls, and flowers, are recognizable, there is a dream-like quality to most of the painted scenes. The walk to the cemetery is laid out like a map, almost a flower-laden stained-glass window. Both the humor and reverence of the holiday are evident.

Garay, Luis. *The Kite*. Toronto: Tundra, 2002. 32pp. Grades 1–4.

The life of a poor boy in a Nicaraguan *barrio* is clearly depicted. Fran-cisco's father has died and his mother expects a baby, so he works hard sell-ing newspapers to earn money. Acquiring the beautiful kite he admires in the toy stall seems impossible. Yet there is joy and hope for him and his fam-ily at the end of the story. Because of the book's design, lengthy text page facing full-page illustration, this is more an illustrated book than a picture-book. The textured paintings of Francisco's life emphasize the solidity of characters and objects; like snapshots they show the busy town, his neigh-borhood, and the delights that crowd his favorite toy store.

Garcia, Guy. *Spirit of the Maya: A Boy Explores His People's Mysterious Past*. Illus-trated by Ted Wood. New York: Walker, 1995. 48pp. Grades 3–6.

Kin, a twelve-year-old descendent of the Maya, and his family are the focus of the color photographs. Along with his depiction of their daily lives, Gar-cia delves deeply into Kin's Mayan heritage. Kin's father shows him how to make traditional clay figures, bows, and arrows. Then they visit Palenque, where his father sells the figures to tourists. We tour the site with Kin, gain-ing a sense of his people's past. The color photographs dominate the pages showing the buildings with impressive clarity.

Geeslin, Campbell. *How Nanita Learned to Make Flan*. Illustrated by Petra Mathers. New York: Anne Schwartz/Atheneum, 1999. 32pp. Grades K–3.

As her First Communion approaches, Nanita worries that she has no shoes. Her father, the shoemaker, is too busy to make her any. So she makes her own, which magically lead her to a large house. There an old woman takes her shoes and puts her to work. She learns to make flan so good that she must make it every day. One day, a parrot she has befriended says he will take her home if she frees him. Nanita's father is so happy to see her that he makes her beautiful white shoes for her Communion. He also celebrates with a fiesta, where she serves her well-appreciated flan. The watercolors simplify and eliminate details, leaving those that add humor or specific action. Body posture and especially facial expressions drive the emotional content. There are sufficient colonial Mexican objects to determine the locale. There is a recipe for the famous flan.

Johnston, Tony. *Day of the Dead*. Illustrated by Jeanette Winter. San Diego, CA: Harcourt, 1997. 48pp. Also Voyager paper, 2000. Grades 1–4.

Just a sentence or two serve as captions in this hand-sized introduction to the Mexican holiday. The family has prepared for weeks. The children are eager to taste the many foods, to see what their father has bought and hidden in the closet, but are told they must wait. After everything is ready, including the flowers, the family makes its way with all the other people to the cemetery for the traditional celebration. Size limits the detail in each small acrylic painting framed in black with appropriate symbols. Yet Winter manages to show the essentials for each part of the preparations. Including the hungry children adds a bit of humor to this attractive, informative sequence of pictures. The typical paper cut-outs are part of the decorations. Further notes on the holiday are appended.

Keister, Douglas. *Fernando's Gift / El Regalo de Fernando*. Boston: Little, Brown, 1998 paper. 32pp. Grades 1–4.

This dual language story about the Costa Rican rain forest uses information-packed color photographs of a real family, the jungle, and the author's experiences there as the basis for the tale he tells. Fernando relates the routines of his daily life and his appreciation of the beauty around him. When his friend's favorite tree is cut down, he asks his grandfather why. Told about the harm done by the careless destroyers of the forest, Fernando asks his father, whose job is growing more trees in a nursery, to find a safe place for him to plant his gift for his friend, the tree of her choice. This is a quiet plea to halt the destruction of the rain forest and for reforestation.

Kleven, Elisa. *Hooray, a Piñata!* New York: Dutton, 1996. 32pp. Grades K–3.

Clara goes shopping with her mother and friend Samson for a *piñata* for her birthday party. She picks out one in the shape of a small dog whom she names Lucky. She takes him with her on the merry-go-round, on the swing and bicycle, everywhere. When she and Samson are making paper hats for the party, Clara realizes that she doesn't want to break Lucky. Samson solves the problem by buying her another *piñata* as a birthday present. They fill the new one, then break it at the party with a satisfying thwack for great fun. Busy collage and painted scenes describe the frenetic adventures. There are kids having the time of their lives and things all over the place leading up to the two-page spread of the frenzy after the breaking of the *piñata*.

Levy, Janice. *The Spirit of Tio Fernando / El Espiritu de Tio Fernando: A Day of the Dead Story*. Illustrated by Morella Fuemayor. Morton Grove, IL: Albert Whitman, 1995. 32pp. Also paper. Grades 1–3.

   A boy describes the family preparations for the honoring of his uncle who died six months ago. Nando goes shopping in the market, then passes costumed musicians on his way to the cemetery with his family. Nando has worried about whether his uncle's spirit will be there. With his family, he finally feels sure that his uncle is "happy with his fiesta," knowing that they love and remember him. The story is written in Spanish on the top of the pages and in English on the bottom. Details of village life are naturalistically included in the full-page watercolors that focus on the special toys, baked goods, and graveyard events. There is an added brief explanation of the holiday.

Madrigal, Antonio Hernández. *Erandi's Braids*. Illustrated by Tomie dePaola. New York: G. P. Putnam's Sons, 1999. 32pp. Also Puffin paper. Grades K–3.

   Money is scarce for Erandi and her mother, and their fishing net is beyond repair. So when men come from the city to their village of Pátzcuaro, Mexico, to buy women's hair, Erandi fears that her mother will want to sell hers. Since it will soon be her birthday, her mother takes her first to the store and offers her the choice of a new dress or a doll. Thinking of the coming fiesta, Erandi chooses the dress. Then her mother tries to sell her own hair, but it is not long enough. When the barber admires hers, Erandi sacrifices her braids. Her mother feels sorry, but they are soon glad because they now have enough money to buy both a new net and the doll. The author assures us that there is no longer a market for hair, although there was in the 1940s and 1950s. The illustrator paints a tidy Mexican village, Erandi's house, and the butterfly nets on the lake with flat color areas. The double pages have a theatrical quality to their framed design as mother and daughter go about their chores in a sequence of typical settings. The clothing and tortilla making are also typical of the place and time.

McCunney, Michelle. *Mario's Mayan Journey*. Greenvale, NY: Mondo, 1997. 28pp. paper. Grades 1–3.

Young Mario's parents have talked to him frequently about the Mayan people who used to live in the southern part of Mexico. Living in Mexico City, he spends happy hours in the Mayan area of the museum. One night, he dreams that two Mayan children take him down the river through the jungle to the Mayan city of Chichén Itzá. They spend the night in the jungle. When Mario wakes up the next day, he decides to paint in his room what he remembers of his dream so he never forgets it. Detailed scenes place Mario first in his bedroom, then in the jungle. Everything is, of course, far neater than real, but it all serves as an introduction to the Mayan sites. End-papers have a map of the Yucatan with the significant ruins marked. There is a glossary of the Spanish included.

Meunier, Brian. *Pipiolo and the Roof Dogs*. Illustrated by Perky Edgerton. New York: Dutton/Penguin, 2003. 32pp. Grades 1–4.

In a small town in Mexico, guard dogs live on the roofs all their lives, never having a chance to run free on the ground. Lupe, our narrator, vividly describes her sympathy for them, along with her appreciation for the beauty around her. Pipiolo is her perky but clever puppy who enjoys life with her, while also caring about the dogs on the roofs. One night, Lupe discovers that Pipiolo has been regularly watching television. From what he has seen there, he hatches a plan to free the dogs. The townspeople call it a supernatural event, but Lupe knows that her dog is a hero. The end-papers, with their intriguing scattered green imprints of dog shapes on a roughly painted earth-toned wall, produce a mythic impression suitable for this magical narrative. Double-page scenes, also textured and a bit impressionistic, describe both the arid landscape and the humble village with special attention to the action. They provide enough local detail to frame the story. Both Lupe and Pipiolo are very appealing characters. The author and illustrator live in the village where the story is set.

Reiser, Lynn. *Tortillas and Lullabies / Tortillas y Cancionitas*. Illustrated by "Corazones Valientes." Coordinated and translated by Rebecca Hart. New York: Greenwillow/Morrow, 1998. 40pp. Grades PreS–2.

There are four sections to this book, each one in a repeating pattern of few words about family life. The first concerns tortillas. "My great-grandmother made tortillas for my grandmother; my grandmother made tortillas for my mother; my mother made tortillas for me; and I made tortillas for my doll.

Every time it was the same, but different." Part 2 concerns gathering flowers, Part 3 is washing dresses, and Part 4 is singing lullabies. The houses, people, and clothing change, but the love remains the same. The acrylic paintings that accompany the captions also show the intergenerational affection. The scenes are crowded with objects associated with the activity, for example, a farm with corn plants, the cooking utensils with tortillas, over the years. There is a use of saturated colors; the people who look straight out at us display a kind of innocence. The artists are a group of women in a Costa Rican village who were taught to paint by a Peace Corps volunteer. "Their art celebrates their heritage, their rapidly changing lives . . . and the love in their families. . . ." The music of the lullaby is included.

San Vicente, Luis. *The Festival of Bones / El Festival de las Calaveras: The Little-Bitty Book for the Day of the Dead.* Translated by John William Byrd and Bobby Byrd. El Paso, TX: Cinco Puntos, 2002. 30pp. Grades 1–4.

The Mexican celebration of the Day of the Dead is both elaborate and joyous. It is a difficult concept for non-Mexicans to accept; that when the spirits of the dead come back to visit it is a joyful time for them and for the families who go to great lengths to prepare a welcome. Brief verses here in English and Spanish reflect the excitement as the skeletons dance their wild dance. Eight pages of extensive notes add information on the holiday, with instructions on building an altar, baking special bread, and making a sugar skull. The white drawings on black paper on the end-papers introduce the pictures inside. Delightful sketchy drawings with touches of collage and color offer skeletons dressed in funny clothes with huge top hats and flapping scarves, singing, riding bikes, or dancing. These playful characters can help us better understand the Mexican attitude toward the holiday.

Te Loo, Sanne. *Little Fish.* La Jolla, CA: Kane/Miller, 2003. 26pp. Grades K–2.

The text of this imaginative story says nothing about its location, nor is it based on any specific traditional tale. Bored, Rosa is watching the pelicans by the sea when a small fish leaps into her lap. She takes him home carefully, places him in a bowl of water, and bakes him some crusty corn rolls. The next day he is too big for the bowl. With Grandmother's help, she moves him to a tub. As she cooks her favorite dishes for him, he keeps growing, until finally he is so big that she and the other children carry him back to the sea. Then they can all enjoy the cake Grandmother had baked for him. Although tortillas and other ethnic dishes are mentioned, it is in the illustrations that we get a picture of Mexican or Central American life. The cheerful paintings include cactus, birds in cages, peppers, village streets, enough to set the stage for the magic adventure of the charming Rosa.

Winter, Jeanette. *Josefina*. San Diego, CA: Harcourt Brace, 1996. 36pp. Grades 1–4.

The story is inspired by Josefina Aguilar, a Mexican folk artist who makes clay figures in Ocotlan, Mexico. This Josefina is born into a family of figure makers. She makes her own from her childhood until she has nine children. The author then turns the story into a counting book of the many kinds of figures Josefina creates, from one sun and two angels to nine skeletons and ten stars. The full and half-page illustrations define a range of real clay statues along with the woman who makes them. Acrylic paints exploit the pastel tints of the region with an inventive range of page layouts that keep the visuals fresh throughout.

Winter, Jeanette. *Niño's Mask*. New York: Dial/Penguin, 2003. 34pp. Grades K–3.

Hand-carved masks play a key role in the village celebration of the Mexican Fiesta of the Tigre. Impatient to be old enough to participate, a young boy finally decides he wants to be a *perro,* or dog, and cuts a tree by the light of the full moon to carve a mask of the dog he is sure is hiding there. In a costume made by his mother, he joins the traditional chase to catch the tiger, and surprisingly and happily, he wins. Folk-art style pictures with black outlines and translucent hues catch the flavor of contemporary Mexico. Perspective is flat, the sun has rays, the text is totally projected in hand-lettered speech balloons. The story begins on the front end-papers, with a morning scene of a village and people chatting together; it ends at night after the fiesta with our hero gazing up at the stars on a now-deserted street. There is a glossary of the Spanish along with brief notes on masks in Mexico.

Ziefert, Harriet. *Home for Navidad*. Illustrated by Santiago Cohen. Boston: Walter Lorraine/Houghton Mifflin, 2003. 34pp. Grades K–4.

Rose lives with her grandmother in Mexico. She hasn't seen her mother since she went to work in the United States three years ago. Before school, Rosa goes to pick corn with her Uncle Pancho, who says her mother has been working hard to afford to come home for Christmas. The separation has been difficult; money is a constant worry for the family. Rosa's happy dream is seeing her mother again. There is a child-like freshness to the illustrations, created in Mexico, which are more colored drawings than paintings. They loosely depict the corn picking, the clothes washing, even breakfast and dinner making, along with the Christmas festivities at the church. The endpapers are scattered with colorful Mexican stamps. A glossary explains the included Spanish words. This book offers a different point of view about the workers from Mexico in the United States.

MEXICAN AMERICANS AND THE IMMIGRANT EXPERIENCE

ORIGINAL TALES AND FOLKTALES

Hayes, Joe. *Estrellita de Oro / Little Gold Star: A Cinderella Cuento.* Illustrated by Gloria Osuna Perez and Lucia Angela Perez. El Paso, TX: Cinco Puntos, 2000. 32pp. Also paper. Grades K–3.

This traditional Hispanic tale told in the Southwest has the usual girl mistreated by her father's new wife and her two daughters. Here, the magic is performed by a hawk, who puts a gold star on Arcía's forehead but a green horn and a donkey ear on those of the nasty sisters. The prince finds her with the help of a cat, for the happy ending. The full-page paintings have a look associated with folk art: solidity of form, frozen postures, details limited mainly to those needed to move the narrative. These are brown-skinned and dark-eyed men and women probably modeled on Mexico's indigenous people. The text is in both English and Spanish. Details on the background and versions of the story in the Southwest are added.

Hayes, Joe. *Juan Verdades: The Man Who Couldn't Tell a Lie.* Illustrated by Joseph Daniel Fiedler. New York: Orchard/Scholastic, 2001. 32pp. Grades 1–4.

In the old Southwest, don Ignacio is so confident in the truthfulness of his foreman that he bets his ranch that don Arturo can't make Juan Verdades tell him a lie. Don Arturo begins to worry about losing, but his clever daughter Araceli tells him that if they can get invited to stay at don Ignacio's ranch, they will figure out how to win. Araceli tries to make Juan fall in love with her. She also makes some plans, since she finds that she loves him too. She asks Juan for all the apples from don Ignacio's special tree. At first he tells her he cannot do that. When he finally gives in, he has figured out what to say that makes for a happy ending for all. Notes explain how the author has changed the original tale. The full-page alkyd paintings describe the Southwestern landscape, the costumed characters, the cattle, etc., with a studied restraint. But the emotions of unexpressed love and anxiety are enhanced by the use of appropriate colors in backgrounds.

Hopkins, Jackie Mims. *The Horned Toad Prince.* Illustrated by Michael Austin. Atlanta: Peachtree, 2000. 32pp. Grades K–4.

The fairy tale of the Frog Prince is moved to the American Southwest. Our heroine, Reba Jo, can sing in the wind or race her horse across the prairie, but her favorite occupation is roping. So despite her daddy's warning about *arroyos,* she can't resist trying to lasso a vulture, losing her new cowboy hat down a well as a result. A horned toad offers to fetch it in return for three favors. When Reba Jo rides away without granting them, the toad has her daddy force her to keep her promises. The traditional story takes an unusual and amusing twist after the kiss and transformation. The slickly painted, framed scenes employ unusual, comically exaggerated perspectives that frequently seem like toad's-eye views. The landscape is dry and vast as the Southwest; Reba Jo is outfitted in cowboy gear. Best of all, the toad is portrayed as one crafty character. There's fun for all. A Spanish word list is included.

Kimmel, Eric A. *The Runaway Tortilla.* Illustrated by Randy Cecil. Delray Beach, FL: Winslow Press, 2000. 34pp. Grades K–3.

The saucy runaway here is a Southwestern Gingerbread Man. In their *taquería,* Tía Lupe and Tío José make the best Mexican dishes in all of Texas. Lupe's special tortillas are so light that she is warned that some day they will run away. And of course one tortilla, who says she is too beautiful to eat, rolls right out the door. Her repeated rhyme begins, "Run as fast as fast can be. You won't get a bite of me." Soon she is chased by two horned toads, three donkeys, four jackrabbits, five rattlesnakes, and six buckaroos. When they give up, the tortilla is triumphant, until she encounters the wily Señor Coyote, who ends her story with a snap! The real fun is in the oil paintings spread across long double pages to hold the accumulated parade of chasers. The animals are comic in their aggressive behavior, but the coyote is the epitome of a slick con man. The visuals add spice to the classic tale.

MEXICAN AMERICANS TODAY AND THE IMMIGRANT EXPERIENCE

Ada, Alma Flor. *Gathering the Sun: An Alphabet in Spanish and English.* Illustrated by Simon Silva. New York: Lothrop, 1997. 40pp. Also RAYO paper, 2001. Grades 1–3.

We move from A to Z in English and Spanish with English translation and notes, describing the word for each letter briefly as it relates to the migrant harvest workers and their lives. In addition to the names of the crops harvested, words like "honor," "pride," and "love" are shown as important in the lives of the workers. Double pages depict the farms and the activities on them, along with the people of the farm community, in gouache paintings that seem to radiate the sun's warmth. There is an attempt to create attractive patterns of flowers, orange trees, and especially the cultivated fields with their ribbon-like rows stretching to the horizon.

Altman, Linda Jacobs. *Amelia's Road*. Illustrated by Enrique O. Sanchez. New York: Lee & Low, 1993. 32pp. Also paper. Grades 2–4.

Amelia hates her life on the road with her migrant family and longs for a permanent home. One day, she finds a sturdy old tree on a back road. After a day of work or school she finds security imagining her home by that tree. When it's time to move on to the next harvest, Amelia fills a box with items meaningful to her and buries it by the tree to have a place she can come back to and call her own. Then she can go. The illustrations depict appealing characters in well-defined settings on the migrant worker road.

Ancona, George. *Barrio: José's Neighborhood*. San Diego, CA: Harcourt, 1998. 48pp. Also paper. Grades 2–5.

We follow young José Luís through his days in school and at play and through the year in his San Francisco neighborhood, where the inhabitants bring their Spanish language and Hispanic culture to their homes in the Barrio. The streets have stores where the food reflects that culture. The walls display murals that portray the history of the immigrants. The celebrations through the year include the riotous *Carnaval*, Halloween, the Day of the Dead, and José's birthday party, complete with *piñata*. Large, clear color photographs give ample visual evidence of the activities and participants, including mariachi musicians, skeletons of many sizes, José in soccer uniform kicking the ball, etc. There is a Spanish word list.

Argueta, Jorge. *Xochitl and the Flowers / Xóchitl, la Niña de las Flores*. Illustrated by Carl Angel. San Francisco: Children's Book Press, 2003. 32pp. Grades 1–4.

Young Xochitl, whose name means "flower" in Nahuatl, misses her home and the relatives left behind in El Salvador, particularly the flowers. She is very happy when they move to an apartment with a yard where they can grow and sell plants. But the owner doesn't want them doing any business there. Luckliy their friendly neighbors are able to persuade him to let the flowers grow. And Xochitl's mother adds a bit of soil brought from El Salvador so "no one can say we don't belong here." Intense colors of acrylic paint, color pencil, and photo collage are used to add emotional content to the picture of the family creating fresh life. The illustrations, loaded with flowers, portray the neighborhood and friends with simple directness. The bilingual text is based on a real experience in the San Francisco Mission District.

Bertrand, Diane Gonzales. *Uncle Chente's Picnic / El Picnic de Tío Chente.* Houston, TX: Piñata Books/Arte Público, 2001. 32pp. Also paper. Grades 1–4.

His family in Texas is awaiting Uncle Chente's visit on July 4, planning a splendid picnic. Unfortunately, just as he arrives, the rain begins. By the time they have moved everything inside, the lights go out. But the picnic continues. Uncle Chente tells stories of his childhood in Mexico, teaches everyone how to make shadow animals and to sing his favorite Spanish song. It becomes a family picnic to remember. There is a snapshot quality to the full-page pictures of the party, with images created with a variety of textures that have the effect of looking through a screen. But the details of *frijoles* and *jalapeños* are clear.

Bunting, Eve. *Going Home.* Illustrated by David Diaz. New York: Harper-Collins, 1996. 34pp. paper. Grades K–3.

It's Christmas time and Mama and Papa are excited to be going back to visit the family in the village of La Perla. But the children don't consider Mexico "home" and are not so sure about the trip. As they drive south into Mexico, Papa reminds the children why he and their mother went to the United States, for the "opportunities." When they reach La Perla, the narrator and his sister find it strange, but as they watch their mother and father dance happily in the street, they begin to realize what their parents sacrificed in love and family security to give them "opportunities." Black-framed blocks of text and sculpturesque pictures of people give visual form to the words. Heavy black outlines are filled with bright, naturalistic colors. The sky spins with snake-like constellations and, to add further commotion, the pictures and text are superimposed on photographs of Mexican Christmas ornaments and decorations. This is a visual as well as a verbal trip to Mexico.

Chavarría-Cháirez, Becky. *Magda's Tortillas / Las Tortillas de Magda.* Illustrated by Anne Vega. Houston, TX: Arte Público, 2000. 32pp. Grades K–2.

Magda thinks she is ready for her first tortilla-making lesson with her grandmother. But it is not as easy as it looks. Each attempt turns into something different from the circle she wants to make. Her grandmother is encouraging her, telling her that a heart, or a star, is fine. But Magda doesn't want to make a banana, or a football, while her grandmother rolls one perfect circle after another. When it is time to eat, Magda is ashamed of her efforts. To her surprise, her tortillas are the most popular. She is declared a tortilla artist. Next year perhaps she will learn how to mix the dough. Full-page opaque paintings exaggerate a bit in displaying the changing emotions as Magda gets involved in the flour-y world. Family affection is conveyed particularly in later pages when her baking artistry is appreciated.

Cohn, Diana. *Sí, Se Puede! / Yes, We Can: Janitor Strike in L.A.* Illustrated by Francisco Delgado. Essay and poem by Luis J. Rodríguez. El Paso, TX: Cinco Puntos, 2002. 32pp. Grades 2–4.

The story of the successful strike by the Service Employees International Union in Los Angeles in 2000 is made more understandable for young readers as told by Carlitos, the son of one of the working janitors. The difficulties faced by so many Latino and Latina immigrants occur not only in the more commonly covered areas of migrant farm work but also in those urban jobs where the wages do not allow a decent standard of living. Large colored drawings provide many of the details not in the brief text: youngsters making posters, heavenly angels playing in Carlito's dream, workers organizing. Unsophisticated, almost crude in places, the illustrations express conviction stronger than words. The inside of the dust jacket is an informative poster. Further information on organizer Dolores Sánchez follows the story.

Córdova, Amy. *Abuelita's Heart.* New York: Simon & Schuster, 1997. 32pp. Grades K–3.

A young girl describes her visit to her grandmother in the Southwest, which is rich with her Hispanic heritage and the love of the land and its creatures. Under the stars at night, wrapped in her grandmother's *rebozo,* she feels the light of the *corazón,* or heart of her family and friends, the love everywhere. Included is a recipe for her grandmother's Happiness Meal, the secret ingredient of which is to share it with someone you love. There is a spiritual strength in these double-page acrylic, oil pastel, and colored pencil illustrations done on the site; a folk-art directness to the representation of the characters and objects in the story. The scenes in a cave and subsequent dream are mystical but in keeping with the notion of the power of love. The included Spanish words are easily understood in context.

Jiménez, Francisco. *La Mariposa*. Illustrated by Simón Silva. Boston: Houghton Mifflin, 1998. 40pp. Also paper. Grades 1–4.

Francisco begins first grade knowing no English. School gives him a headache, except for art class. The other students are not friendly. As time passes, he notices that the caterpillar he has been watching in a jar has woven a cocoon. Meanwhile, he learns a bit of English, but school is still very difficult for him. Just before school ends in May, he is thrilled to receive the blue ribbon prize for his drawing of a butterfly. And he is also pleased to be able to set free the beautiful butterfly that emerges from the cocoon. He sees hope for a brighter future. With the somewhat lengthy text, the many full-page gouache paintings are important in setting the tone for the narration. The sequence of visuals makes a strong story line. There is a glossary of the included Spanish words.

Johnston, Tony. *Uncle Rain Cloud*. Illustrated by Fabricio VandenBroeck. Watertown, MA: Talewinds/Charlesbridge, 2001. 32pp. Also paper. Grades 1–4.

Carlos's uncle has been as gloomy as a black cloud since the family moved to Los Angeles. When they go shopping, he seems particularly angry as he mutters the few English words he knows, but he doesn't want any help from Carlos. Still, in the evenings, as he tells Carlos the tales that Carlos enjoys of the gods of ancient Mexico, he seems calmer. When he goes to Carlos's conference with his teacher, Carlos must translate back and forth. Uncle Tomás seems angry then but later admits that his pride is broken because he is afraid to speak English. Carlos tells him that he used to feel that way also. Together they plan to work on both English and Spanish in the future. The "action" takes place between nephew and uncle, showing them together in various situations. Several scenes have Mayan paintings on the wall as Tomás tells an ancient story. The textured paintings in acrylics with colored pencils have a rough but animated appearance. The names of the Mayan gods are listed; the Spanish in the text is not translated.

Lomas Garza, Carmen, as told to Harriet Rohmer. *In My Family / En Mi Familia*. Edited by David Schecter. Spanish translation by Fracisco X. Alarcon. San Francisco: Children's Book Press, 1996. 32pp. Grades 2–4.

The artist has painted a series of pictures of her memories of growing up in Kingsville, Texas, near the Mexican border. Opposite each picture she describes in English and Spanish the aspect of her life that she has painted. We learn about important events like birthday barbeques and weddings, plus more ordinary items like cleaning cactus pads or making *empenadas*.

We meet La Llorona and the Virgin of Guadelupe in this rich slice of Mexican American life. The full-page scenes are like dioramas carefully set with the objects needed to illustrate the text. Typical of much native painting, they are full of personal insights, crowded with local detail, and executed in a somewhat odd perspective.

Lopez, Loretta. *The Birthday Swap.* New York: Lee & Low, 1997. 32pp. Also paper. Grades PreS–1.

Lori wants to find a present she can give her older sister for her birthday. She and her mother go across the border to Mexico to shop. She looks at many possibilities in the market, but nothing seems right. They stop at the *piñatas,* but her mother says that her sister is too old for one. On Sunday, the birthday, Lori's mother dresses her in a new dress. After church they go to *Tío* Daniel's house, where there is quite a surprise. Her sister has given Lori her birthday, to be celebrated with a big party, *piñata* and all. Having a winter birthday, Lori has never been able to enjoy one like this. The party and her present make it the "best birthday party ever." The child-like simplicity of the text is matched by full-page gouache paintings with colored pencil, portraying the church, market, etc., with details of the locale. Around each text page are scattered more appropriate articles. A glossary of the included Spanish words is added.

Markel, Michelle. *Gracias, Rosa.* Illustrated by Diane Paterson. Morton Grove, IL: Albert Whitman, 1995. 32pp. Grades 2–4.

Kate relates how Rosa arrives to take care of her, speaking almost no English. Rosa brings her a doll from Guatemala. Playing with her, Kate learns about Rosa's difficult life on the farm, about her daughter Juana, and along with it all some Spanish. When Rosa goes back home, Kate sends a doll for Juana with her. She misses Rosa but has learned a lot. A glossary explains the Spanish in the text. Full-page watercolors depict Kate and Rosa interacting realistically as they become friends.

Mora, Pat. *Tomás and the Library Lady.* Illustrated by Raul Colón. New York: Alfred A. Knopf, 1997. 32pp. Also Dragonfly paper. Grades K–3.

Tomás and his migrant working family travel to Iowa, where they work in the fields picking corn. His grandfather tells Tomás that he is old enough to go to the library for more of the stories he loves. At first, he finds the building intimidating, but then the librarian helps him find the books that take him far away. All summer he enjoys books and brings them home to read to the family. When they have to leave, he takes with him a precious new book of his own, a gift from the librarian. The story is based on the childhood experience of Tomás Rivera, who became chancellor of the University of California at Riverside. Colón scratches through the paint with a comb-like tool to create textured surfaces on his full-page pictures of migrant life. The overall effect of the story is to enhance the significance of books for children on the move.

O'Neill, Alexis. *Estela's Swap*. Illustrated by Enrique O. Sanchez. New York: Lee & Low, 2002. 32pp. Grades 1–3.

At a "Swap Meet" Estela hopes to get enough money for lessons with the Ballet Folklórico, but no one seems to want her music box. After a flower stand nearby is blown down, Estela offers the owner her music box. This generous gesture leaves her with nothing to sell. But the owner brings her a beautiful dancing skirt as a "swap." Estela still hopes that next week she can sell something so she will be able to dance in the beautiful skirt. The blocks of text are integrated into double-page scenes of the Southwest that take Estela through the market with its many stands, as well as the wind storm. We see her final dance in the brilliant, flouncing red skirt. There is a folk art look to the illustrations, a style that conveys the vitality of the characters. A few easily understood Spanish words occur throughout.

Pérez, L. King. *First Day in Grapes*. Illustrated by Robert Casilla. New York: Lee & Low, 2002. 32pp. Grades 1–3.

We experience with Chico, moving through California with his family as the crops ripen, what it is like to start school always in a new place, an outcast teased by other children. With the help of some friendly students and a sympathetic teacher, as well as his own ability, Chico finds this first day not so bad at all. Watercolor, pencil, and pastel illustrations are rather literal in showing Chico's new home and the several school-related settings. The actions are portrayed in a believable sequence of naturalistic scenes in the California farm country.

Ryan, Pam Muñoz. *Mice and Beans*. Illustrated by Joe Cepeda. New York: Scholastic, 2001. 32pp. Grades K–3.

Rosa María spends a week preparing in her small house for a family birthday party for her youngest grandchild. She believes what her mother always said, "When there's room in the heart, there's room in the house, *except* for a mouse." So each day of the week she prepares. And each day she sets a mousetrap. The next day it is missing, so she sets another. Other things seem to come up missing as well. The text says nothing about it, but in the illustrations the mice have been as busy as Rosa María. So on the day of the party, when it's time to break the *piñata*, she realizes she has forgotten to fill it. But it is full of goodies. Back in her kitchen, she begins to think that perhaps there is room in her small house "even for a mouse." Cepeda makes room for the mice in the visual tale while also showing the details of the house and garden. Of course the anthropomorphic mice steal the fun-filled show. The two double-page scenes of them filling the *piñata* come right out of animated cartoons. The final scene of their party is priceless. There is a glossary with pronunciation.

Soto, Gary. *Chato and the Party Animals.* Illustrated by Susan Guevara. New York: G. P. Putnam's Sons, 2000. 32pp. Also Puffin paper. Grades K–4.

Chato, feline hero of *Chato's Kitchen* below, doesn't understand why his friend Novio Boy isn't enjoying Chorizo's great party. When he learns that Novio Boy, an orphan, has never had a birthday party, he decides to make one for him. He prepares all the food and decorations and invites everyone. But then he realizes that he has forgotten to invite Novio Boy. All the friends worry when they can't find him, fearing the worst. When they finally locate him, it's party time, complete with *piñata*. Thickly painted acrylic on scratchboard pictures are designed expressionistically with so much thrown together that we must linger to extract the significant details. The anthropomorphic cats and other animals are wildly in motion into the spirit of the party. There's a directness to the imagery that borders on crudeness. There is a glossary of the included Spanish.

Soto, Gary. *Chato's Kitchen.* Illustrated by Susan Guevara. New York: Putnam, 1995. 26pp. Also Puffin paper. Grades 1–4.

Using anthropomorphic cats and mice for characters allows for word-play fun with the "cool, low-riding cat" hero, Chato. When the hungry cat spies a group of plump mice, he invites them to dinner. The suspicious mice, giving him the benefit of the doubt, accept on the condition that they bring a friend. Meanwhile, Chato and his friend get to work in the kitchen, making a variety of *latino* foods. When the mice's friend turns out to be a large dog, expectations must be revised. Luckily there's enough good food for all. Thickly applied, brightly colored paints create strong, larger-than-life personalities in detailed settings that almost fill the double pages with action, leaving just a bit of white space for the short bursts of text. A glossary of the Spanish words and a menu with translation are included.

Soto, Gary. *Snapshots from the Wedding.* Illustrated by Stephanie Garcia. New York: Putnam, 1997. 32pp. Also paper. Grades K–3.

Maya, the flower girl, guides us through the festivities of a Latin American wedding. Clay figures in costume and appropriate settings, all framed in open boxes, are photographed in the activities suggested in the text. The illustrations are placed on an appropriate lace background. There is a glossary of the Spanish words.

Soto, Gary. *Too Many Tamales.* Illustrated by Ed Martinez. New York: G. P. Putnam's sons, 1993. 32pp. Also paper. Grades K–3.

Maria loves being grown-up enough to help her mother make tamales for the family Christmas gathering. She puts her mother's ring on just for a bit, admiring its shine. Then her father comes to help roll the mixture into the husk wrappers. While playing with her cousins, Maria suddenly remembers the ring. Thinking that it must have fallen into the tamale mixture, she asks her cousins to help her eat the twenty-four tamales and find it. They all eat until it hurts, but no ring is found. Ashamed, Maria goes to tell her mother the bad news. To her surprise, her mother is wearing the ring. When she tells the story, everyone laughingly agrees to help make more tamales. A charming Maria is shown in scenes of domestic detail. Not quite photographic, the illustrations are like snapshots of the events of the text. There is a genuine sense of family celebration.

FIVE

ABORIGINAL AND NATIVE CULTURES OF NORTH AMERICA

ORIGINAL TALES AND FOLKTALES EVOKING THE PAST

Bouchard, David. *Qu'appelle*. Illustrated by Michael Lonechild. Vancouver, British Columbia: Raincoast, 2002. 32pp. Grades 1–4.

This sad folktale of lost love, retold in blank verse, comes from the Cree. Ikciv and Witonia grow up together and declare their love. When he rides off to war, they swear they will always be together. But Witonia falls ill. While Ikciv is riding back after the battle, he seems to hear her calling. By the time he reaches home, she is dead. Angry in his grief, he rides off "in search of the love of his life." Legend says you may hear him out on the prairie calling, "Qui appelle?"—"Who is calling?" The formal design of the book sets the serious tone. The several lines of poetic text are set with very wide margins on white pages faced by paintings in equally wide margins. These are detailed naturalistic landscapes with small figures acting out the events of the story. These mood-provoking "story pictures" use light to enhance drama. Notes are added on the various versions of the legend.

Bruchac, Joseph. *Crazy Horse's Vision*. Illustrated by S. D. Nelson. New York: Lee & Low, 2000. 34pp. Grades 1–4.

The story begins with the youth of the legendary Native American who was already a leader and fine hunter called Curly. When the settlers move into Lakota land, the army comes also, and conflict begins. Curly, troubled by the slaughter, seeks a vision. "Keep nothing for yourself," he hears as he sees a warrior riding into battle. When he finally describes it to his father, he is told that the rider is himself, destined to defend his people. His father gives him his own name for that destiny: Crazy Horse. The acrylic painted scenes combine interpretations of ledger-book style with that of conventional perspective and naturalistic representation, offering direct emotional impact plus information about the landscape and the conflict. End-papers replicate pictures from Lakota ledger books further described in the Illustrator's Note. The author also fills in the known facts about Crazy Horse in an extensive note.

Bruchac, Joseph. *Gluskabe and the Four Wishes.* Illustrated by Christine Nyburg Shrader. New York: Cobblehill/Dutton, 1995. 32pp. Grades 2–4.

This native Abenaki tale teaches a lesson. Four men go to see Gluskabe, the Great Spirit's helper, because he has promised to grant a wish to those who do. Each man wants something different, and each helps along the difficult journey. When they arrive at their destination, Gluskabe gives each a pouch that they are not to open until they reach home. The first, who wanted many possessions, opens it while still in a canoe, and the weight sinks him. The second, who wanted to be taller than all others, is turned into the tallest pine tree when he opens his pouch too soon. The third, who wanted to live forever, becomes a boulder. The fourth, who wanted only to feed his people, finds nothing in his pouch but the understanding of animals and their ways, "the best of the gifts" for finding food. End-papers depict a misty evening sea with far-off islands. Pastels accentuate their smeary quality, while realistic and believable three-dimensional characters in close-ups on double pages integrate well with the text.

Bruchac, Joseph, and James Bruchac. *Turtle's Race with Beaver: A Traditional Seneca Story.* Illustrated by Jose Aruego and Ariane Dewey. New York: Dial, 2003. 32pp. Grades PreS–3.

One spring, Turtle comes up from the mud in the bottom of her pond to find that a beaver has moved in. Turtle is willing to share, but not Beaver. Beaver challenges Turtle to a race to see who will stay. The excitement builds as all the other animals come to watch and cheer. Clever Turtle fastens on to Beaver's tail, then bites down hard at the end, causing Beaver to toss her off over the finish line. Having learned his lesson, Beaver moves on to another pond, this time to share. The artists create very engaging double-page pen and ink, pastel, and gouache scenes in which their characters confront each other. There's a cartoon-like quality, a style which emphasizes profile views and flat shapes, is decorative, only vaguely naturalistic, with little relevance to anything Native American. Notes on the many versions of this tale include references to the Aesop "Tortoise and the Hare."

Bunting, Eve. *Moonstick: The Seasons of the Sioux.* Illustrated by John Sandford. New York: Joanna Cotler/HarperCollins, 1997. 32pp. Also paper, 2000. Grades K–4.

In succinct poetic prose we are taken through the thirteen moons of a year, beginning with the spring. A young boy's father cuts a notch in a moon-counting stick for the first month as the sweetness of spring arrives. Each moon is named for the signs of nature it displays, and the activities of the people are described. At the Cherry-Ripening Moon, the boy is too young to dance the Sun Dance or to hunt. By the Moon When the Grass Comes Up, the snows melt and it is time to cut a new moonstick. At the end of the story, the narrator looks back over the years and the changes in his life. His father is gone; so are the buffalo; the people do not hunt any more. But he can still cut a moonstick to mark the months for his grandson. Each moon has a dou-ble-page textured painting that pictures the specifics in the text by present-ing naturalistic scenes with landscapes, tipis, and above all, the people going about the seasonal activities. There's a spiritual quality to the trees and fields in muted colors.

Bushyhead, Robert H., and Kay Thorpe Bannon. *Yonder Mountain: A Chero-kee Legend.* Illustrated by Kristina Rodanas. New York: Marshall Cavendish, 2002. 32pp. Grades 1–4.

Feeling his age, Chief Sky sets a test for three young men to see who should succeed him as chief. They must go the top of the mountain and bring back what they find. Black Bear brings valuable stones from the lower path; Gray Wolf discovers healing herbs further up. Soaring Eagle does not return for seven days; then he brings nothing but a story. From the top of the mountain, he has seen a signal asking for help. He tells Sky Chief they must go to those in need. Chief Sky gives him the chief's robe, for he has climbed to the top of the mountain and has shown that he can lead his peo-ple to help others. The detailed colored pencil and watercolor scenes across double pages visualize the landscape and the village with clarity and atten-tion to dress and natural history. There are even some basket-weave decora-tive borders. The foreword by Joseph Bruchac fills in the background of the Cherokee and of the tale itself. There is also a glossary.

Dominic, Gloria. *Coyote and the Grasshoppers.* Illustrated by Charles Reasoner. Vero Beach, FL: Rourke, 1996. 48pp. Grades 1–4.

In a time of terrible drought, locusts also eat every blade of grass. Thirsty Coyote asks the Great Spirit for help. He is told to eat grasshoppers until he is ready to burst, then to follow the few that are left. At the spot where the Clear Lake has dried, he must dig. The waters of the lake return. Then Coyote must follow the grasshoppers into the lake, where they become fish to feed the people. He has been brave and unselfish, earning the love of the Pomos. Smooth, stylized paintings of Coyote, Pomos, and landscape tell the visual tale in a decorative manner but without any particular emotion. The final sixteen pages of the book are rich with factual information about the Pomos and their history, plus many photographs, unfortunately not all clear. From the "Native American Lore and Legends" series.

Dominic, Gloria. *Song of the Hermit Thrush: An Iroquois Legend*. Illustrated by Charles Reasoner. Vero Beach, FL: Rourke, 1996. 48pp. Grades 1–4.

According to the story Grandmother tells, the animals long ago agreed to live peacefully by dividing the forest, with the animals on the ground and the birds above. But the noise of them all greeting the sunrise is dreadful, so they have a contest to find the best song. Trying to reach the Great Spirit where the sweetest songs must be, only one little bird can make it. He hides until evening, then sings the song he remembers. So still, at daybreak, there is the noise of all the creatures. But at night, it is the hermit thrush singing alone that is the sweetest. Stylized pictures of animals and trees done in flat color areas combine with more naturalistic interpretations of birds to illustrate the very brief text. The final sixteen pages offer a wealth of factual information about Iroquois life and history, with many clear photographs and drawings. This is another volume in the series "Native American Lore and Legends."

Drucker, Malka. *The Sea Monster's Secret*. Illustrated by Christopher Aja. San Diego, CA: Gulliver/Harcourt, 1999. 32pp. Grades K–4.

A young man traps and kills a sea monster, then having wrapped himself in its skin, finds himself swimming underwater to the monster's splendid home. But he misses his wife and returns home. There his complaining mother-in-law derides him for not providing well for them. So he begins to hunt as the monster, leaving ever-larger fish by their door. When his mother-in-law has invited the villagers to share the whale he has left, and she is hoping that he has gone, he returns as the monster. His wife recognizes him inside the skin, but her frightened mother runs away. The author describes a sea monster totem pole that inspired her to seek out this story. The double pages are dark, but the characters are painted in acrylics and gouache as if spotlights illuminate their faces. Cultural symbols are used as backgrounds in many scenes. The sea monster is truly a creature to fear; emotions are strongly portrayed. Some totem poles are shown.

Duncan, Lois. *The Magic of Spider Woman*. Illustrated by Shonto Begay. New York: Scholastic, 1996. 32pp. Also paper, 2000. Grades 2–5.

In the fall, Wandering Girl returns from the mountains with her sheep to a cold world. Spider Woman takes pity on her and teaches her how to spin and weave, changing her name to Weaving Woman. The girl is told to "walk the Middle Way," warned not to try too much or weave too long. Weaving Woman forgets this, and in her attempt to create the most beautiful blanket in the world, weaves her spirit into the blanket and is trapped there. When Spider Woman pulls a strand to make the blanket less perfect, a path is open for Weaving Woman to escape. Having learned her lesson, Weaving Woman teaches all weavers to make that path in their borders and not try for perfection. Striking naturalistic paintings of the Southwest are set on sand-toned pages. Sometimes the artist breaks the border with a tree branch, thread, or gesturing hand. Illustrations include much detail of costume and artifacts plus some landscape; many emphasize the mystical qualities of the story by using amorphous backgrounds.

Dwyer, Mindy. *Coyote in Love*. Seattle, WA: Alaska Northwest/Graphic Arts Center, 1997. 32pp. Grades PreS–3.

Here Coyote, the traditional trickster, falls in love and is responsible for the formation of Oregon's Crater Lake. The "song" of coyotes is the inspiration for this mother's telling of a story of long ago. Coyote stays up all night watching the stars, for he has fallen in love with a blue star. Because she seems to be close to the top of a mountain, he runs and climbs until he reaches the top. There he begs her to take him with her and be his wife. She takes him to a far, dark part of the sky, calls him a fool, and lets him drop. He crashes into the top of a mountain, broken-hearted. The blue tears he cries form Crater Lake. Very stylized pictures of a purple coyote and decorative landscape with five-pointed stars in the sky are opposite the text, which gives us some colored words all set in wide borders with geometric patterns. The scene of Coyote's crash is agitated by swirling lines of reds and yellows against billowing purple clouds. This light-hearted interpretation of the legend includes no reference to the exact background.

Goble, Paul. *Iktomi and the Boulder.* New York: Orchard/Scholastic, 1988. 32pp. Also paper. Grades K–4.

This is only one of the several tales Goble has written about the clever but also sometimes stupid Sioux trickster. Among those still in print include *Iktomi and the Ducks* (1990) and *Iktomi !   His Eyes* (1999). Goble gives Iktomi's brash or rude comments printed in one typeface and/or color with the author's asides in a different one, leaving room for spontaneous remarks or reader response. All are filled with humor and take careful reading. The ink and watercolor illustrations are based on the life style of the Plains peoples; clothing, ornaments, and weapons reflect tradition. The action usually takes place against a white background with only the most necessary landscape and the varying texts. Usually there are many added bits of information.

Goble, Paul. *The Legend of the White Buffalo Woman.* Washington, DC: National Geographic, 1998. 32pp. Also paper. Grades 1–4.

After a great flood and the marriage of a Woman of the Earth and the Eagle of the Sky, the nation of people return. An attack by enemies sends the sad people to treeless plains. While hunting buffalo one day, two young men encounter a beautiful mysterious young woman. She asks for the people to gather at an altar, where she brings a pipe from the Great Spirit to join all the people together in love and peace as the smoke sends prayers up to the Great Spirit. Then the woman becomes a white buffalo calf who joins the herd of buffalo that surround them. Red stone, traditionally from the people drowned in the flood, is uncovered by the traveling buffalo and used to make the traditional pipes used for the prayers. Characters are pictured in the clothing of the 19th century and set on the plains. There is a mythic look to the static double-page scenes, which resemble Lakota paintings. The author adds a summary of the legend, the sources, and information about the pipestone quarry and the meaning of the parts of the pipe.

Goble, Paul. *Storm Maker's Tipi.* New York: Richard Jackson/Atheneum/Simon & Schuster, 2001. 34pp. Grades K–3.

Before the story begins, we are taken back to when the Great Spirit made the first man and woman. He tells his helper Napi to look after their needs. For shelter, Napi gathers the materials and teaches them how to pitch their tipi and direct it to catch the first rays of sun. Detailed drawings and instructions are given on how to make and pitch one. Then the tale of the hunter Sacred Otter and his son Morning Plume begins. After Morning Plume has killed his first buffalo, Storm Maker brings a blizzard upon them.

Covered by a skin, Sacred Otter dreams that he encounters Storm Maker, who shows him how to make a tipi that will be safe from storms. Thus Sacred Otter can teach his people how to survive storms in the future. Very small black and white drawings describing the making of a tipi contrast with pencil overdrawn with pen and India ink and painted with watercolor and gouache images that tell the snowy tale. The scenes of massed running bison and galloping horses vitalize the narrative. The end-papers are from Blackfoot tipi covers; there is also an informative introduction with photographs.

Goldin, Barbara Diamond. *Coyote and the Fire Stick: A Northwest Indian Tale.* Illustrated by Will Hillenbrand. San Francisco: Gulliver/Harcourt Brace, 1996. 40pp. Grades 1–4.

This traditional tale begins before people had fire. They ask Coyote how they can get it from the three evil spirits on the top of the mountain. His plan has a role for each animal in a line from the mountaintop to the village. Coyote steals a stick with fire and passes it in turn from one animal to another as the evil spirits chase them. The fire ends up inside a tree. Then Coyote shows the people how to rub dry sticks to make sparks for fire. The lively telling has many added details depicted with verve in a seriocomic style that creates real characters, whether spirit, animal, or even tree. Double-page mixed media scenes vivified by brushed black outlines tell an even more animated tale than the text. Both author and illustrator have added notes about their work. Compare with another version of this story by London below, *Fire Race.*

Haley, Gail E. *Two Bad Boys: A Very Old Cherokee Tale.* New York: Dutton/Penguin, 1996. 32pp. Also Puffin paper. Grades 1–4.

Boy has always listened to First Hunter Kanati and Corn Mother Selu, until he meets a boy who claims to be his wild brother. Happy to have company, he does not tell his parents. When they finally meet the other boy, they cannot tame him. He leads Boy into all kinds of mischief. When the boys find out where Kenati gets his meat, they release all the animals he has kept there. Now people will have to track and hunt for meat. When the boys follow Selu to see where her corn comes from, they make her lose her source; henceforth they must plant and grow their food. So all people's work since "was caused by those two bad boys." Melodrama unfolds in fancy-bordered gouache scenes that emphasize movements in swirls of steam, twisted strands of hair, and bold body gestures. Stylization contributes to the mythic presentation.

Hall, Amanda. *The Stolen Sun: A Story of Native Alaska.* Grand Rapids, MI: Eerdman's, 2002. 32pp. Grades 1–4.

When the people Raven had placed on earth begin to argue and rage, he hides the sun and vows never to return, leaving behind one small feather. When a woman swallows this feather, she gives birth to a child named Little Darkness, who grows wings, flies up to Raven, and finds the sun. Aided by Raven, he then brings the light back to earth. The visual story, which parallels the brief mythic telling of this folktale, is produced in tones of blue and purple across double pages. Details of landscapes, a few animals, some costume, and starry skies set Little Darkness's adventures in an eerie light, adding emotional impact to the melodramatic events. The gradual evolution from the dark hues to the final rosy sky conveys hope for a brighter future. This makes an interesting comparison with McDermott's *Raven* and other tales of stolen light.

Harrell, Beatrice Orcutt. *How Thunder and Lightning Came to Be: A Choctaw Legend.* Illustrated by Susan Roth. New York: Dial/Penguin, 1995. 32pp. Grades 1–3.

In this tale the author heard from her family, the busy Great Sun asks two silly birds to devise a way to warn the Choctaw when a storm is coming. Big, slow-moving Heloha and her swift but clumsy husband Melatha try various ways with humorous results. Finally, when Heloha lays her eggs in the clouds, they roll away, and Melatha zips around, setting off sparks, trying to catch them. The thunder and lightening they produce are the signs the Great Father is pleased with to announce the wind and rain he sends. According to legend, the foolish birds are still trying to find the warning as they continue to lay eggs and chase them around the sky. This entertaining story includes information on the Choctaw Green Corn Dance along with the humor. Complex collages pick up the vitality of the narrative, with inventive use of all sorts of papers, sometimes depicting nature clearly and sometimes creating suggestive abstract settings. The "great, silly birds" are a special delight.

Hausman, Gerald. *The Story of Blue Elk.* Illustrated by Kristina Rodanas. New York: Clarion/Houghton, 1998. 32pp. Grades 1–4.

A boy born in a Pueblo village cannot make a sound. On the same day, a great elk enters the village and seems to ask to see the baby. It stamps twelve times and leaves. When the boy, called Blue Elk, is twelve, the great elk reappears, spends time with Blue Elk, then says he must leave but Blue Elk must plant his antlers. The elk is killed by a hunter; Blue Elk plants his antlers.

They grow twined around a red cedar tree. Blue Elk understands from a dream that he must cut a flute from the cedar. With it he can speak with music for all to listen, "a gift of power from the great elk." Scenes of Pueblo life created with oil-based color pencil on watercolor wash include portraits of Blue Elk and naturalistic representations of the other characters. Landscapes include scenes of the tranquil life style and Pueblo houses. The overall tone is spiritual and as silent as the mute boy is until he makes his flute. A double-page scene of his playing while birds circle with open wings creating arabesques is the most emotional of the narrative. The author adds a note on the sources and versions of the story.

Hobbs, Will. *Beardream*. Illustrated by Jill Kastner. New York: Atheneum, 1997. 32pp. Grades 1–3.

One spring, when the Great Bear is still dreaming in his den, a young boy named Short Tale climbs the mountain to find him. In a dream, the boy locates and wakes him. To thank him, the Great Bear takes him in the dream to see the bears dance the end of winter and tells him to go back and show his people how to do the dance. As the people dance, the boy seems to see the bear watching approvingly. The unity of boy and bear is depicted in a painterly double portrait on the jacket. Oil paints are used somewhat impressionistically in double-page scenes that depict the forest and episodes by moon or campfire light. The tale of religious mystery is based on the Ute Beardance.

Lewis, Paul Owen. *Frog Girl*. Hillsboro, OR: Beyond Words, 1997. 34pp. Grades K–4.

The youngest daughter of a village chief is surprised when a frog speaks to her. The frog takes her under the lake, becomes a young woman, and leads the girl to her old grandmother, who asks her where all her frog children are. The girl remembers seeing boys with nets at the lake. The young frog/woman tells her that she must return home to find them. There she finds an erupting volcano has set a fire that will destroy her village. No one seems to be there except for a box of the frogs. She runs to set them free in the lake so that they can go back to their grieving grandmother. As the girl returns to the village, rain puts out the fires; her people come back in canoes. She reminds them that the frogs are their sisters and brothers and should be treated as such. The end-papers set the stage with a scene of the tops of totem poles in front of a snow-capped mountain and a forest. The illustrations are intense in design and use of color; realistic in details of forest and clothing and of the village houses and carvings. The interior of the grandmother's house makes a very impressive double page. The original story is based on native story elements. There are copious notes on the relationship of this story to mythological themes and on the motifs seen in the illustrations.

Lewis, Paul Owen. *Storm Boy.* Hillsboro, OR: Beyond Words, 1995. 34pp. Also Tricycle paper, 2003. Grades K–4.

When the chief's son is caught in a storm and washed ashore, he finds himself in a strange village where everything is very large. He is welcomed to a feast in the chief's house, where he joins the dances and teaches them some from his people. But he misses his home and family. The chief tells him how he can get home. With his eyes closed, he is carried back to the beach near his village. Strangely, he has been missing for a year and presumed lost. Everyone celebrates his return as he tells his strange tale. Illustrated in the same manner as *Frog Girl* above, it also has an underwater adventure and return. The pictures of costume and carvings on walls and totem poles are based on existing examples. Visually melodramatic, with figures in masks, fire-lit dances, a ride on a whale's back, and a bird's-eye view of his village at night, the tale has a powerfully mystic impact. The role of the whales is implied rather than stated. Extensive notes are like those in *Frog Girl.*

London, Jonathan, with Larry Pinola. *Fire Race: A Karuk Coyote Tale about How Fire Came to the People.* Illustrated by Sylvia Long. San Francisco: Chronicle, 1993. 40pp. Also paper, 1997. Grades 1–5.

Wise Old Coyote devises a plan to steal fire from the Yellow Jacket sisters for the cold and miserable animal people. When he tricks the sisters and runs away with the fire, they are in close pursuit. As planned, each animal in turn picks up the fire as the other flags: eagle, mountain lion, fox, bear, worm, turtle, and finally frog, who swallows it until the Yellow Jackets tire of waiting for him to give it back. When frog spits the remaining hot coal into the willow, which swallows it, the animals fear all is lost, until Coyote shows them how to coax fire from the willow sticks over dry moss. Then they have fire when they need it. In addition to the simply but excitingly told story, there is an after word about stories and storytelling in his tribe by Karuk Julian Lang and a useful bibliography. The double-page lively ink and watercolors first realistically depict the northern California landscape with the shivering animals. Later pictures show the adventures in detailed close-ups and several multiple images. The text is integrated in panels at the tops or bottoms of the pages, separated with linear borders that are displayed on the end-papers, on Coyote's cap, and on objects in the Yellow Jackets' house. Compare this with Goldin's version of the tale above.

McDermott, Gerald. *Raven: A Trickster Tale from the Pacific Northwest.* San Francisco: Harcourt Brace, 1993. 32pp. Also Voyager paper, 2001. Grades K–4.

Raven, the cultural hero of many moods and powers, here searches for light for the men and women of the world who live in darkness. He finds it at Sky Chief's house. Raven transforms himself into Sky Chief's grandchild, tricks the chief into giving him the ball of the sun to play with, then turns back into Raven to bring it to the people. Notes on Raven as a character and an art motif draw connections among the many stories in which he occurs. On large double pages with mixed media, McDermott begins with a misty dark landscape and concludes with a bright one illuminated by the liberated sun. Classical decorative forms, clean-cut shapes such as those in brilliant reds and greens on Raven's body, more muted in the wood carvings and clothing of the Sky Chief's family, all are set against solid color backgrounds. The illustrations have great eye appeal as they project the quality of such art forms in the life of the people of the Pacific Northwest.

McLerran, Alice. *The Ghost Dance.* Illustrated by Paul Morin. New York: Clarion/Houghton, 1995. 32pp. Grades 2–4.

Rather than retelling a legend, the author is evoking in emotional and poetic cadence first the beauty of the life of the People, then the blight after the arrival of the Europeans, and finally the voice of the prophet Tavibo, who first preached the dancing of the Ghost Dance. Belief in this magical dance, which was supposed to vanquish the white invaders, swept through Native Americans at the end of the 19th century. Of course it was not successful. The author concludes on a hopeful note: that all people will join in a dance of harmony with nature. From the end-papers, scumbled pitch-dark hues with mysterious shapes, we move on to a photograph of a steer's skull on the title page. Morin uses both paints and photographs of objects to make the succinct text come alive.

Murphy, Claire Rudolf. *Caribou Girl.* Illustrated by Linda Russell. Boulder, CO: Roberts Rinehart, 1998. 32pp. Also published in Inuit and Inupiak. Grades K–4.

This original story is based on some myths of the Inupiak and resembles other transformation tales of the Inuit. "Long ago in the far north" the caribou herd that the people hunted has disappeared. A young girl named Caribou Girl decides to seek help from Tatqiq, the Moon Man, while wearing an amulet that had belonged to her shaman great-grandmother. The Chief of the Caribou offers to carry her on his back to Tatqiq, who tells her she must live with the caribou to find out why they have gone away. With the help of her great-grandmother's spirit, she survives and then becomes a girl again as the herd returns to the people. Painted illustrations fill the long double pages with mystical images. The pictures flow in sweeps of colors, yellows, greens, purples, on which naturalistic animals and people interact. There is a dream-like quality to the visual narrative, which intermixes symbols with natural history. Notes add facts along with mythic background.

Nelson, S. D. *Gift Horse: A Lakota Story*. New York: Harry N. Abrams, 1999. 32pp. Grades 1–4.

A Lakota warrior recalls when he was young and his father brought him as a gift a special horse, "the horse for a boy who is becoming a man." He names the horse Storm, decorates her, and rides her so fast that he is called Flying Cloud. Once when lost in a snowstorm, the horse brings him safely home. His mother feels it is time to make his Warrior Shirt, for which he must collect quills. Next, he goes to the sweat lodge, then off on his Vision Quest, and joins the buffalo hunt. He not only shoots a buffalo but also saves a fellow-rider. His last task is to fight a battle. Successful in battle, he is given the shirt of a Lakota warrior. On it his mother and sister have quilled the image of the Gift Horse, his faithful companion. Nelson uses his own "contemporary interpretation of traditional Lakota art" from drawings in old ledger books here and in his other illustrations (see Bruchac, above, and the next entry.) They combine some naturalistic representation with stylization adding mythic qualities. There are full notes on the background of the story.

Nelson, S. D. *The Star People: A Lakota Story*. New York: Harry N. Abrams, 2003. 34pp. Grades K–4.

Sister Girl and her younger brother Young Wolf have wandered away from their village, watching the shapes of people in the clouds. They even think they see their beloved grandmother, who died in the spring. Suddenly, a thunderstorm surprises them. It is followed by a fire started by the lightening. Just before the flames catch up to them, they find a stream to immerse themselves in. But after the fire, they find that they are lost in the dark. From the stars, their grandmother seems to take and embrace them. She then sees them safely home. Nelson's visual narrative, using the same interpretation of the traditional Lakota ledger-book art that he has in his other books, depicts the fire in swirling acrylic yellows and reds that contrast with the star-dotted deep blue of the subsequent night sky. The dream sequences with animals and grandmother maintain the mythic atmosphere. His notes add information on his sources and art.

Oliveiro, Jamie. *The Day the Sun Was Stolen*. Illustrated by Sharon Hitchcock. New York: Hyperion, 1995. 32pp. Grades 1–3.

In this story from Haida folklore, it is Bear, bothered by the heat in his heavy coat, that has stolen and hidden Sun. A boy decides to trick Bear into letting Sun go. He disguises himself as a fish to be carried back to Bear's cave. He then shaves Bear's fur off so Bear feels the need for Sun's warmth and releases it. This also explains why some animals grow thicker coats in winter while others hibernate. The text is set along the bottom fifth of each page. The illustrations are produced in flat, untextured gouache and acrylic within thin black lines. The stylizations are derived from the Haida style of encapsulating forms within forms as seen in the totems on the end-papers and in the borders on each page.

Orie, Sandra De Coteau. *Did You Hear the Wind Sing Your Name? An Oneida Song of Spring*. Illustrated by Chris Canyon. New York: Walker, 1995. 32pp. Also paper. Grades K–3.

The author asks a series of poetic questions about the changes in nature from morning to night. A note details the symbols important to the Oneida along with the signs of spring in the simple text. Each question of the text gets a bordered double-page scene. Canyon renders birds, animals, and flowers in naturalistic fashion set in an appropriate landscape but a bit frozen. The illustrations are attractive in a hard-edged way, answering the questions as poetically as posed.

Rosen, Michael. *Crow and Hawk: A Traditional Pueblo Indian Tale*. Illustrated by John Clementson. San Diego, CA: Harcourt Brace, 1995. 32pp. Grades 1–3.

Crow gets tired of sitting on her eggs and flies away. Hawk takes over. When the eggs hatch, she feeds and cares for the baby crows. Crow comes back and wants her little ones, but Hawk refuses to give them up. They go to the King of the Birds to settle the dispute. He asks the babies, who say that Hawk has been their mother. Crow left them, and so has lost them. The cut-paper illustrations won't stay still on the pages. Hyperactive borders, decorated spaces for the text, and scenes with multiple images all imply motion. The tone is set by the rich blue end-papers with gyrating black birds.

Sabuda, Robert. *The Blizzard's Robe.* New York: Atheneum/Simon & Schuster, 1999. 32pp. Grades K–3.

This original tale depicting the origin of the Northern Lights is set "far to the north by the great Arctic Sea." It is told about the so-called "People Who Fear the Winter Night," because they are so afraid of Blizzard, the destructive force that comes during the long period of winter darkness. Here a young girl named Teune makes the finest of robes. One night Blizzard's robe is burned by the fire from Teune's *yaranga.* The people are happy, but she feels sorry for him. She works with difficulty to make him a magnificent new robe. The village leader orders it destroyed. But Blizzard comes to take it and sends as his promised gift the beauty of Northern Lights. Batik pictures flood the double-page scenes with multiple layers of color: dark blues of the Arctic night, reds and yellows of the people's fires that burn bright against them. Shapes of habitations and people tend to meld with the settings. But Blizzard's new cloak is brilliantly displayed with its large and handsome symbols, mask-like images. No references are given for the derivation of the symbols nor the exact location of the story.

San Souci, Robert. *Two Bear Cubs: A Miwok Legend from California's Yosemite Valley.* Illustrated by Daniel San Souci. Yosemite National Park, CA: Yosemite Association, 1997. 32pp. Grades K–3.

Two bear cubs take a nap one day on a flat rock. While they are sleeping, the rock rises to a great height. Their worried mother asks many other animals about them, but no one has seen them. They all offer to help, however. The Red-Tailed Hawk tells them where the cubs are, but none of the animals can climb the steep mountain. Tiny Measuring Worm offers to try. After days, he finally reaches the cubs and leads them down. The raised rock, named after the brave Measuring Worm, is now called "El Capitan." Full-page watercolor paintings reflect the Miwok belief in the ancient "animal people" by depicting anthropomorphic animals in the clothing and ornaments of that time. The settings are scenes of Yosemite. Vignettes on the text pages add informative events to the appealing visual narrative. There is a wealth of additional information on sources, the legend, and the Miwok people, with words from the Miwok language in the text as well.

Shaw-MacKinnon, Margaret. *Tiktala*. Illustrated by László Gál. Toronto: Stoddart, 1996. 32pp. Grades 1–4.

Tiktala bravely offers to go on a journey to find her spirit at a time when her village elders fear that their soapstone carvings no longer have the spirit of the animals. She wishes to be able to carve a harp seal; in this original tale she magically becomes a seal. When she returns as a girl the many emotional experiences she has had enable her to carve a seal that can bring back her father's lost belief. Double-page scenes are naturalistic but in shades of blues and greens that enhance the spirituality of the story. The typical Arctic landscapes and seascapes dominate, providing dramatic environments for the few animal and human characters, all appropriately dressed.

Taylor, Harriet Peck. *Brother Wolf: A Seneca Tale*. New York: Farrar, Straus, 1996. 26pp. Grades K–3.

After an argument with Wolf, Raccoon plasters mud over Wolf's eyes while he sleeps. When Wolf wakes up, he begs the birds to peck off the mud, promising them a reward. But first he must pay back Raccoon. Finding him asleep in a hollow log, Wolf rolls him down the hill. Then in answer to their request, he paints the previously dull-colored birds all the beautiful colors they have today. He even paints the black rings around Raccoon's tail, making him so happy that he promises never to tease Wolf again. The light-hearted text is paralleled in the simplified, white-outlined animals in the double-page batik illustrations. The colors are bright; the birds painted by Wolf are much closer to anatomical correctness than the animals. There are notes on sources, on the Seneca, and on the traits of the animals.

Taylor, Harriet Peck. *Coyote and the Laughing Butterflies*. New York: Macmillan, 1995. 26pp. Grades K–3.

Coyote is tricked by the butterflies in this story based on a Tewa legend. On his way to fetch some salt, he takes a nap and the butterflies take him home again. His wife is angry, but he promises to go the next day. Again he falls asleep, and the butterflies take him home. On the third day, he finally gets the salt. The butterflies take pity on him and fly both him and the salt home, to his wife's delight. Taylor uses the batik technique here as in her other books for illustrations outlined in white. Coyote and the other characters are placed here on the butte-filled landscape.

Taylor, Harriet Peck. *Coyote Places the Stars.* New York: Bradbury, 1993. 27pp.
Also Aladdin paper, 1997. Grades PreS–3.

Coyote manages to reach the moon in search of the secrets of the heavens. He finds that he can rearrange the stars by shooting them with his arrows. He sets them there to form the shapes of himself, his animal and bird friends. Then he makes a Big Road with the leftover stars and returns to earth. With his howling call, he assembles the creatures to admire his handiwork in the heavens. They celebrate, as should we as we gaze at them. Batik pictures outlining objects in white exploit the colors of the desert landscape. Coyote's actions are a reasonable prelude to the parade and assembly of the animals on land and in the sky. Sources of the tale are given.

Taylor, Harriet Peck. *Secrets of the Stone.* New York: Farrar, Straus, 2000. 32pp.
Grades K–3.

Taylor fashions a story of Coyote and Badger chasing Jackrabbit, bringing them to a cave where there are traditional paintings done by the inhabitants of the old Southwest. Other animals join them there, finding representations of themselves. When they fall asleep, Coyote encounters in his dream spirits dancing to the traditional flute player, just like the figures depicted in the caves. Taylor's typical batik illustrations here tend toward the decorative. Natural objects in the landscape are symbolic, while the pictographs in the cave suggest some that exist. Traditional designs run down the sides of the text pages. There are notes on petroglyphs, pictographs, and cults of the Southwest.

Taylor, Harriet Peck. *Ulaq and the Northern Lights.* New York: Farrar, Straus, 1998. 32pp. Grades K–3.

Ulaq, a very curious fox, wonders about the strange ribbons of light that pulse across the dark winter sky. He sets out to discover what they are. Each animal he meets has a different explanation relating to his own life. But Ulaq cannot accept any of them. Rabbit persuades him to join the other rabbits to celebrate their belief, that the lights mark the return of the magic Sky Rabbit heralding the end of winter. Ulaq finally climbs on Owl's back when he promises to show him the northern lights. Ulaq flies up to them, wishing he could touch them. All too soon he is back on the ground with the sun rising. He decides that "maybe the northern lights were put there simply for everyone to enjoy, to light up the long dark night with their magic and beauty." The author notes the sources from which she has spun her story. Taylor's usual batik illustrations here are of soft snowy landscapes, icebergs, animals with just enough naturalism, and with the northern lights represented with different swirling colors in a smooth black sky.

Taylor, Harriet Peck. *When Bear Stole the Chinook: A Siksika Tale.* New York: Farrar, Straus, 1997. 32pp. Grades K–3.

One winter long ago, it seemed as if the warm wind called the chinook would never blow. A poor young orphan boy asks his animal friends where the chinook is. When the magpie reports that a huge Bear has taken the chinook to keep him warm, the boy and his friends set bravely out into the snow and cold to find him. Together they manage to snatch the chinook from the Bear's den and release it. Then they must outrun Bear to escape down the mountain. The warm wind brings the blue sky and the end of winter to the happy people. And since then, unable to endure the cold, bears stay in their dens and sleep all winter. Taylor's batiks are decorative here, with landscape in pastel colors and intriguing patterns on native robes and teepees. Sources and background are explained.

Van Laan, Nancy. *Shingebiss: An Ojibwe Legend.* Illustrated by Betsy Bowen. Boston: Houghton Mifflin, 1997. 32pp. Also paper, 2002. Grades K–4.

In the "way-back time," Shingebiss the small merganser duck has always managed to find fish in Lake Superior for food. But one bitter winter, when the lake freezes over, Shingebiss challenges the Winter Maker, managing to get food despite the storms, ice, and snow. This infuriates the Winter Maker, who enters Shingebiss's lodge, preparing to finish him. Instead, he begins to melt and must go out to regain his strength. When spring arrives and he must return to the far north, he declares Shingebiss to be "a very singular being." He promises to leave him alone in the future, and he has. Told in an oral history storyteller style, the text is sprinkled with native words and expressions, explained in the glossary. Colored wood block prints tell the story melodramatically, symbolically rather than realistically. The Winter Maker in particular, with his mask, string-like body, and blue twisted ribbons of cold is chillingly effective. Our duck hero is portrayed with appealing strength. The use of different colored pages adds to the attractiveness. An introduction includes information on the Ojibwe and their beliefs. The illustrator explains her printing process and additions in detail, including colored pencils and basket borders.

Vidal, César. *Gray Feather and the Big Dog: A Legend of the Plains Indians.* Columbus, OH: Peter Bedrick/McGraw Hill, 2002. 32pp. Grades 1–4.

Gray Feather's tribe cannot keep up with the buffalo they need for food and clothing before winter arrives. The animals are moving quickly in their search for food in a time of drought. In desperation, Gray Feather seeks help from the Great Spirit. The answer is in the form of the promise of a strange animal with wonderful qualities. These "big dogs" are the horses that enable them to hunt successfully. The people are eternally grateful for this gift. The visual narrative is expressionistic in its depiction of multicolored swirling clouds that fill the sky and eventually become the horses. The canyons in the landscape look like rugged building blocks, formidable land for Gray Feather to cross. The clothing is appropriate for the time.

Wargin, Kathy-Jo. *The Legend of Leelanau.* Illustrated by Gijsbert van Frankenhuyzen. Chelsea, MI: Sleeping Bear, 2003. 48pp. Grades K–4.

A county on Lake Michigan is named for the main character, a young girl who loves the woods and nature. In this Ojibwe legend, the Native Americans fear the fairies who live in the Spirit Wood, but Leelanau enjoys playing with the Pukwudjininees. Her parents, wanting her to grow up, arrange her marriage, but on her wedding day, she goes off into the forest to be a child forever. This mystical tale, perhaps with psychological undertones about adolescence, is visualized in a rather naturalistic series of scenes heavy with dark forest greens and contrasting bright fairy yellows. With her parents, Leelanau is an introspective child, but in the forest, she is a freely dancing spirit. The visual contrast in the textured paintings helps predict her eventual flight from impending adulthood. There is a useful map and additional background on the legend.

Wisniewski, David. *The Wave of the Sea-Wolf.* New York: Clarion/Houghton, 1994. Also paper. Grades 2–6.

Tlingit culture and mythology underlie this lengthy, original story. A Tlingit princess, Kehokeen, has a vision of Gonakadet, the sea-wolf spirit, at a bay with sudden, dangerous waves. After her experience with a wave, she can predict them and save lives. She also has the spirit help her people when European explorers threaten them. Wisniewski's intricate paper-cut illustrations create complex and emotionally charged scenes across double pages as he incorporates Tlingit artifacts and landscapes. The scene of a ferocious tidal wave is particularly striking. Extensive notes put the tale into mythological and historical context.

Wood, Audrey. *The Rainbow Bridge*. Illustrated by Robert Florczak. San Diego, CA: Harcourt Brace, 1995. 32pp. Also Voyager paper, 2000. Grades 1–4.

The Chumash of the southern California coast inspired Wood's retelling of this legend, which she notes is still very much alive. She has expanded it and added characters, making it more vivid. The tale recounts the creation of the Chumash by the Earth Goddess and their growth until they have over-crowded their island home. The goddess tells them that half of them must leave the island for the mainland. A magic rainbow bridge appears, but as they cross, some look down and fall into the sea. The goddess turns them into dolphins. A girl, whose friend has fallen, joins him in the sea, for "the dolphins of the sea are brothers and sisters of their tribe." Romantic, lush oil paintings portray naturalistic anatomy, with human figures set against smooth, almost airbrushed skies. The illustrations, in frames, include lots of dramatic action, almost overshadowing the brief, simple text.

Wood, Douglas. *The Windigo's Return: A North Woods Story*. Illustrated by Greg Couch. New York: Simon & Schuster, 1996. 32pp. Grades 1–3.

The legendary Windigo is a terrible creature, made of stone so he cannot be wounded, who eats people and can change shape. In this version of the tale told by many groups, it is young Morning Star who thinks of trapping the Windigo. As he is burned, he promises to eat people forever. A cycle of seasons goes by before early summer brings the return of his ashes as mos-quitoes. Double and single-page paintings enhance a mysterious mood, de-picting people and settings merging together, illuminated by dim campfires and night skies. The Windigo is portrayed as a frightening creature of the imagination while the people display humanity.

Yolen, Jane. *Sky Dogs*. Illustrated by Barry Moser. San Diego, CA: Harcourt Brace, 1990. 32pp. Also Voyager paper, 1995. Grade 1–4.

Drawing on several stories and legends of the Blackfeet people as de-scribed in her notes, Yolen has constructed a story as told by an old man. Ex-plaining why he is called He-Who-Loves-Horses, he tells of long ago, when his people had to walk everywhere. When they first saw horses, they called them Sky Dogs, gifts from the Blackfeet creator figure, the Old Man. A woman who came with the horses married the father of the old narrator, and taught him how to care for these new creatures. Transparent watercolors il-lustrate the action on double pages that depict the vast plains under a re-lentless sun. Oval-framed portraits and rectangular-shaped illustrations are saturated with browns and yellows. Realistic pictures showing blades of grass and the curly texture of a fur hat are also visions of a vanished people as conceived by a skillful and sensitive artist.

NATIVE AMERICAN LIFE TODAY AND IN THE RECENT PAST

Bouchard, David. *The Song within My Heart*. Illustrated by Allen Sapp. Vancouver, British Columbia: Raincoast, 2003. 32pp. Grades 1–4.

The artist's impressionistic paintings inspired the text, which in brief blank verses with occasional rhyme tells of childhood memories of the Cree reservation, the beloved grandmother, the pow-wow. The repeated "boom" of the drum and the "Hey hey hey hey Hi hey hey hey" make for continuity and background. The paintings are informative as they describe the various pow-wows and the grandmother going about her mundane activities like making bannock, feeding the chickens, or telling her stories. The painter adds a note about his personal background and his relationship with his grandmother, including black-and-white photographs.

Bruchac, Joseph. *A Boy Called Slow: The True Story of Sitting Bull*. Illustrated by Rocco Braviera. New York: Philomel, 1995. 32pp. Grades 2–5.

The author recreates the childhood of the boy called Slow, who tries to be "both brave and wise." When he is fourteen, Slow fights his first battle and is a hero. Finally, he earns his new name, Sitting Bull, from his father. Shadowy darkness is maintained in most of the textured acrylic paintings. Landscapes are simplified, herds of bison hinted, warriors on horseback blend into the night sky, producing emotional intensity.

Cumming, Peter. *Out on the Ice in the Middle of the Bay*. Illustrated by Alice Priestly. Richmond Hill, Ontario: Annick/Firefly, 1993. 32pp. Grades K–4.

Leah lives where ice and snow cover the land by November. One day as the sun is setting, while her mother is away and her father naps, Leah goes exploring. On the other side of the iceberg in the bay, while his mother sleeps, Baby Nanook polar bear also goes exploring. While her father and his mother wake and begin frantically searching, girl and polar bear meet at the iceberg and, amazingly, cuddle together. Then his mother and her father meet; luckily both paw and gun miss their targets. Reunited with their children, the parents back away from confrontation. Leah goes happily home to end this simple tale of wonder written by a resident of Canada's eastern Arctic. Colored pencils create a visual tone poem, a blurry reaffirmation of the innocence of all nature's young. Scenes are lit by the sky-blue pinks of the near-polar North. The people are properly in parkas, the landscape is suitably vast, and the iceberg handsomely sculptured.

Dupre, Kelly. *The Raven's Gift: A True Story from Greenland*. Boston: Houghton Mifflin, 2001. 32pp. Grades K–4.

The author describes the difficult, 3,200 mile, fifteen-month journey made by her husband and a companion to and around the coast of Greenland. Most impressive is his encounter with a raven whose foot is badly entangled. Although tired and depressed by the difficulty of his travels, he takes strength from the raven as he sets it free. After varied experiences with the Inuit, traveling by both kayak and dogsled, the journey ends. Throughout the succinct but exciting tale, there are small sidebars with additional factual information on Greenland and its inhabitants. Naive linoleum block prints with touches of watercolor suggest the rugged life. Landscapes have symbolic mountains; the sea is full of broken bits of icebergs. The sequence of scenes with the raven helps keep the story more personal than the distant pictures of the kayak's watery adventures. The almost crudely drawn images convey clearly the deep cold and icy land, uninviting for all but the most adventurous.

Edwardson, Debby Dahl. *Whale Snow*. Illustrated by Annie Patterson. Watertown, MA: Tailwinds/Charlesbridge, 2003. 32pp. Grades K–4.

When Amiqqaq's father and his whaling crew return, it is time to go through the snow and ice to where the bowhead whale's body is, to prepare for the big feast that celebrates the capture. The tradition of the Iñupiaq culture involves the whales allowing themselves to be taken to reward the worthy crews in a spiritual relationship. Amiqqaq asks about the "spirit-of-the-whale" but finally realizes that it is all around them. It may go back to the sea, but they will "still have happiness." Double-page watercolors emphasize the spirituality of the event, ignoring the factual cutting up and rendering of the whale. The story is projected by a young boy who listens to the traditional accounts and asks the questions about the whale's spirit. The naturalistic illustrations display the snowy village and vast white landscape as well as the villagers in their white parkas. There is a glossary along with notes on the Iñupiaq language, history, and their continued interaction and connection with the whales.

Hoyt-Goldsmith, Diane. *Apache Rodeo*. Illustrated by Lawrence Migdale. New York: Holiday House, 1995. 32pp. Grades 3–6.

Felecita is a ten-year-old Apache living on a reservation today. She tells about life there and some history of her people. The focus of her story is the annual rodeo, the preparations and the events. There are many lengthy caption notes throughout on the people, customs, and daily life, including recipes. Clear color photographs, two or more to a page, show the people and actions described in the text.

Hoyt-Goldsmith, Diane. *Potlatch: A Tsimshian Celebration*. Illustrated by Lawrence Migdale. New York: Holiday House, 1997. 32pp. Grades 3–6.

Young David invites us to his father's boyhood home in Metlakatla, Alaska, for a potlatch "to honor our heritage and celebrate our traditions." After filling us in on the history of the Tsimshians, he details the tradition of the potlatch. Having faded with the arrival of the Europeans, the potlatch was revived by David's father. The one they are preparing for will honor his great-grandfather Albert. We follow the planning of the feast, the raising of the poles, the dedications, the dances, and the gifts, in this revival of culture and tradition. Clear color photographs illuminate all the stages and events relating to the ceremonies. We see the creation of the crafts and the rehearsals of the performances along with the landscape and contemporary dwellings. The collection of informative photographs helps in understanding more about the Northwest Coast peoples. A glossary is included.

Hunter, Sara Hoagland. *The Unbreakable Code*. Illustrated by Julia Miner. Flagstaff, AZ: Northland, 1996. 32pp. Grades 1–4.

When young John doesn't want to leave his grandfather and move to Minnesota, Grandfather reassures him in Navajo by telling him about his earlier life. He had to go away to school and speak only English there. He ran away and enlisted in the army in World War II with other Navajos. They were needed to devise a code that the Japanese couldn't break. The key to their success was the Navajo language they had been told to forget. Grandfather believes that he was kept safe by the medicine man's corn pollen in his wallet. He gives the wallet to John who now feels confident enough to leave. Oil paintings, mainly full page, illustrate the dramatic episodes literally without needless detail. The original code is included at the end.

Joosse, Barbara M. *Mama, Do You Love Me?* Illustrated by Barbara Lavallee. San Francisco: Chronicle, 1991. Grades K–3.

In answer to the universal question asked in the title and those that follow, Mama uses the world of nature around and the traditional objects of an Arctic home to reassure her child that her love is there "forever and always," no matter what the questioner might do or turn into. The questions and answers are simple and rhythmically reassuring. Visualizing the loving relationship with hugs and other appropriate gestures, the artist creates mother and daughter figures who, page after page, keep changing costumes. They are mainly set against a bare white background that shows off the dress patterns and the fancifully pictured animals of the verbal game. Watercolors and colored pencils create engaging personalities as well as providing local details of outdoor gear, sealskin boat, sled, and a series of circular masks based on traditional models, including four large ones on the end-papers. As an added bonus, there are two pages of information on the Inuit and the items and creatures in the story.

Kroll, Virginia. *The Seasons and Someone.* Illustrated by Tatsuro Kiuchi. San Diego, CA: Harcourt Brace, 1994. 32pp. Grades K–3.

This poetically written story evokes the mood of the changes of seasons in the far North through the eyes of a young girl called "Someone" because it is bad luck to speak one's own name. We see the family life as well as the animals, birds, and related surroundings throughout the year. Thickly applied oil paints in lively, lyrical vertical scenes emphasize the vastness of the landscape in snowy winter and verdantly green summer. Single pages enhance the intimacy in the snowbound interiors.

Kusugak, Michael Arvaarluk. *Baseball Bats for Christmas.* Illustrated by Vladyana Krykorka. Richmond Hill, Ontario: Annick, 1990. 24pp. Paper. Grades 2–5.

This may be autobiographical; the subject is a seven-year-old asthmatic boy named Arvaarluk living at Repulse Bay at Christmas in 1955. To that barren place an airplane has brought six strange-looking "stand-ups," which we recognize as Christmas trees, but which the local people have seen only in books. The Christmas tradition there is to give your favorite thing to your best friend. Arvaarluk receives a rubber ball. Everyone there loves to play ball, but bats in a treeless area are not readily available. Now, however, there is an obvious use for those "stand-ups." So the kids can play ball all year, until they get more baseball-bat trees next Christmas. Detailed watercolor-like scenes illuminate the various activities of the story. Several double-page paintings in particular establish the feeling of the northern environment.

Kusugak, Michael Arvaarluk. *Hide and Sneak*. Illustrated by Vladyana Krykorka. Richmond Hill, Ontario: Annick/Firefly, 1992. 32pp. Also paper. Grades 1–5.

In this contemporary story, Allashua meets a character from traditional tales when she plays hide-and-seek, a game at which she is not very good. Fortunately the Ijiraq she encounters who, her mother has warned her, may hide her so that no one will ever find her, is not very good at the game either. Allshua is frequently distracted by butterflies, fish, birds, and other animals. When the Ijiraq offers to hide her, she thinks her mother was wrong and goes to a cave with him. But then he won't let her out. Luckily she outstares the shy creature but still is lost. This is when she finds out what the strange stone man-like constructions seen in the landscape called *inuksugaqs* are for: to help you find your way home. The vital stone sculpture is pictured significantly in an early scene at the water's edge and on the cover. Watercolors create windswept cloudy skies and clear waters; mixed media detail the flowery fields, Allashua's family, and the mythical sprite. Each scene is bordered with a band of black rubbings of relevant objects. A few Inuit words are included but not translated.

Littlechild, George. *This Land Is My Land*. San Francisco: Children's Book Press, 1993. 32pp. Grades 3–6.

This Native American artist combines his paintings with single-page reflections on his life, his ancestors, his Plains Cree tribe, and how they are reflected in his art. The illustrations are painted in flat shapes with no concern for perspective. Shapes are grossly simplified, surfaces highly decorated. Sometimes photographs are integrated into the strong design.

Luen, Nancy. *Nessa's Fish*. Illustrated by Neil Waldman. New York: Atheneum, 1992. 32pp. Also Aladdin paper. Grades K–4.

In the Arctic of today, Nessa and her grandmother have caught fish for themselves and everyone in camp. But Grandmother becomes ill while they are fishing. Many animals come after the fish while grandmother rests during the long day. Remembering what her parents have taught her, Nessa protects herself and Grandmother along with the fish until rescued. Double pages are designed with a thin rectangle on the left edge and a large rectangle on the right page. The watercolor illustrations sweep from the left edge to the right, missing only the small section of the simple text, as if to emphasize the vastness of the Arctic ice fields, with undulating bands of pastel colors breaking out of thin black frames on left and right. Nessa and her family are dressed in parkas; the clouds and fish sequences are neatly arranged.

Smith, Cynthia Leitich. *Jingle Dancer.* Illustrated by Cornelius Van Wright and Ying-Hwa Hu. New York: Morrow, 2000. 32pp. Grades 1–4.

Jenna daydreams about the *tinks* made by the cone-shaped jingles on her grandmother's dress as she dances to the beat of the powwow drum. But Jenna needs four rows of jingles for her dress if it is to "sing" at the next powwow. Her Great-aunt Sis is happy to give her a row of jingles from the dress she doesn't dance in any more. Mrs. Scott gives her a row because she will be too busy to dance. Cousin Elizabeth can't make the powwow so she offers one row. Grandmother gives her the fourth row. Together they sew them on her dress. Jenna practices and finally fulfills her dream; she dances at the powwow as promised for all of them. Double-page naturalistic watercolors provide a detailed picture of Jenna's life and her relatives. The final four pictures are action shots of the charming heroine dancing in her beaded moccasins and jingle dress. Information is included on the Creek Nation, the folktale her grandmother tells, and details on the making of a jingle dress and the Jingle Dance. There is also a glossary.

Spalding, Andrea. *Solomon's Tree.* Illustrated by Janet Wilson and Victor Reece. Victoria, British Columbia: Orca, 2002. 32pp. Grades K–3.

Young Solomon is very upset when his beloved maple tree is uprooted in a storm. With the help of his uncle, a carver, he fashions a mask from the wood, beginning with a traditional song and dance. As they work, Solomon thinks of what he remembers about the tree. The finished mask brings hope of a "new beginning." Victor Reece, a Tsimpshian master carver, created the mask shown in a photograph at the end for the story, as well as the designs for the strips that run under the text. Details on the carving and the meaning of the designs are included. The naturalistic full-page oil paintings animate the story of a tradition that is still practiced. The pictures focus on each step from the cutting of the tree trunk to the final oiling as they show the boy's involvement.

Waterton, Betty. *A Salmon for Simon.* Illustrated by Ann Blades. Toronto: Groundwood/Douglas & McIntyre, 1996. 32pp. Also paper, 1998. Grades K–3.

Simon has been hoping all summer to catch "the king of the fishes" that his grandmother calls Sukai, but he hasn't caught any salmon at all. One day, as he is digging clams on the beach, an eagle drops a salmon it has been carrying right into the hole Simon has dug. The fish is still barely alive in the shallow water. Determined to save it, Simon works hard to dig a channel to the sea so the salmon can be free. Satisfied, Simon will not fish for salmon any more. Full-page watercolors simplify with enough details of beach, gulls, and Simon's gear to hold interest. The scene of the salmon leaping free against a scarlet sunset is a sentimental climax.

Watkins, Sherrin. *White Bead Ceremony.* Illustrated by Kim Doner. Tulsa, OK: Council Oak Books, 1996. 36pp. Also paper, 1997. Grades 1–3.

Mary Greyfeather is preparing for the White Bead Ceremony and her mother is trying to teach her Shawnee words, although Mary prefers playing with her Barbie dolls. The family is gathering for the traditional naming ceremony, when Mary will receive the necklace of white beads. There is a crisis when her aunt Laura, who is supposed to bring the necklace, has car trouble. Grandma saves the day with a makeshift necklace, as the family debates possible names and their meanings. "Wapa iyeshe" is selected; it means a white-necked moving horse. The naturalistic illustrations are a bit on the "cute" side. Transparent watercolors and ink line create almost sterile scenes of family activities. A brief history of the Shawnee and flash cards of Shawnee words are included.

Six

MULTICULTURAL AND CROSS-CULTURAL EXPERIENCES

Bernhard, Emery. *A Ride on Mother's Back: A Day of Baby Carrying Around the World*. Illustrated by Durga Bernhard. San Diego, CA: Harcourt Brace, 1996. 32pp. Grades K–3.

The universal theme of carrying baby takes us from early morning to evening in time while we travel from one two-page spread to the next, each in a different part of the world where another young child is being carried as the other folks go about their usual activities. Information on life in parts of South America, Africa, and Asia is given in the two paragraphs on each, along with climate and customs. Additional facts are provided in notes at the end, all to provoke curiosity, while the universal theme shows commonality. Full-page gouache paintings describe the activities in the text. Naturalistic but quite decorative, with an emphasis on flat patterns of vegetation and dress, the illustrations offer a generalized sense of place. A world map on the end-papers aids in location.

Dooley, Norah. *Everybody Cooks Rice*. Illustrated by Peter J. Thornton. Minneapolis: Carolrhoda/Lerner, 1991. 32pp. Also paper. Grades K–4.

Carrie's quest to round up her mooching brother for dinner takes her, in this wordy text, to the homes of families from Barbados, Puerto Rico, Vietnam, India, and Haiti. In each kitchen, native dishes with rice are being cooked and/or eaten, and Carrie samples them all. When she finally arrives home, where her mother is cooking a rice dish from northern Italy, her brother is there ready to eat more, but Carrie is full. Full-page illustrations show interiors and street scenes of an American suburb. Pastels create rather detailed scenes of middle-class Americans at routine tasks. Recipes for the mentioned dishes are an added plus. Note that this same team has also produced the similar *Everybody Bakes Bread*, *Everybody Brings Noodles*, and *Everybody Serves Soup*.

Fox, Mem. *Whoever You Are*. Illustrated by Leslie Staub. San Diego, CA: Harcourt Brace, 1997. 32pp. Also Voyager paper, 2001. Grades PreS–2.

Simple statements, with regular repetitions, are addressed to "little ones." It is reassuring to remind them that "there are little ones just like you all over the world." Despite differences of skin, homes, schools, even words, "their hearts are just like yours." So are their smiles, and their hurts, even when you are grown, "all over the world." Set in hand-carved frames, these unsophisticated oil paintings of people in different locales, wearing different clothes, engaged in different activities, still exemplify each aspect of the text. A quartet of youngsters carried by a mysterious man appears in several backgrounds, perhaps as a symbol of the unity of humanity.

Jackson, Ellen. *It's Back to School We Go! First Day Stories from Around the World*. Illustrated by Jan Davey Ellis. Brookfield, CT: Millbrook Press, 2003. 32pp. Grades 1–4.

A composite child from each of eleven countries describes a day at school in his or her country. On the other side of the double-page spread are additional facts about the country and its children. The places included are Kenya; Kazakhstan; Nunavut, Canada; Australia; Japan; China; Peru; Germany; India; Russia; and California in the U.S. This brief introduction, with the appropriate visuals, should provoke interest in further study. Detailed colored drawings start on the bottoms of the title pages, giving previews of the illustrations in the stories that follow. There are bits of architecture, clothing, typical activities, a few adults; all in lively scenes in and surrounding the text. A world map showing locations and a bibliography with Web sites add to the usefulness.

Katz, Karen. *The Colors of Us*. New York: Henry Holt, 1999. 28pp. Grades PreS–2.

Seven-year-old Lena tells us that she is the color of cinnamon, while her mother is the color of French toast. As her artist mother teaches her how to mix colors, she learns that there are many shades of brown. She introduces her friends, who range from peanut butter and chocolate brown to peachy tan, honey, reddish brown, cocoa brown, and butterscotch. Other adults are other shades. She decides that all the colors are beautiful and sound delicious, and she paints them all. Large portraits of the different folks, flatly painted in gouache with colored pencils and collage, are set against some details relating to the person's occupation or activity. Heads are round, doll-like, with the simplest of features. Patterns are everywhere. The examples make clear how a word like "brown" can have many visual meanings.

Lewin, Ted. *Market!* New York: Lothrop, 1996. 48pp. Grades K–4.

Lewin takes us to specific markets in Ecuador, Nepal, Ireland, Uganda, New York City, and Morocco. His words fill in some background information, but it is the illustrations that bring us right into the markets. His almost photographically realistic double-page watercolors put us right there. We can almost smell the fish in the market, or hear the stomping horses in the Irish gathering.

Mandelbaum, Pili. *You Be Me: I'll Be You.* La Jolla, CA: Kane/Miller, 1989. 36pp. Also paper, 1993. Grades 1–3.

In the simplest of terms, the Belgian author deals with profound questions. Anna's father is "white;" Anna is "brown," and convinced that she is not pretty. She wants to look like her father. Anna decides that her mother is like the coffee they make, her father like the milk, and she's the coffee-milk or *café au lait*. She prefers her father's hair as well. If you can accept the fact that they go out to meet mother with father's hair in pigtails, his face covered with coffee grounds, and Anna's with powder, then this foolishness, which simply embarrasses mother, can lead to a provocative discussion on self-esteem. The author also has the characters comment on how everybody seems to be curling their straight hair or straightening the curly or tanning their white skin; nobody seems happy with what they have. Collage using fabrics and papers against faintly spatter-painted backgrounds create believable characters and everyday objects. The full-page illustrations comfortably include the few lines of caption-like text.

Morris, Ann. *Hats, Hats, Hats.* Illustrated by Ken Heyman. New York: Lothrop/HarperCollins, 1989. 32pp. Also paper. Grades K–3.

This is only one of the author's books about common items and events that occur in many places and cultures. She uses few words, sometimes rhymed, to explain similarities and differences. More details on place or culture are offered at the end, along with a map. Clear color photographs focus on the people in action while also providing considerable contextual information. Others in this series still in print include *Shoes, Shoes, Shoes,* and *Weddings.*

Polacco, Patricia. *Chicken Sunday*. New York: Philomel/Penguin, 1992. 32pp. Grades 1–5.

In this story from her childhood, the author tells of her African American "brothers," Stewart and Winston, and their gramma Eula Mae Walker. The children are saving money to buy Miss Eula a hat she admires in Mr. Kodinski's shop. The shopkeeper helps them earn money by selling the *pysanky* Easter eggs that Polacco's mother helps them make. Miss Eula proudly wears the hat to church on Easter Sunday. She lives on in memory, and the brothers remain friends of the author today. The loving African American family, their acceptance of the "white" narrator, Mr. Kodinski's prickly behavior after eggs are tossed at his shop perhaps because of his Russian-Jewish background, all this is woven into a lengthy narrative of the loving acceptance of difference. Lively illustrations in sketchy pencil and paint depict portraits of real individuals with added specific objects for the ethnic settings. Polacco's deft pictures put us into her world.

Raschka, Chris. *Yo! Yes?* New York: Orchard/Scholastic, 1993. 32pp. Also paper. Grades 1–6.

Raschka's "story" here is so much more than its one monosyllabic word per page. Two male characters from different cultures meet. One is dark-complexioned and "hip," confrontational down to the loose laces on his athletic shoes. The other is lighter-skinned, trousered and jacketed, wary. Equally "monosyllabic" pictures created with charcoal and watercolors depict the boys' reactions to each other. Each appears on facing pages with tinted backgrounds and the word painted boldly in black above them. The gestures and actions tend to be exaggerated. They convey their meanings in the manner of caricature while maintaining their personalities and fundamental humanity. The final page, showing them holding hands and leaping off the top edge of the pages together, is pure joy.

Rosa-Casanova, Sylvia. *Mama Provi and the Pot of Rice*. Illustrated by Robert Roth. New York: Atheneum/Simon & Schuster, 1997. 32pp. Also Aladdin paper. Grades K–3.

When Mama Provi's granddaughter Lucy gets the chicken pox, she can't come down from the eighth floor to the first to visit and hear stories about Mama Provi growing up in Puerto Rico. So Mama Provi decides to cheer her up by cooking her a big pot of her rice with chicken, *arroz con pollo*. Walking up the stairs, Mama Provi stops at 2B, where she smells Mrs. Landers's crusty white bread. She trades some of her dish for a chunk of bread. On the third floor, she exchanges for some of Señor Rivera's *frijoles negros*, black beans. From 4G she receives tossed salad in trade, from 5A it's collard greens, from Mrs. Woo on the sixth floor it's tea, and from 7C it's apple pie. She and Lucy can then share an international feast. Double-page scenes illustrate not only the culinary delights but also the surroundings and personality of each cook. Fine line drawings and thoughtfully applied transparent watercolors produce a delicate reality.

Rosen, Michael J. *Elijah's Angel: A Story for Chanukah and Christmas.* Illustrated by Aminah Brenda Lynn Robinson. San Diego, CA: Harcourt Brace, 1992. 32pp. Also paper. Grades K–4.

The barber and self-taught African American woodcarver Elijah Pierce was known to both author and illustrator, who have made this story true to his character and spirit. Nine-year-old Michael, a regular visitor to Elijah's barbershop, tells how he received the angel of the title the year that Christmas Eve and the first night of Chanukah coincided. Elijah and his carvings are concerned with Jesus and the Bible, while Michael is Jewish. When Elijah gives him a Christmas guardian angel, a "graven image" not allowed in some Jewish homes, Michael is afraid his parents will be upset. But they assure him that it is an angel of friendship. Michael gives Elijah a menorah in exchange, which Elijah lights in the barbershop window each night of Chanukah. Information on the artist Elijah Pierce is included. In keeping with Pierce's use of house paints on his carvings, Robinson uses them here on cloth in many textless double-page scenes, as well as for a variety of vignettes in the lengthy text. Black outlines blend with the opaque intensities of these paints to produce detail-crammed scenes of the barbershop and the neighborhood as well as of several of the carvings. Expressionistic in their exaggeration of forms, like those of Pierce's hands, the illustrations are full of good feelings shared.

Sis, Peter. *Madlenka.* New York: Frances Foster/Farrar Straus, 2000. 42pp. Grades PreS–2.

Charming Madlenka sets off from her New York City apartment with her tooth loose, to tell her friends around the block. Mr. Gaston, the French baker, is her first stop. Through a cut-out window in his shop we can see the Eiffel Tower, while on the left page Madlenka is in the middle of the sketched block, surrounded by Mr. Gaston's baked goods and their dialog, going around the squared page. Turning the page, the Eiffel Tower is on a two-page spread of Paris at night, with Madlenka seen through the window now on the left. As she goes on to tell her news to her friends from India,

Italy, Germany, Latin America, Africa, and Asia, we get see-through windows and glimpses of each country. She has indeed been "around the world" in her walk around the block, and lost her tooth along the way. Beginning on the end-papers, we see a small earth, next a globe with a dot on New York City. A street map of lower Manhattan, a bird's-eye view of city blocks, then Madlenka's block and a picture of her looking out her window follow. Her journey begins and is told in the main with muted colors; objects are built up with tiny lines. A world map locates the native lands of Madlenka's friends in this world voyage.

Steptoe, John. *Creativity.* Illustrated by E. B. Lewis. New York: Clarion/ Houghton, 1997. 32pp. Also paper. Grades 1–4.

Our narrator tells the story of the arrival of a "new dude" in his class. Hector is from Puerto Rico and speaks only Spanish. He puzzles Charles, the narrator, because he is the same color but with straight black hair. His teacher explains that Hector also has African ancestors. Charles agrees to walk Hector and his sisters home. He would like to learn to swim from Hector and to teach him English in turn. Charles's father, however, calls his use of English "creative." Charles tries to help Hector fit in at school by giving him a pair of his sneakers that are "the right kind." Hector reciprocates with the special T-shirt his grandmother gave him, a "creative" gift for sure. Because of the lengthy text, the watercolors tend to be mainly snapshot illustrations that add information. The teacher's-eye view of the classroom epitomizes the comment that "everybody in this room is mixed-up together." These naturalistic scenes of genuinely individual characters offer a hopeful note on the growing friendship between strangers.

Vyner, Tim. *World Team.* Brookfield, CT: Roaring Brook, 2001. 32pp. Grades K–3.

In our "big round world" right now, "more children than you can possibly imagine are playing soccer." And around the world we go, one double page at a time, each with the name of the country and the time along the side and a few sentences about the player and how he (or she) practices while sharing the same dream: winning the World Cup. The double-page paintings incorporate regional settings such as Rio's Sugarloaf Mountain, a fisherman by the sea in Mexico, a makeshift goal on a Kenyan plain, an empty school arena in France. All have at least one youngster and a soccer ball in common to make the unwritten but hopeful case that despite regional differences, the game at least is universal.

BOOKS ANNOTATED IN OTHER CHAPTERS THAT
ALSO HAVE CROSS-CULTURAL THEMES

Akio, Terumasa. *Me and Alves: A Japanese Journey.*
Kroll, Virginia. *Pink Paper Swans.*
Pinkney, Andrea Davis. *Fishing Day.*
Say, Allan. *Grandfather's Journey.*
———. *Tea with Milk.*
Torres, Leyla. *Liliana's Grandmothers.*
Wiles, Deborah. *Freedom Summer.*
Woodson, Jacqueline. *The Other Side.*

Appendix

ADDITIONAL RESOURCES

BOOKS

Freeman, Deena. *How People Live.* New York: DK Publishing, 2003.

SERIES WITH BACKGROUND INFORMATION, BY PUBLISHER

Compass Point Books, 3109 W. 50th St. #115, Minneapolis, MN 55410-2102
    Many Cultures, One World series, Grades 3–5
    Coming to America series, Grades 3–5
Crabtree Publishing, 350 Fifth Ave., Suite 3308, New York, NY 10018
    Lands, Peoples, and Cultures series, Grades 3–6
    Kid Power: Multicultural Meals, Grades 3–6
    We Came to North America series, Grades 3–6
Franklin Watts, 90 Old Sherman Turnpike, Danbury, CT 06816
    A to Z series, Grades 2–4
Lerner Publishing, 1251 Washington Ave. North, Minneapolis, MN 55401-1036
    Visual Geography series, Grades 5 and up
    Colors of the World series, Grades 1–3
Millbrook Press, 2 Old New Milford Rd., Brookfield, CT 06804
    Grandma . . . Remembers series, Grades K–3
Picture Window Books, 7825 Telegraph Rd., Bloomington, MN 55438
    Country ABCs series, Grades 1–3. For information only; illustrations not helpful.
    Meals Around the World series, Grades K–3. Illustrations not helpful.
Raintree, 100 North La Salle, Suite 1200, Chicago, IL 60602
    Living Religions series, Grades 4–6
    Culture in . . . series, Grades 4–6

Rosen Publishing Group, 29 E. 21st St., New York, NY 10010
    Coming to America series, Grades 2–4
    Crafts of the World series, Grades 2–4

FREE PERIODICALS

Saudi Aramco World, Box 469008, Escondido, CA 92046-9008
Teaching Tolerance, PO Box 548, Montgomery, AL 36177-9622

PUBLISHERS SPECIALIZING IN BOOKS FROM OTHER CULTURES

Arte Publico Press, University of Houston, 452 Cullen Performance Hall, Houston, TX 77204-2004
Asia for Kids, PO Box 9096, Cincinnati, OH 45209; www.afk.com
Bess Press, 3565 Harding Ave., Honolulu, HI 96816
Children's Book Press, 2211 Mission St., San Francisco, CA 94110
Cinco Puntos Press, 701 Texas Ave., El Paso, TX 79901
Good Minds, www.goodminds.com
Jewish Lights, Sunset Farms Offices, Rte. 4, Woodstock, VT 05091; www.jewish lights.com
Kane/Miller, PO Box 8515, La Jolla, CA 92038-8515; www.kanemiller.com
Kar-Ben, 1251 Washington Ave. North, Minneapolis, MN 55401-1036; www.karben .com
Lee & Low Books, 95 Madison Ave., New York, NY 10016; http://leeandlow.com
Shen's Books, 40951 Fremont Blvd., Fremont, CA 94538; www.shens.com
Turtle Books, 866 United Nations Plaza, Suite 525, New York, NY 10017; www.turtle books.com

PUBLISHERS WHO HAVE OFFERED MULTICULTURAL BOOK LISTS

Harcourt Children's Books, 525 B St., Suite 1900, San Diego, CA 92101; www.HarcourtBooks.com
Penguin Young Readers Group, 345 Hudson St., 15th floor, New York, NY 10014; www.penguin.com
Simon & Schuster Books for Young Readers, 1230 Avenue of the Americas, New York, NY 10020; www.SimonSaysKids.com

SOURCES OF ARTS AND CRAFTS FROM MANY LANDS

American Museum of Natural History, Central Park West & 79th St. New York, NY 10024-5192

Art Institute of Chicago, Michigan & Adams Sts., Chicago, IL 60603

Crizmac, PO Box 65928, Tucson, AZ 85728-5928; www.crizmac.com

Metropolitan Museum of Art Store, 255 Gracie Station, New York, NY 10028-9998; www.metmuseum.org/store

Museum of Fine Arts, Boston, PO Box 244, Avon, MA 02322-0244; www.mfa.org/shop

Smithsonian Institution, Dept. 0006, Washington, DC 20073-0006

INDEX

ABOUT THE AUTHORS

Sylvia Marantz has been involved with books, children, and libraries for over fifty years. For most of them, she was a school librarian—at the University of Chicago Laboratory School, and in the Worthington Schools, at Wellington School, and at St. Michael School, all in the Columbus, Ohio, area.

She is currently a picturebook reviewer for *The Five Owls*, the *Columbus Dispatch*, the Children's Literature Comprehensive Database, and MeltonArts. org, and an interviewer/writer for CLDB and *Book Links*.

Her books include *Picture Books for Looking and Learning: Awakening Visual Perceptions through the Art of Children's Books* (Oryx) and, with her art educator husband, Kenneth, *The Art of Children's Picture Books: A Selective Reference Guide* (Garland), *Artists of the Page: Interviews with Children's Book Illustrators* (McFarland), *Multicultural Picture Books: Art for Understanding Others*, volumes I and II (Linworth), and *Creating Picturebooks: Interviews with Editors, Art Directors, Reviewers, Booksellers, Professors, Librarians, and Showcasers* (McFarland).

She offers presentations and workshops for groups of librarians, library aides, and teachers, and at the annual Children's Literature Conference in Columbus, the Ohio Educational Library Media Association conference, and the American Association of School Librarians conference.

Mother of two daughters and a son, she is now enjoying grandmothering three grandsons and a granddaughter, book lovers all. She also volunteers in a local school library and as a teacher of English as a Second Language for immigrants.

Dr. **Ken Marantz** was an art teacher in grades K–12 in public and independent schools, as well as a professor of art education at Pratt Institute, the

University of Chicago, and the Ohio State University, where he chaired the department for sixteen years before retiring.

He has had book reviews published in the *New York Times*, and currently reviews regularly for *School Arts, Choice, Artline,* and *The Five Owls.* He has edited several professional periodicals, had articles printed in many professional art education and library publications, given too many talks to specify, and served on the nominating committee for the Hans Christian Andersen Award and twice on the Caldecott Award Committee. He was World Counsellor for the International Society for Education through Art.

He is the author of *The Picturebook: Source and Resource for Art Education* (National Art Education Association) as well as five other volumes with his librarian wife, Sylvia, with whom he has traveled extensively nationally and internationally.